RECREATION FACILITY MANAGEMENT

Design, Development, Operations, and Utilization

Richard F. Mull, MS
Indiana University

Brent A. Beggs, PhD
Illinois State University

Mick Renneisen, MS
Director of Parks and Recreation
City of Bloomington, Indiana

Human Kinetics

Library of Congress Cataloging-in-Publication Data

Mull, Richard F.
   Recreation facility management : design, development, operations, and
utilization / Richard F. Mull, Brent A. Beggs, Mick Renneisen.
       p. cm.
   Includes bibliographical references and index.
   ISBN-13: 978-0-7360-7002-7 (soft cover)
   ISBN-10: 0-7360-7002-8 (soft cover)
   1. Recreation centers–United States–Management. 2. Sports
facilities–United States–Management. I. Beggs, Brent A. II.
Renneisen, Mick. III. Title.
   GV429.M85 2009
   796.06'8–dc22

   ISBN-10: 0-7360-7002-8
   ISBN-13: 978-0-7360-7002-7

The Web addresses cited in this text were current as of October 2008, unless otherwise noted.

Acquisitions Editor: Gayle Kassing, PhD; **Developmental Editor:** Amy Stahl; **Assistant Editor:** Lauren B. Morenz; **Copyeditor:** Alisha Jeddeloh; **Proofreader:** Anne Meyer Byler; **Indexer:** Andrea J. Hepner; **Permission Manager:** Martha Gullo; **Graphic Designer:** Fred Starbird; **Graphic Artist:** Dawn Sills; **Cover Designer:** Keith Blomberg; **Photographer (cover):** Top: Human Kinetics/Tom Roberts; middle: Mick Renneisen; bottom: Human Kinetics; **Photographer (interior):** Mick Renneisen, unless otherwise noted; Photos on pages 30 (top), 32, 42, 44, 73, 87, 96, 108 a,b, 116, 117, 118, 126,128, 138, 180, 195, 208, 212, 227, 228, 229, 232, 234, 256, 261 © Human Kinetics. **Photo Asset Manager:** Laura Fitch; **Photo Production Manager:** Jason Allen; **Art Manager:** Kelly Hendren; **Associate Art Manager:** Alan L. Wilborn; **Illustrator:** Keri Evans; **Printer:** Total Printing Systems

Printed in the United States of America   10 9 8 7 6 5 4

The paper in this book is certified under a sustainable forestry program.

Human Kinetics
Web site: www.HumanKinetics.com

United States: Human Kinetics
P.O. Box 5076
Champaign, IL 61825-5076
800-747-4457
e-mail: humank@hkusa.com

Canada: Human Kinetics
475 Devonshire Road Unit 100
Windsor, ON N8Y 2L5
800-465-7301 (in Canada only)
e-mail: info@hkcanada.com

Europe: Human Kinetics
107 Bradford Road
Stanningley
Leeds LS28 6AT, United Kingdom
+44 (0) 113 255 5665
e-mail: hk@hkeurope.com

Australia: Human Kinetics
57A Price Avenue
Lower Mitcham, South Australia 5062
08 8372 0999
e-mail: info@hkaustralia.com

New Zealand: Human Kinetics
P.O. Box 80
Torrens Park, South Australia 5062
0800 222 062
e-mail: info@hknewzealand.com

E4177

This book is dedicated to the memory of Linda S. Mull for her patience, understanding, tolerance, and cooperation during the early stages of thinking, writing, and rewriting the content.

Contents

Preface   xi
Acknowledgments   xiii

Part I   **Foundations of Recreation Facility Management** 1

Chapter **1**   **Understanding Recreation Facility Management**.......................3

Managing the Product   4
Defining Management   6
Managing Resources   10
Understanding Marketing   12
Setting Goals   13
Summary   15

Chapter **2**   **Managing Recreation Facilities**.................17

Fundamentals of Recreation Facilities   18
Recent Changes in Recreation Facility
  Management Responsibilities   21
Influences on Management Responsibilities   22
Key Responsibilities of Recreation Facility Management   24
Career Implications of Recreation Facility Managers   25
Summary   27

Chapter **3**   **Learning the Basics of Recreation Facilities**......29

Structure   30
Product Influence   32
Developmental Stages   33
Indoor Recreation Facility Characteristics   34
Outdoor Recreation Facility Characteristics   40
Summary   44

Part II   **Design and Development of Recreation Facilities.....................47**

Chapter 4   **Assessment....................49**

Influencing Factors in Facility Assessment   50
Influencing Techniques in Facility Assessment   54
Initial Proposal   55
Summary   56

Chapter 5   **Planning 57**

Planning Options   58
Planning Committee Members   58
Master Plans   60
Planning Considerations   61
Development Options   62
Project Statement   64
Summary   66

Chapter 6   **Designing Recreation Facilities and Reading Blueprints....................67**

Design Team   68
Design Considerations   69
Blueprints and Design Documents   75
Reading Blueprints   77
Summary   83

Chapter 7   **Funding and the Bid Process 85**

Project Costs   86
Construction Options   90
Bidding the Project   91
Contract Arrangements   93
Funding Options   95
Summary   99

Chapter 8   **Constructing Recreation Facilities 101**

Construction Documents   102
Construction Management   103
Final Stages   107
Summary   110

Part III Resources for Recreation Facility Management. 111

Chapter 9 Managing Equipment 113

Basics of Recreation Facility Equipment   114
Types of Equipment   115
Purchasing Equipment   119
Receiving and Distributing Equipment   121
Renting and Leasing Equipment   122
Using Equipment   122
Summary   122

Chapter 10 Managing Finances 123

Expenses   124
Income   127
Fiscal Practices   130
Summary   131

Chapter 11 Managing Employees .133

Job Classification   134
Job Description   135
Hiring Procedures   135
On-the-Job Training   137
Performance Appraisal   137
Types of Employees   139
Work Environment   144
Employee Relations   145
Summary   145

Part IV Utilization of Recreation Facilities 147

Chapter 12 Circulation, Safety, Control, and Security 149

User Circulation   150
Safety   152
Control   159
Security   162
Summary   164

Chapter **13** **Coordinating and Scheduling**. **165**

Coordinating   166
Scheduling   168
Summary   176

Chapter **14** **Maintenance**. **177**

Facility Image   179
Safety   179
Maintenance Categories   180
Maintenance Types   181
Maintenance Systems   183
Other Maintenance Considerations   186
Summary   188

Chapter **15** **Emergencies and Emergency Responses** **189**

Disruption in Facility Activities   190
Emergency Responses   194
Summary   198

Part Ⅴ **Auxiliaries of Recreation Facilities** **199**

Chapter **16** **Parks and Playground Facilities** **201**

Parks   202
Playgrounds   214
Summary   219

Chapter **17** **Aquatic Facilities** **221**

Types of Aquatic Facilities   222
Aquatic Facility Construction and Accessibility   223
Aquatic Facility Operations   224
Aquatic Facility Product Delivery Areas   231
External Support   233
Summary   235

Chapter **18 Ancillary Spaces** 237

    Parking   238
    Reception Area   243
    Locker and Shower Area   247
    Summary   249

Chapter **19 Core Product Extensions and Areas** 251

    Commodity Outlets   252
    Food Services   256
    Child Care   259
    Equipment Checkout or Rental   266
    Summary   269

Appendix A: Associations and Accredited Academic Programs   271

Appendix B: Accreditation Standards and Certified Park and Recreation Professional Study Guide Criteria   275

Glossary   279

Bibliography   286

Index   288

About the Authors   296

Preface

Today's recreation professionals find themselves responsible for a variety of recreation facilities that vary in type, scope, size, budget, and condition. These facilities may also have vastly different goals and expectations according to the setting and location. Recreation facility management is an expansive and complicated subject that can vary greatly with the nature and objective of each facility.

Recreation Facility Management: Design, Development, Operations, and Utilization focuses on recreation facilities and the products and services they provide. Recreation facilities include schools, stadiums, fitness centers, sports complexes, recreation centers, golf courses, water parks, public pools, convention centers, parks, playgrounds, tourism facilities, and theme parks. Tourism facilities, including resorts, hotels, and cruise ships, are included in the definition of recreation facilities because these facilities are used by people in their leisure time.

Recreation administrators and those who use the facilities often don't appreciate the complexity of responsibilities associated with recreation facility management. The material in this text is based on a logical model incorporating information that prepares students to perform the responsibilities required of a recreation facility manager. Rather than take a theoretical approach to recreation facility management, this text analyzes and synthesizes the practical applications that recreation professionals should be aware of in facility management.

Recreation Facility Management is arranged into five parts. The content reflects a progression of concepts that aid in retention of information for practical application. Part I covers foundations of the profession, including the definition of management and the description of duties of managing recreation facilities. Part II examines the development of recreation facilities, including needs assessment, planning, design, reading blueprints, funding, and construction. Parts III and IV include discussions about managing resources related to efficient and safe use of a facility. Part V examines various types of auxiliary spaces that enhance a facility, such as parks and playgrounds, aquatic areas, ancillary spaces, and core product extensions.

Each chapter includes objectives and summaries. A glossary at the end of the book defines the terms boldfaced throughout the chapters in the book. Students using *Recreation Facility Management* will also have access to the online student resource that ties the information in the book to practical matters on the job. Forms appearing in this book in thumbnail size appear full sized in the online student resource, are indicated with a 🖱 on the page, and are from the files of actual facility managers. The online student resource also contains learning activities, discussion questions, and Web sites to help students further explore the ideas found in the book.

By using this text and the resources that come with it, students will develop a better understanding of the different types of facilities that exist in recreation and leisure services and the responsibilities associated with planning, designing, operating, and utilizing these spaces.

Acknowledgments

We are grateful for the assistance and support of many people along the way in the development of this publication. In particular, special thanks to the following people:

Donna Beyers, administrative assistant, who efficiently and tirelessly edited and assisted with the original publication and ensuing phases of this book

Kian Lam Toh, graduate assistant, for his resourcefulness and dialogue with the initial outlines

Mike Williams, graduate assistant, for his analysis of content and discussions providing valuable feedback

Nancy Brunton for her assistance with the content, analysis, and PowerPoint development

Sylvia Tosi, graduate assistant, for the original PowerPoint presentations and critique of content

Chris Crume, aquatics assistant, for his original draft of the aquatics chapter with the advisory assistance from Bill Ramos, director of aquatics at Indiana University

City of Bloomington Parks and Recreation for charts and forms

Support from the department of recreation, park and tourism studies in the School of Health, Physical Education and Recreation at Indiana University

Foundations of Recreation Facility Management

All recreation services and core products are delivered in spaces known as facilities. To deliver these core products, recreation facilities must be managed efficiently. Management of a recreation facility includes influencing agency resources such as employees, money, and equipment so that users have a positive experience. The management of a recreation facility varies based on the type of facility and the types of services and products provided at a facility. Facilities can be natural or manmade; they can also be indoor or outdoor spaces. Each facility is unique in how it provides core products and how it is managed. Regardless of the type of facility, there are numerous factors that can influence the ability of a recreation facility manager to deliver products and services. Understanding these factors and how to manage resources is the foundation of facility management and requires extensive education and training.

Understanding Recreation Facility Management

L E A R N I N G   O B J E C T I V E S

At the completion of this chapter, you should be able to do the following:

1. Define the term *management*.
2. Understand the administrative functions and operational functions of a recreation administrator.
3. Recognize the resources available to a recreation administrator in managing a facility.
4. Understand methods of marketing the leisure service product.
5. Recognize the various types of goals in place for the various types of recreation agencies.

If you are running an amusement park or supervising a local senior citizen center, you are managing a recreation facility. Whether you are supervising staff, operating a facility, maintaining equipment, or running a softball tournament, you are applying **recreation facility management** practices in one way or another. All leisure service organizations use some form of recreation facility management. **Management** is a concept that takes on several meanings and, therefore, may be employed in a variety of ways. However, all management functions share a common process of working with people and resources to achieve goals. This chapter represents a practical understanding of terminology and concepts that can provide direction to management as it applies to facilities.

MANAGING THE PRODUCT

In management, a person or a group wants to accomplish a specific directive. A stated vision, mission, values, goals, and objectives that explain the intended direction usually exist to represent the concept of management. Organizational directives such as a vision and mission are communicated from the higher-level administrators throughout an organization and are vital to establishing the role of the organization and putting policies in place. Lower-level directives such as goals and objectives are created within specific divisions of an organization and are shaped by the vision or mission. As directives move from a higher level to a lower level, they become more specific. For example, the mission of an agency may be to provide outdoor facilities for its community. A specific goal related to the mission may be to design and operate a community skate park. Objectives within that goal would establish a timeline for the development of the skate park.

The organizational directive is considered a **product** and in overall management, it is the **core product**. This core product is the primary interest of the organization, and it is why management exists. Management seeks to accomplish something with the core product such as success, profit, satisfaction, and participation. For example, a campus recreation organization at a university may seek to increase participation and provide opportunities for students to be physically

▶Softball games and leagues are examples of core products, which are an organization's main interest.

active. Quite often, auxiliary directives exist that supplement the core product. These **core product extensions** usually support the core product and add to its success. Let's consider an example from an outdoor recreation agency that provides rafting excursions. Core product extensions might include instructional programs that teach participants how to use equipment or improve certain skills. Another core product extension could be a retail area where participants can rent or purchase

▶Retail areas, such as a golf course pro shop, and food service areas are two examples of core product extensions.

equipment or clothing that will allow them to participate in activities.

DEFINING MANAGEMENT

The basic premise of management can vary from field to field and from profession to profession. In this section, we attempt to give a meaning to management that is logical and reasonable and can withstand the diversity and extensiveness of management.

Management is often confused with concepts such as *administration* and *operation,* which are two components of management. *Leadership* is another term that is often discussed in the context of management; however, it also is another component within management. Management represents a goal-oriented system where leadership places emphasis on the people in the process of achieving organizational goals or those people who participate in the core product.

Modern understanding of management is based on human interpretation and the capacities to share, coordinate, and cooperate. This understanding can be applied to recreation facility management by engaging people in the process of striving to achieve organizational goals. Taking both goals and people into consideration allows the establishment of a working description of management that is practical and applicable to all of its facets.

These various understandings of management can best be simplified into a description that works for all systems where management is required: Management is influencing resources to obtain a goal. This definition describes the human element in the functions and activities that are involved in striving to accomplish a goal.

Probably the most important term in describing management is *influence.* It incorporates the ideals of leadership, representing a modern interpretation of management instead of traditional interpretations involving terms such as *administer, direct,* and *control.* **Influence** means the power to affect an outcome. It is applicable to both personal as well as professional responsibilities.

It is important to understand the full meaning of influence as a key concept for management. If a product exists, management needs to find a way to make the product accessible and successful, bringing about satisfactory results for the organization as well as those who use the product. There are two broad areas where this is accom-

plished: **administrative functions** and **delivery operations.** These distinct systems of influence represent the various functions and operations in recreation facility management that bring about a desired result.

Administrative Functions

All professional and personal management starts with the responsible person or system having some type of authority. This administrative person or system represents the executive or upper-level personnel in charge of producing a product. Most authoritative systems include four administrative functions: planning, organizing, directing, and controlling. These administrative functions can be described as the ultimate executive system that influences the desired outcome of an organization. The four functions encompass a number of activities that help to influence everything that takes place.

Planning

Very little takes place without some degree of planning early in the effort. In its simplest description, **planning** is anticipating through thought and, when appropriate, documentation, all facets that should take an organization to an expected level of success. A plan is a predetermined and theoretical way to accomplish set goals and objectives. Planning can be short term (1-3 years) or long term (3 years and beyond). It may be simple, such as a conversation among a few people that establishes tasks and direction, or it can be a detailed, comprehensive process with several people, referred to as **strategic planning.**

Planning is a critical aspect of recreation facility management. The importance of planning can be observed in a number of areas in recreation facility management, including facility development, risk management, emergency and evacuation instructions, equipment purchasing and distribution, preventive maintenance, and budgeting. Evidence of planning can almost always be observed where there is successful recreation facility management, and lack of planning is just as evident in unsuccessful recreation facility management.

Organizing

Organizing involves recognizing and assigning specific responsibilities to employees and resources, as well as designing areas and time assignments that relate to the product. Much of this organization is included in scheduling. In scheduling, certain steps are taken to efficiently allocate human and physical resources; it thus involves an appreciation for all facets of managing the core product. Resources can be categorized into the areas of information, equipment, human resources, and organizational resources so that management can coordinate the efficient delivery of a product and take appropriate steps for this process to occur in a methodical and timely fashion.

The organizing function incorporates more than the assignment of areas for specific activities. It also includes establishing a flowchart that reflects the authority structure of an organization (see figure 1.1), developing policies and procedures, and creating facility signage that designates areas and provides information. Organizing a facility uses all the elements of the facility to implement a meaningful process that influences the success of the product.

Directing

Directing is the process of guiding people or groups within an overall management system. It is a managerial function to ensure that employees understand the importance of their position and how they help the organization achieve its goals. Staffing, which includes recruiting, hiring, and training employees, is important, but the real test is creating an environment where employees fulfill their role as intended.

Directing incorporates elements such as leadership style, training, delegation, communication techniques, coordination, and motivation. Having employees in place and fulfilling their obligations correctly is the foundation of ongoing success in recreation facility management. The directing function requires that employees be in place and fulfilling their obligations as outlined in their job description.

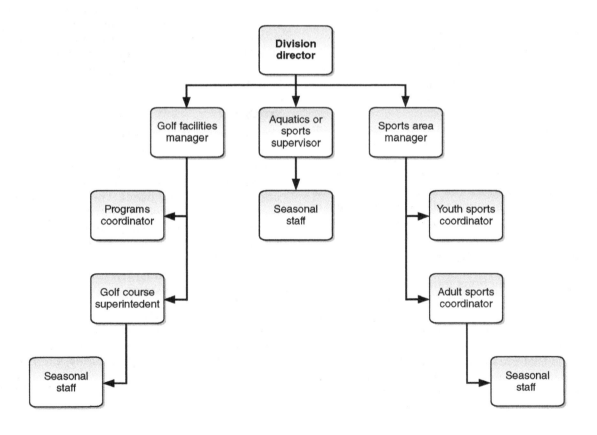

Figure 1.1 Sample organizational chart.

Controlling

Ideally, employees will perform every function in their job description in a timely and professional manner, but this does not always occur. Additionally, things often do not go as planned by management. Therefore, employees, funds, facilities, equipment, and resources need to be monitored to ensure that they have a positive influence on the product and meet the expectations of management. This effort, described as **controlling,** is similar to the process of directing, except it focuses more on monitoring resources. Controlling can be defined as the process of supervising, assessing, and correcting employee performance and resources to ensure successful product delivery.

Putting various controlling methods into practice can reduce or eliminate negative occurrences and can help deliver a product efficiently. Some examples of controlling methods include

- establishing expected performance standards,
- creating an evaluation system,
- implementing an award and recognition program,
- developing corrective procedures,
- formulating grievance procedures,
- using financial statements, and
- recording inventory.

Many factors are involved in the interpretation and performance of responsibility. In addition, management uses checks and balances to monitor efficient use of resources. However, even the best plans, organizational structure, direction, and control can't eliminate all problems, which is where delivery operations come into play.

Delivery Operations

Administrative functions initiate ideas and influence the product. In recreation facility management, presenting the product to the user is referred to as **delivery operations.** Delivery operations integrate the resources and administrative functions that create interest leading to product participation or purchase, which results in a user experience that affects the success of the product. Delivery operations have four functions: production, support, auxiliaries, and maintenance.

Production

Arguably the most important area of delivery operations is the production function. **Production** is the basis of how the product is delivered. It includes communicating information to recreation facility users and allocating the human and physical resources and other elements critical to the delivery of the product. Production represents the detailed knowledge of employees and the responsibilities they perform to deliver a product.

In the recreation profession, production takes the form of **programming,** or providing various activities so that participants gain a sense of satisfaction from their experience. Programming is the designing and manipulating of leisure environments in an effort to promote the desired experiences of participants. Programming is not necessarily the responsibility of recreation facility managers but is often the responsibility of other employees. In the tourism model, programming is often referred to as *event planning.* In the entertainment field, it is the effort to show a movie, create an event, or produce a television show, play, or musical that spectators enjoy. In business, it could be the creation of a retail outlet or food and beverage outlet that brings the product to the customer for purchase. In the educational field, it is the delivery of information by the educator, including the methods for ensuring that students acquire knowledge.

Support

Support is another important delivery operation that has an impact on the production effort. **Support** represents activities that take place behind the scenes by personnel who are typically not in contact with facility users. The support function is often not recognized as contributing to management efforts in relation to product delivery, but in reality, support includes essential activities that are critical to the success of the product. These activities can be considered either internal or external support systems.

Internal Support Systems **Internal support systems** take place within the organization. For instance, many organizations employ staff members to handle support duties, such as

- clerical support (typing, record keeping, appointment scheduling),
- payroll and benefit management,

- communications,
- bookkeeping,
- supply purchasing and distribution, and
- mail service.

Internal support staff are employees hired by the agency and play an important role in the operation of facilities.

External Support Systems The support function can also take place externally. **External support systems** can involve outside contractual services and may include

- legal services,
- medical assistance,
- accounting, and
- consultants.

These services are usually specialized and not within the basic activities of daily agency operations. Outside services are brought in to help with specific tasks where existing personnel lack expertise.

Auxiliaries

As mentioned earlier, certain product management needs outside the primary production effort can be thought of as auxiliary or supplemental to the primary product and are often called *core product extensions* or *ancillary spaces*. Core product extensions are spaces in a facility that generate revenue through the provision of additional products or services. Ancillary spaces can be defined as spaces in a facility that support the core product, but are not designed to generate additional revenue. Essential to overall management, auxiliaries may represent only a small percent of product delivery.

Auxiliary activities may not be part of the primary product delivery, but in many instances their elimination would have a negative impact on the success of the product. One example of a core product extension is parking, which is a critical convenience feature for recreation facility users. Another consideration could be the provision of child care for users while they are benefiting from the recreation product. Food and beverage outlets, including vending machines, snack

© Scott Boehm/Getty Images Sport

▶External support from medical assistance personnel is sometimes required at a recreation facility when an injury is too severe to be handled by the internal facility staff.

▶One example of an ancillary area in a recreation facility is the reception area.

bars, or full-service restaurants, are core product extensions that could enhance users' experiences and meet management goals. Another example is a reception area that is used for communicating information, controlling access, distributing schedules, collecting fees, registering participants, and receiving visitors. Some management systems may also have an equipment checkout system and shower and locker areas as extended functions. These auxiliary functions, although not usually as encompassing as the core product, could be significant enough to require their own production and delivery effort.

Maintenance

In the delivery operation of recreation facility management, **maintenance,** or keeping facilities and equipment in proper and safe condition, can be considered a support function. However, maintenance is such a significant part of recreation management that it is considered a separate function. Maintenance functions can vary greatly. As organizations increase in size, maintenance responsibilities increase proportionately, making this effort more complicated. The day-to-day responsibilities can vary from simply cleaning areas to a full system of delivery incorporating repairs and preventive and cyclical maintenance.

Maintenance can incorporate specially trained staff who are either part of the agency or an outside source contracted in a situation requiring certain expertise. Some of the tasks that relate to the maintenance function include facility and equipment repair, cleaning, mowing, watering, safety measures, inventory management, electrical controls, and equipment setup and takedown. The lack attention to maintenance can have a negative short-term effect on the perception of a recreation facility as well as serious implications from a long-term perspective. Some settings require emphasis on maintenance when appearance is important and especially when the health and safety of users and employees may be compromised if proper maintenance practices are not observed, such as at an amusement park or even a playground.

MANAGING RESOURCES

Administrative functions and delivery operations rely heavily on **resources.** The most obvious management resources in the recreation environment are employees, money, equipment, and facilities.

© iStockphoto/Inger Anne Hulbækdal

▶Examples of maintenance functions associated with outdoor recreation facilities include mowing, care of turf, and maintenance of ball field surfaces.

Each plays a significant role within management. Being able to effectively and efficiently use these resources is a recreation administrator's greatest challenge.

The capacity of management to influence these resources as they pertain to the core product and core product extensions cannot be overemphasized. Management resources are of considerable importance to facilities and will be discussed in greater detail in later chapters. The following material summarizes how each can be interpreted as part of the recreation facility management process.

Employees

Human involvement and the management of that involvement is essential in the delivery of a product. A critical function of management is the capacity to influence **employees** to fulfill their obligations in the production or delivery of a product. This process is called **staffing** and includes the recruitment, hiring, and training of appropriate people to facilitate the requirements of a successful product.

A variety of formal and informal considerations are incorporated in the staffing function. A more formal staffing process is necessary as job complexity increases. Some of the steps in providing proper staffing include

- classifying employees,
- establishing levels of authority,
- establishing a hiring timetable,
- creating a search-and-screen process,
- establishing selection criteria,
- announcing the position,
- interviewing potential employees,
- negotiating salaries, and ultimately,
- hiring staff.

Each of these activities is significant in the appropriate placement of people within the management system. Allocating the appropriate responsibility to the right people can be critical to meeting the product expectations of recreation facility users and management.

Money

As either a source of income or an expenditure, money is a critical component of any management system. The proper management of fiscal resources can have a significant impact on the viability of a recreation facility. Other terms relating to this resource include *funding, financing, fiscal, budgeting,* and *accounting.* The management of money, which is referred to as **budgeting,** must be planned in advance. The use of money must

▶The most important recreation facility resource is the facility's employees.

also include **accounting,** which is the documentation of income and expenditures associated with operating a facility. Money is a complicated resource that often requires specialized applications or processes.

Equipment

Equipment includes any item, mechanical or otherwise, that enhances the production and delivery processes. There are a number of ways to describe and classify equipment, which will be addressed in later chapters. Equipment is an extensive resource that carries a great deal of responsibility, including purchasing, inventorying, receiving, storing, distributing, and maintaining. Often, equipment is taken for granted, yet it represents a significant expense as well as a potentially labor-intensive problem when it does not work as expected. The ability of management to influence proper use and care of equipment can contribute to the efficiency and effectiveness of delivery operations.

Facilities

The **facility** is a resource that is critical to the production and delivery of the product. Recreation facilities, which can be indoor or outdoor

structures, vary greatly. As a resource, facilities are initially the most expensive element in the provision of a recreation product. It is essential that management recognize the nature and scope of facilities in planning. The ability to understand the value of facilities to the product is the basis of this text.

UNDERSTANDING MARKETING

No matter what the product or how the resources are allocated, a process needs to be in place that brings the product to potential users. Whether a person enjoys the product as an experience or makes a purchase, a system is needed to create interest in the product. The effort to reach an audience to deliver them a product is called **marketing.** This process involves assessing a targeted population and developing a strategy to create product awareness and availability, which is essential in meeting management goals for success.

Several methods and techniques are involved in marketing. Marketing is a complete field of its own that can be divided into the four Ps: product, promotion, price, and place. Each represents a different aspect of creating product awareness.

▶Recreation facilities can include anything from a fitness center to a community outdoor theater.

© Rhoda Peacher

- **Product** is what the consumer receives from the business transaction. The product can be a tangible good or intangible service.
- **Promotion** is the advancement of the status or value of a product or idea. Promotion includes strategies to deliver information, such as public relations, personal selling, sales promotions, publicity, and advertising.
- **Price** is the cost to the consumer to acquire a product. This expense goes beyond the sticker price and may also include time and opportunity costs, psychological costs, personal effort costs, and indirect financial costs.
- **Place** is where a product is distributed to target consumer markets.

Marketing also involves a process to evaluate the demographic characteristics of a population, establishing a **target market** to help ensure the success of a product. Some characteristics that can be evaluated in establishing the target market include age, sex, socioeconomic background, and geographic location. Lifestyle information, known as **psychographics,** can also be incorporated and assessed to reflect the influence of a product on the potential user. Marketing also uses **market segmentation,** which targets specific segments of users by recognizing their particular needs and interests and then attempting to meet them. Marketing has proven to be extremely important to product delivery and ultimately to accomplishing management goals for success.

SETTING GOALS

In describing the concepts involved in recreation facility management, we have reviewed administrative functions and delivery operations, resources required to deliver the product, and marketing techniques for reaching potential users. No matter the product, management always wants to accomplish a predetermined goal. Ultimately, the desired outcome is reflected in the values, vision, and mission of an organization and will be evaluated using criteria that depend on the setting of the recreation facility. This desired outcome or goal can be thought of in broad terms as service oriented or profit oriented; however, these categories are not exclusive.

Service-Oriented Goals

Management in the service category exists when an organization provides a meaningful experience for users without the incentive of profit. These types of services are often delivered in the **public sector.** Federal, state, and local taxes support the administration and delivery of services in the public sector, although the current economy is requiring that service agencies become less reliant on tax dollars and generate their own revenue to support their operations.

Usually, public recreation agencies operate under the guidance of service-oriented goals, which are outcomes motivated by the idea that services should not be profit driven but should be based on the needs of society and made available to all. Many services in the public sector are recognized as necessary for the well-being of society. Examples of agencies that have service-oriented goals include schools, correction facilities, the military, and community agencies such as hospitals and fire, police, and park and recreation departments. The delivery of services in the public sector may involve charging fees to meet operational costs; however, the motivation is not to make a profit but to provide a public service and contribute to society.

Profit-Oriented Goals

Recreation facility management systems in the **private sector** provide products based on profit-oriented goals. Management with profit-oriented goals has traditionally operated very differently from service-oriented enterprises. In private management systems, all efforts are focused on the **bottom line,** an end result that hopefully shows a net profit. Products may be produced and delivered, but without **profit,** or generating sufficient net income to exceed expenses, the recreation facility management system usually is unable to continue. All efforts within this type of management system are focused on the profit-oriented

▶ The Boys & Girls Club is an example of a public sector agency or organization.

© RC Hall

▶The exercise equipment room at a country club is an example of a private sector facility.

goal because it ultimately affects administration, delivery, resources, and the product itself. Positive user experiences and good service are expected if a net profit is to be accomplished. Whether the production is the sale of an item or the use of a recreation environment for an experience, the ultimate goal is generating income that exceeds expenses. Entities of this nature are privately operated and include businesses, factories, corporations, and franchises that receive no tax support in delivering a recreation product.

SUMMARY

Management is a complicated process that can be described as influencing resources such as employees, money, and equipment to obtain a goal. The goal for a recreation facility manager is to deliver the core product to users. The recreation facility manager must utilize internal and external support systems in delivering the core product and auxiliary spaces to users. Ultimately, the goals of management are established through understanding the values, vision, and mission of an organization. These goals are used to establish administrative functions, delivery operations, resource utilization, and marketing in the recreation facility.

Managing Recreation Facilities

LEARNING OBJECTIVES

At the completion of this chapter, you should be able to do the following:

1. Define the term *facility*.
2. Understand the concept of sustainability in relation to recreation facilities.
3. Recognize the various influences on the responsibilities of recreation facility management.
4. Understand the background and training required for becoming a recreation professional.

The delivery of the core product in leisure services can be done in a variety of ways depending on the service or product being provided. Regardless of what the core product is, it must be delivered in a space. The space where product delivery occurs is referred to as a facility. The facility is essential to the quality of the leisure experience. Despite the tremendous importance of facilities in providing leisure opportunities, the importance of managing recreation facilities is often underappreciated. The ability of recreation professionals to oversee a facility can have a significant impact on the success of product delivery. By acquiring proper training and education, such as by reading this book, recreation professionals can enhance their knowledge of recreation facility management.

FUNDAMENTALS OF RECREATION FACILITIES

Many activities that are part of everyday life take place in some type of facility. In this book, **facility** particularly refers to the environments where leisure activities occur. Facilities can include naturally occurring resources, such as park areas and lakes, or they can be man-made structures, such as museums and health clubs. A facility can be indoors or outdoors. It can be as simple as a playground or as complex as an amusement park. The point is that facilities can take many forms, and they are of great importance to recreation professionals. To understand more about recreation facility management and its importance, we must first examine the fundamentals of the facilities themselves, including structures, facility management, extensiveness, uniqueness, and complexity.

Structures

Recreation facilities exist in two broad categories of **structures.** One category is **natural environments,** where little about the attraction has been constructed by people. The other category of recreation facilities includes **man-made structures** that are conceived, planned, designed, constructed, and occupied by a management system to deliver a recreation product. In simplest terms, structure type refers to whether a facility is a natural environment or is a man-made structure.

Natural Environment

Visitors to the Grand Canyon, Niagara Falls, or even local wildlife areas experience a recreation facility in a natural environment. In this type of facility, little to no adjustment is made to the natural environment. A natural environment facility might include a lake, stream, cave, or other natural resource. The ski slopes at a ski resort are another example of a natural environment that is used in a recreational setting. These natural environments often have a management component that regulates use of the area in addition to providing auxiliary services to facility users, such as boat, canoe, kayak, or ski rentals. These types of facilities may be managed by a local, state, or federal agency or private entity for use by the general public.

© Sergio Piumatti

▶Natural recreation areas have little or no change from their natural evolutionary state and can include settings such as waterways and caves.

Man-Made Structures

A man-made facility is a designated area that facilitates a process, operation, or course of activities and is conceived, planned, and built by people to deliver a particular recreation product. Man-made structures can be either indoors or outdoors and designed to deliver a specific product. An outdoor man-made facility can range from local playgrounds or tennis courts to large water parks and sport stadiums. An indoor man-made structure also can be observed in many forms, ranging from bowling alleys or fitness centers to indoor arenas or major resorts. Some structures may consist of both indoor and outdoor facilities, such as a swimming pool with a concession building and locker room. Structures can be multifaceted with many designated areas for many activities.

Facility Management

Creating and maintaining a recreation facility as a functional space requires significant management effort. A variety of responsibilities and functions help make a product available. Of particular importance is the facility, or space, where that product is produced or delivered. **Synthesizing,** or bringing the recreation product and space together as a useful experience for the user, forms the basis of recreation facility management, a support process aimed at enhancing the success of the core product and its extensions. A more direct definition of recreation facility management is coordinating a physical workplace with the employees and goals of the agency while integrating the principles of management, architecture, and behavioral and engineering sciences. Facility management is just

▶ A softball complex is a man-made recreation facility, which can vary greatly in diversity and complexity.

one component of the recreation environment, functioning in an indirect but crucial fashion by providing significant support to the delivery of the product.

Extensiveness

The responsibilities of managing a recreation facility vary greatly because of the unique requirements of each facility. Recreation facilities serve a multitude of purposes and may vary in size, volume, and square footage. As each of these grows, so does the responsibility in managing the facility. The **extensiveness,** or number of products provided at a facility, indicates the complexity of recreation facility management, which encompasses everything from risk management to maintenance, not to mention unexpected disruption in product delivery (see figure 2.1). The extensiveness of responsibilities in facility management can be demanding, and it often creates the greatest purpose of facility management.

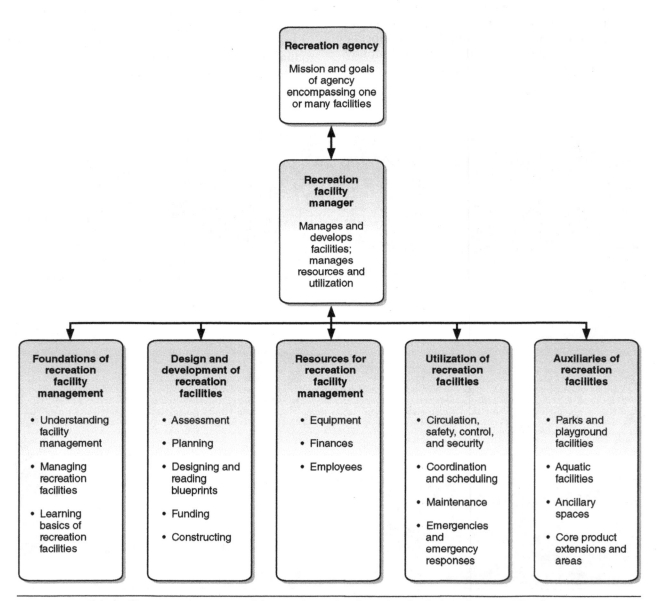

Figure 2.1 This facility management model provides a visual guide of relating the variables that create or relate to the extensiveness of a recreation facility.

Uniqueness

Each recreation facility is unique as a result of the facility design and the product being delivered. In addition, administrative styles, management philosophy, staff composition, and leadership qualities all contribute to the **uniqueness** of a facility. Although the functions of a facility manager may remain the same, it is the unique characteristics of each facility that create the diversity.

Complexity

Technology has created a more complicated work environment for management where operating equipment, efficiency systems, registration applications, and maintenance functions all affect the production and delivery processes. In many respects, facilities and equipment have evolved into a science of human behavior and structural and mechanical technology, making the daily duties of recreation facility managers more complex than ever.

RECENT CHANGES IN RECREATION FACILITY MANAGEMENT RESPONSIBILITIES

In the past, recreation administrators acknowledged that recreation professionals were responsible for managing the facilities; however, not much emphasis was placed on effective management and utilization of resources toward production or delivery. Recently, the role of facilities in the operation of organizations has taken on new meaning. Today the emphasis is on utilizing a facility to its capacity while maximizing revenue and minimizing expenses. The better a facility is utilized, the more it is perceived as beneficial to the mission of an organization. Some of the reasons for this change in emphasis include the demand for functional space, advancing technology, legal code interpretation, cost savings, protection against liability, and interest in sustainability.

Sustainability refers to operating a facility while minimizing its long-term impact on the environment. **Being green** is another term referring to ways that a facility can be more efficient and lessen its negative influence on the environment. Many leisure service organizations serve as stewards for the environment. Because of this, recreation facilities are being designed and operated using technological advancements in materials and efficiency systems that minimize their effect on the environment.

Demand for Functional Space

Unutilized space in a facility is not only inefficient; it also has negative fiscal repercussions. Today, recreation professionals are placing more importance on analyzing and assigning space to maximize its use. Functionality of space is critical to administrative plans and expectations because few facilities can afford to have space that is not being used or is creating expenses without producing revenue. In an effort to maximize resources, recreation professionals are constantly analyzing the product and seeking to make all facility areas a functional part of the production process.

Advanced Technology

With population growth comes the evolution of industry and technology. Recreation professionals 20 years ago had little concern for facility and equipment technology. A recreation professional, most times a facility manager, is responsible for coordinating, facilitating, and maintaining all systems of a facility. Properly functioning and successful facilities require highly automated systems along with technological applications integrated with human capacities. This can include anything from computer-oriented efficiency systems to technologically complicated equipment that must remain operational to meet demands. Recreation professionals face constantly changing technology that emphasizes obtaining and assessing information to enhance the efficiency of human resources and any equipment that delivers a product.

Code Interpretation

In recent years, recreation professionals have put even greater emphasis on providing equal opportunity and a safe and healthy environment to users and employees. State and federal governments have written codes that protect the welfare of all users and employees. Interpreting and applying these regulations requires professional attention to protect a recreation agency and its users.

Recreation professionals, especially facility managers, have the responsibility of ensuring that all codes are observed in the design and operation of facilities. The Americans with Disabilities Act (ADA) and the Equal Employment Opportunity Act are just two examples of legislation that influence recreation professionals. In addition, risk management policies must be considered in facility design and operations. Negligence in this responsibility can have serious consequences resulting in formal reprimands, lawsuits, termination of employment, or even the demise of an organization.

Cost Savings

Maximizing revenue while minimizing expenses has become a demanding requirement in all areas of the recreation profession. All costs related to the operation of recreation facilities have come under scrutiny by facility managers, including utilities, maintenance, labor, and facility financing. Close analysis of these expenses has resulted in far-reaching implications in terms of maintaining environments and equipment. The concept of sustainability, which has already been discussed, also has cost implications. By finding ways to more efficiently use resources, facility managers can lower the costs associated with operating a facility.

In short, recreation agencies are required to be financially accountable for their operations. Financial inefficiency can result in lost income, decreasing profits, and negative perceptions of an agency.

Protection Against Liability

In today's society, it is common for people to take legal action against anything or anyone that negatively affects their lives. Lawsuits can be expensive and time consuming and may even lead to the demise of an organization. Recreation administrators have responded to this challenge by attempting to prevent such actions. They emphasize the need to have a safe working environment for employees to protect their health, and the same consideration is extended to the people who use the recreation product. Recreation professionals must take every precaution to protect users of their product. They must establish risk management strategies and provide facilities and equipment that are free of both mental and physical dangers. Sound recreation facility management practices play a major role in protecting the administration from legal consequences while delivering a product.

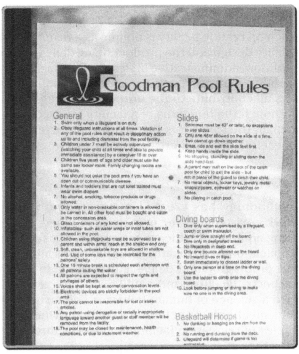

© Mary Langenfeld

▸ To provide both employees and users with equipment that is free from danger, recreation facility managers should include detailed instructions for using equipment in addition to warnings for hazards that may occur when equipment is used incorrectly.

INFLUENCES ON MANAGEMENT RESPONSIBILITIES

The responsibilities of recreation facility management can be greatly influenced, both positively and negatively, by the functionality of a facility, the employees, and the users of the facility. These factors play an important role in product delivery.

Facility Functionality

A **recreation facility** is a structure that provides space for the production of the core product and its extensions. Administrators and employees facilitate the functions and activities that occur in the facility and result in users receiving benefits from a product.

Positive Influences

The mere existence of a facility has no significance until the product production and delivery occur. If the doors were locked, there would be no use and thus the facility would not have any inherent value. However, once a management system is functioning within a facility, the facility has a reason to exist. In addition, a recreation facility and its equipment must be functional and coordinated with the production process for efficient and effective product delivery.

Negative Influences

In many respects, a recreation facility is only as good as it is designed to function. A poorly designed facility can hinder the ability to produce a product to fulfill the expectations of employees and users. In some instances, expectations are not met, time schedules fall short, equipment breaks down, delays occur, and any number of other situations arise. Some specific examples of negative occurrences include doors being locked when they should be opened, not having proper signs to direct users, dead trees not being removed, snow left on a sidewalk, malfunctioning or unclean restroom facilities, limited or no security system, missing fire extinguishers, design flaws, and unclean spaces. Some of these situations are regular occurrences that have to be monitored and controlled.

Employees

Recreation agencies strive to create an experience that is rewarding and achieves the mission and goals of the organization. Employee efforts significantly contribute to creating positive or negative experiences in relation to the product delivery.

Positive Influences

The primary goal of a recreation agency is to do everything possible to produce and deliver a product that is valued by users, and employees are a key component to achieving this goal. Agencies want employees who are competent in fulfilling their responsibilities, including providing good customer service, completing assignments in a timely manner, being organized, maintaining an attractive environment, avoiding hazards and injury, and following established risk management plans. Employees are trained to be competent through their education, certification, training, and professional development. Competent recreation professionals have the ability to anticipate problems and avoid them while presenting the product in a positive way. This competency requires a large amount of time and effort from rec-

reation professionals, and its importance should not be underestimated.

Negative Influences

Unfortunately, in some instances employees can have a negative influence on a facility as well. Employees not showing up for work, displaying inappropriate attitudes or behaviors, and performing poorly on the job can lead to users having an unsatisfactory experience.

Users

All agencies emphasize the importance of people coming to their facility to have a positive experience while using their product. These people are called **users** and can be described by any other number of terms, including *clients, customers, patients, students, children, adults, participants, spectators,* or *members.* It is important for recreation agencies to appreciate and understand the users of their facility. Understanding the users involves learning **user patterns** and using **needs assessment** strategies to better serve them. User attitudes, behavior, and ability can affect operations both positively and negatively in a recreation environment. Needs assessment strategies are discussed in more detail in chapter 4.

Positive Influences

The success of a recreation agency depends on bringing users to a facility to enjoy an activity, purchase something, or watch an event. Hopefully, the users take part in an activity of their choice and present no problems while using a facility. The goal is to provide an experience that meets users' expectations and encourages a return visit. The users' capacities, including behaviors and attitudes, will help them to fulfill their reason for visiting the facility. Recreation professionals plan for the user to have a positive experience while causing minimal distractions that are disruptive to the experiences of other users.

Negative Influences

Facility use is not always positive, and a facility user who exhibits negative behavior can become a serious disruption. User behaviors or attitudes can negatively affect operations in many ways. Users may violate rules or policies, such as smoking in undesignated areas, using foul or abusive language, initiating physical altercations, or vandalizing or damaging equipment. Or, they may just have an unpleasant attitude toward other users or employees.

More serious user behaviors could include drug and alcohol use, physical altercations, or health problems including stroke, heart attack, or seizures (see chapter 15). Recreation agencies would like to think that everyone entering a facility can be trusted to behave properly. Unfortunately, that is not always the case. Recreation professionals must recognize their responsibility to respond to negative user attitudes and behaviors. By being prepared for these concerns, they can help all users have a better leisure experience.

KEY RESPONSIBILITIES OF RECREATION FACILITY MANAGEMENT

The information presented thus far in this chapter has covered the complexity and extensiveness of facility management responsibilities. A recreation facility can no longer simply exist without regard for serving the mission, goals, and objectives of the responsible agency. Facilities must be managed to support the core product and the core product extensions. This is true whether it is small facility with part-time facility employees or a large facility that requires not only a professional administrator but various types of staff to support the overall operation. This section describes the roles and responsibilities of recreational facility managers in greater detail in relation to product delivery and human resources.

Ensure Delivery

Ensuring delivering of the core product and core product extensions involves coordinating facility areas and space. Recreation professionals assist in supporting the core product and its extensions by properly coordinating all spaces. This coordination of space includes scheduling the areas for the appropriate use and assigning the appropriate equipment and staff resources to those areas. Employees must recognize their role as part of a team in bringing together all activity and functions with the smallest amount of resistance and disruption in the production and delivery of the product. Employees should report any activity that can negatively affect the delivery of the product and then take the necessary steps to ensure proper delivery.

Operate Efficiently

Facilities and equipment play a key role in the production process. Recreation professionals have to be cognizant that the facility and equipment are functioning efficiently. They have the responsibility to make sure that space, equipment, and weather do not negatively affect delivery. Employees keep a comfortable environment with proper ventilation, maintain clean and attractive spaces for users, and apply preventive measures to areas and equipment in order to efficiently deliver the product. Other areas that require attention to operate efficiently include mechanical systems, vehicles, and electrical and plumbing components.

Be Flexible

Flexibility is crucial in managing a recreation facility. The delivery of a product can require so much attention that recreation facility managers sometimes unintentionally neglect facility-related concerns. Even though facility management responsibilities are important, they often do not receive the same kind of enthusiasm and attention as the efforts associated with product delivery. The ability for recreation professionals to be flexible and aware of the need for adjustment can play a significant role in the success of the agency. Activities that can challenge recreation facility managers' flexibility include administrative-imposed priorities, production difficulties, conflicting interests, last-minute changes, communication problems, politics among employees, and challenging personalities. Sometimes not all demands can be addressed. It is the responsibility of facility managers to address all variables to help the administration recognize how facility operations can be influenced by these demands.

Be Cost Efficient

A critical responsibility of recreation professionals is attending to the finances of the resources assigned to them and accounting for spending. Recreation facility managers find themselves assessing space in order to make it as efficient as possible in terms of revenue and expenses. Typical areas of **cost containment** include controlling utility costs by evaluating use patterns, reviewing labor costs and employee scheduling practices, and monitoring the purchase and use of supplies and equipment. Energy costs in particular have skyrocketed in recent years. Facilities are expensive to operate, and recreation facility managers need the capacity to interpret facility functions from a cost perspective and make appropriate decisions to control costs without affecting the delivery of services.

Maintain Effective Human Resources and Relations

Staffing a recreation facility requires a diverse range of employees to perform the necessary roles associated with product delivery. One of the most important functions of recreation facility managers is managing personnel and working effectively with people, or **employee relations.** Recreation professionals must be able to communicate appropriately, be sensitive, and motivate, coach, mentor, and discipline employees. Interacting well with staff requires more attention than any other aspect of the recreation profession because it is also one of the most critical aspects of a successful facility.

Closely related to employee relations is **user** or **customer relations.** By responding to user needs, maintaining open communications, and enforcing agency policy while maintaining high levels of customer service, recreation professionals can establish a positive relationship with users. The task of addressing human relations, whether with employees or users, can be challenging and

▶Working effectively with people, whether they are employees or users, is a key responsibility of a recreation facility manager because it is one of the most critical aspects of a successful recreation facility.

time consuming. Recreation professionals must have the ability to stay composed, thoughtful, organized, and tactful when it comes to human relations.

CAREER IMPLICATIONS OF RECREATION FACILITY MANAGERS

The wide variety of responsibilities associated with the recreation profession, in addition to the diversity of facilities that exist, indicate a significant demand for qualified people who can fulfill such numerous obligations. Expectations for qualified recreation facility managers vary based on the diversity, complexity, and extensiveness of the agency. Consider the variety of facilities that exist today, including convention centers, professional sport arenas, theme parks, fitness centers, community centers, resorts, cruise ships, aquatic centers, sport complexes, community parks, theaters, museums, galleries, playgrounds, and golf courses. All of these public and private facilities need trained recreation professionals.

There is no question that the role of recreation professionals is necessary and is receiving more and more attention. Career opportunities in the recreation profession have expanded dramatically in recent years due to the proliferation of new facilities in the marketplace and the understanding that there is value in employing personnel with academic training in the recreation profession. This section discusses the professional activity of the field and the numerous responsibilities of recreation facility management.

Employment

The opportunity for employment in the recreation profession is virtually endless considering all the recreation and tourism-related agencies that exist—there are more than 4,000 recreation organizations in the United States alone. Organizations with the responsibility for large populations such as military bases, community systems, colleges and universities, correctional settings, schools, hotels and resorts, stadiums and arenas, recreation centers, and hospitals provide even more opportunities for employment. As an organization increases in size, the need for greater and more formal recreation professional knowledge increases.

Overseeing resources has become a much greater responsibility in recent years. Owners and administrators understand the need for professional management of agency resources. The employment of recreation professionals will increase as organizations grow and more are created to meet the increasing demand for recreation services. Both the public and private sectors are going to continue to hire qualified people as well as contract with professionals for recreation-related services. This will create enormous growth in the profession.

Associations

Most professions have at least one formal membership-based organization consisting of professionals who meet regularly to address issues relevant to their field. People in leadership roles have created a number of associations that work to enhance the management of recreation agencies. One of the most widely recognized associations is the National Recreation and Park Association (NRPA), with a membership of 22,000 throughout the world. Since its formation in 1965, it has been meeting members' needs by conducting research, providing educational opportunities, assisting in the development of strategies for recreation management, promoting advanced technology, addressing structural and equipment needs, and providing other valuable assistance. The NRPA also includes a variety of branches and sections to meet the needs of recreation professionals in areas such as aquatics, armed forces, commercial recreation and tourism, education, and therapeutic recreation.

Many other national associations incorporate the importance of **resource management** within their mission. These associations address facilities and equipment that are specific to their particular field. Their recognition of subjects related to the recreation profession can be observed at their national and regional meetings and within their publications. They address content that reflects trends, research, safety and legal matters, professionalism, and systems of efficiency and effectiveness in facility management. Some examples of associations that are invested in the importance of recreation agencies include the National Education Association (NEA); the International Association of Convention and Visitor Bureaus (IACVB); the Resort and Commercial Recreation Association (RCRA); the American Alliance for Health, Physical Education, Recreation and Dance (AAHPERD); the American Therapeutic Recreation Association (ATRA); the North American Society for Sport Management (NASSM); the Association for Experiential Education (AEE); the International Festivals and Events Association (IFEA); the National Collegiate Athletic Association (NCAA); and the National Intramural-Recreational Sports Association (NIRSA). A complete listing of recreation professional associations and organizations is lengthy and continuing to grow as the need for information increases.

Formal Training

A variety of jobs and levels of employment require training in the delivery of products at recreation agencies. Expectations can range from no training, to on-the-job training, to formal academic learning requirements. Some roles require specific training and certifications, such as electricians, plumbers, landscape architects, golf-course superintendents, lifeguards, youth sport administrators, and personal fitness trainers.

Many agencies seek the services of recreation professionals to meet agency goals and expectations. These professionals usually come from 4-year college or university degree programs. Graduates from these programs have usually been exposed to a body of knowledge that helps guide them to competency in all areas of the recreation profession. Usually, such degrees are broad in nature and are not limited to classroom experience but also include internships, volunteer experience, and practical skills. Schools that offer recreation as a field of study hold the following objectives for their graduates:

- Demonstrate an understanding of the recreation profession and have the skills necessary to manage efficiently and effectively.
- Be able to solve problems in a systematic manner.
- Think clearly and analytically and be able to apply appropriate research information to workplace problems.
- Have effective and persuasive communication skills with a vast knowledge of technology relevant to responsibilities.
- Hold the highest of values and ethics.
- Manage responsibilities in a cost-effective manner.

- Feel equally capable in small agencies as well as large agencies.
- Understand current research and be familiar with information in the profession.
- Apply concepts and ideas in practical situations and learn from experiences.

Many schools achieve these objectives by maintaining accreditation through the Council on Accreditation of the NRPA.

Publications

It is obvious that the subjects related to the recreation profession are extensive. Committed recreation professionals who are involved in the advancement of the profession will review, assess, and research topics that have significance to their responsibilities. Their findings and significant factual or theoretical information are published in a number of formal publications, a list of which is included in appendix B. These publications show the level of involvement by people working in the field, demonstrating the significance of managing recreation facilities. Research and publication is a typical activity in any profession that helps to identify and solve problems, creating a better understanding of the profession.

SUMMARY

Recreation facilities are instrumental in the delivery of the core product in that they are the spaces where core products are available to users. Recreation facilities can take many natural and man-made forms and can be extensive in the variety of products and services they provide. The recreation facility manager must be aware of the positive and negative influences on a facility by users and employees. In order to minimize negative employee influences, recreation facility managers need to properly train employees and have opportunities for professional development. Much goes into the training of recreation professionals as they prepare to administer and deliver a recreation product. Recreation and tourism classes leading to a college degree are designed around understanding facilities in addition to the management functions associated with delivery of recreation products. These degrees help fulfill the need for a fundamental knowledge base about structures and facility management.

Learning the Basics of Recreation Facilities

At the completion of this chapter, you should be able to do the following:

1. Explain facility classification systems.
2. Understand the developmental stages that must occur in order for a recreation facility to exist.
3. Recognize the various characteristics that affect indoor and outdoor facilities.

Recreation facilities vary in diversity, extensiveness, and complexity. The nature of the recreational environment suggests that recreation professionals must have insight into the physical nature of facilities. To the average person, this information may not be evident or considered important, but to recreation professionals, such awareness is fundamentally necessary. Fortunately, many management practices are based on common sense. This chapter will help identify the many details associated with describing and categorizing recreation facilities.

STRUCTURE

For purposes of this material, all recreation facilities will be known as *structures*. As discussed in

▶Outdoor structures, like an outdoor tennis court, and indoor structures, like this dance studio, have unique characteristics and needs that a recreation facility manager must understand to be successful.

chapter 2, there is a differentiation between areas that are composed of natural environments—including mountains, lakes, streams, and forests—and planned, constructed structures. Some natural environments may have constructed facilities to enhance a product that the natural environment offers.

Recreation facilities are created through various stages that involve many people and a great deal of detail. They are designed to best deliver a core product and any core product extensions. Each recreation facility requires structural dimensions and functional design that ultimately contribute to product delivery. The following information is a basic introduction to recreation facilities and how they are classified.

Indoor and Outdoor Structures

Almost everyone uses indoor and outdoor recreation facilities in daily life. More often than not, little consideration is given to the actual structure of the facility, and even less to how and why it was constructed. Recreation structures that are easily defined as indoor facilities include sport arenas, gymnasiums, community recreation centers, dance studios, museums, bowling alleys, swimming pools, and resorts and hotels. Outdoor recreation facilities often have similar structural requirements to indoor facilities and can include recreational sport complexes, outdoor pools, tennis courts, golf courses, playgrounds, stadiums, parks, beaches, and ski resorts.

Unique Designs

No two recreation facilities are exactly alike. Golf courses present a good example of unique facility designs. Although every golf course has tees, fairways, and greens, they all have different designs. The same can be said for health clubs, hotels, theaters, museums—the list is endless. Usually, design reflects the influence of factors such as the core product, architectural interests, environmental considerations, efficiency needs, and legal requirements. The personalities, attitudes, and interests of owners can be reflected in the design as well. The unique structural design of a recreation facility can also reflect the marketing or visual promotion of the product.

© Rhoda Peacher

▶ A unique design for a recreation facility, such as this Rock and Roll Hall of Fame in Seattle, can be used as a visual marketing promotion to make users want to visit the facility.

PRODUCT INFLUENCE

No matter what the structure, fundamental to its existence is the production and delivery of the recreation product. All recreation facilities are built with the delivery of a specific product in mind that involves human creativity and initiative while managing resources efficiently. The following will create awareness of how the product and its production system are incorporated in a recreation facility.

Purpose

Indoor and outdoor recreation facilities are constructed in all sizes and shapes. As the management process becomes more complicated and the facilities become more complex, they require

▶ A golf course is a single-purpose facility and a YMCA is a multi-purpose facility.

more attention. In order to manage a facility well, recreation professionals must understand the purpose or function of the facility.

A **single-purpose facility** typically has only one product that is developed and delivered. The administrative and delivery operations may be less complicated because of the single purpose of the product being delivered. **Multipurpose facilities** incorporate two or more products. Multipurpose facilities may create more complicated management responsibilities because of the diverse applications and requirements of the products being offered.

Another way of looking at the purpose of a recreation facility is to consider the size of the user base that it attracts. Bringing large numbers of people to a recreation facility creates many responsibilities that place various burdens and technical requirements on recreation professionals. These responsibilities can result in additional staffing requirements, increased maintenance tasks, and greater attention to risk management, among other concerns.

Public or Private Recreation Facilities

Another way of determining the basic nature of a recreation facility is to examine how and why the facility came into existence. In other words, what is the primary goal of the facility? One basic premise is that local, state, or federal funds are used to support the construction and management of public recreation facilities. Many factors are involved in the creation of these facilities because of requirements associated with the use of tax dollars to fund them. The basic philosophy behind public recreation facilities is to create a service-oriented operation to meet the needs of the citizens who pay taxes for the operation and construction of the facility. Examples of public recreation facilities include sport complexes of park and recreation agencies, community centers, swimming pools, beaches, and public tennis courts. Funding options to support these types of facilities vary based on the type of facility and the politics involved.

Private recreation facilities usually operate very differently from public facilities. Private facilities rely on the income generated from the product for facility construction and management expenses. Without adequate income, privately managed recreation facilities could not remain open. Some examples of private recreation facilities include private golf courses, fitness centers, sport complexes, hotels, resorts, and marinas.

DEVELOPMENTAL STAGES

In order for a recreation facility to come into existence, a number of developmental stages must occur. Each stage has specific responsibilities and requires the completion of the previous stage before the next step can be undertaken. These steps can be thought of as an evolutionary process of recreation facility development that includes assessment, planning, design, construction, and management. Following is a brief description of these stages. They will be discussed in greater detail in upcoming chapters.

Assessment

Whether a recreation facility already exists or needs to be created, an assessment should be conducted to determine the need for the facility. The assessment stage involves careful review of the space necessary to develop and deliver a product. It includes the recognition of weaknesses such as poor or inadequate lighting, inadequate space to produce the product, accessibility problems, or changing participation trends. These observations can result in recommendations to renovate a facility or design a new facility so the core product can be better delivered. Assessment is discussed in more detail in chapter 4.

Planning

Once it is determined that a recreation facility needs to be renovated or constructed, steps are taken to formally review how the facility can be modified or constructed. Planning often involves politics, prioritizing, and influencing various levels of administration and ownership to support the project. Sometimes these plans can be either short range or long range and relate to a corresponding master plan for the agency. Many components of a plan may be conceptual. This stage is where all needs, functions, and ideas are brought up for discussion. Planning is discussed in more detail in chapter 5.

Design

The design phase recognizes the need for a recreation facility and the acceptance of the proposed plan by the administrators of the agency. This phase also includes the formal process of designing the facility using architects and engineers, who provide guidance and detailed information regarding all aspects of the structure. Consultants often assist in this process to manage the technical details not commonly understood by management. The design phase is complicated and requires a great deal of attention to detail. It culminates in the completion of blueprints and specification books that are placed out for bid to obtain a price for the job from a qualified contractor before initiating construction. The design phase is discussed in greater detail in chapter 6. The funding and the bid process is discussed in greater detail in chapter 7.

Construction

Planning requires thorough review of information to justify the design of a recreation facility and involves the assistance of consultants to provide technical details. A recreation facility begins to take an identifiable form during the construction phase. As the construction phase evolves, it may require the professional assistance of construction management firms, contractors, and subcontractors to install building materials, finishes, and landscaping. It is a complicated stage that can be very rewarding when all facets of the project finally come together. Construction is discussed in greater detail in chapter 8.

Management

A facility is developed for management to produce a product for consumption by customers or users, so once a recreation facility is constructed, recreation professionals provide the expertise to produce and deliver that product. Recreation professionals are challenged to efficiently coordinate the use and care of the facility to meet the goals of the administration. Facility management can be broken down into the management of equipment, finances, and employees. These will be discussed in chapters 9 through 11.

INDOOR RECREATION FACILITY CHARACTERISTICS

A fundamental requirement of recreation professionals is basic knowledge of the specific characteristics of recreation facilities. With that in mind, certain details about the structure should be understood. Following is an overview of basic characteristics of indoor facilities.

Site

All recreation facilities have to be located in a specific place. That location or site receives a great deal of attention as to how it will contribute to the successful delivery of the product. The makeup of the area can have a significant influence on the facility and its development. Typical site issues include natural barriers such as rock formations, drainage areas, weather conditions, and prevailing winds. Issues of site coordination also include the proximity of roads, utilities, and natural energy sources in addition to the proximity of other facilities and product competition. Additional site considerations are discussed next.

Topography

Topography can be defined as the natural condition of the land. Land conditions may be flat, hilly, or mountainous. Topography addresses area elevation, which incorporates water runoff and potential flooding. It also involves the orientation of the proposed facility (direction in relation to sunrise and sunset), layout, and potential access. A site with topographical problems could result in increased excavation costs or other management problems.

Rock

Rock at or around facilities can provide aesthetic appeal; however, in most cases it creates tremendous disadvantages in construction. Rock may require excavation, blasting, and drilling to remove it from a location. It can also create water runoff that can result in soil erosion. Rock excavation can lead to unexpected construction costs.

Water

Unfortunately, recreation facilities are often not designed to protect against the potential impact of water sources. Architects and engineers must be aware of nearby rivers and streams because flooding may result from heavy rain or runoff. Sometimes recreation facilities are built in or near flood zones in order to save on land and construction costs. Other concerns involving water include leaking roofs or facility deterioration because of dampness. Sump pumps can be used to get rid of water seepage in a facility, especially from areas below ground level. Water in and around a recre-

© Dale Garvey

▶ Rock excavation at a construction site can result in higher construction costs for a project.

ation facility can have far-reaching implications if not managed properly as part of the site design.

Production Space

The most important factors relating to the basic nature of a recreation facility are the core product, the core product extensions, and the product delivery. Recreation facilities are developed with the product in mind, and specific areas are designed to enhance the production process. The production space and its characteristics are vital to the success of a recreation facility. This section addresses a number of these factors and should help recreation professionals understand their importance.

Main Areas

The space that is necessary for developing and delivering the core product is essential to any recreation facility. Specific sizes, dimensions, and a variety of technical considerations should be considered when it comes to the design of primary product delivery areas. For example, sport fields or courts have dimension standards that must be followed to create an appropriate area for the delivery of the core product. The nature and efficiency of these areas plays a critical role in the success of the product. In the design as well as in the delivery, all such areas should be planned in a detailed manner.

Surfaces

Recreation professionals should be aware of the variety of **surfaces** that are available and how each surface may affect the production process. Generally, there are three surface areas in a recreation facility: floors, walls, and ceilings. Each surface has unique requirements to help an environment meet its intended purpose. Floors have different characteristics depending on the type of activity that will take place in a space. Common floor surfaces are carpet, hardwood, synthetic, and tile with each having different degrees of elasticity, resiliency, absorbency, and slide characteristics. A wall is a surface that acts as a sound barrier, reflects light, contains heat, and affects moisture and acoustics. Ceiling surfaces may hide conduit,

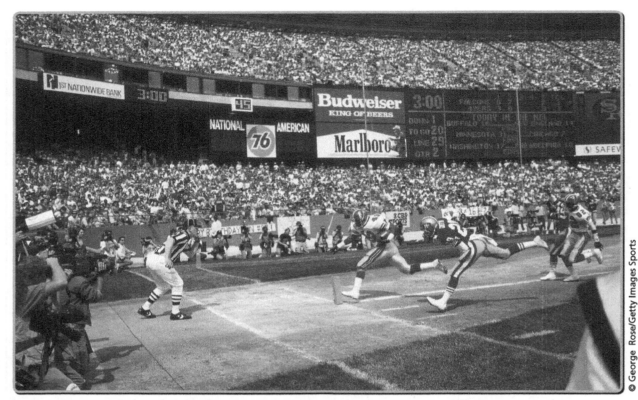

▶Candlestick Park in San Francisco is an example of a professional sports park that has two main areas, one for baseball and one for football.

electrical lines, steam lines, vents, duct work, communications wiring, and security devices. Ceilings often include a wide variety of lighting systems required for recreation facilities. Indoor surfaces will be discussed in more detail in chapter 6.

Illumination

Another factor that influences the production space is the illumination required for the area. The level of lighting can be generated by a variety of lights with different capacity and production requirements. The supply of energy required to brighten an area with light is measured by units referred to as **foot-candles.** Indirect lighting, where light reflects off surfaces, or specialized lighting that is unique to the product or area can also be used. Windows and skylights often provide natural light. These features are popular but can create glare, shadows, and water leakage.

Types of light sources include incandescent, fluorescent, and density lighting. Each source has unique characteristics to meet a variety of product needs and will be discussed at greater length in chapter 6. Supplementary lighting includes emergency lighting, night-lights, and exterior lights for aesthetics. Motion-activated lights and security lights are also important to the security of recreation facilities. The technical requirements associated with selecting the appropriate illumination for a recreation facility often require engineering and consultant assistance.

Electrical Systems

Depending on the recreation product, a variety of electrical systems may be necessary. The wiring required to accommodate these systems can be diverse. Wiring can be the common type used in homes or more specialized types required for computers, laboratory equipment, product equipment, lighting systems, scoreboards, and communication systems. All wiring must meet electrical codes as well as state and local fire regulations. Main service electrical panels should be located in restricted areas where users and employees have limited access. Sometimes secondary control panels are provided for staff members who open and close a facility. Electrical planning, design, and maintenance are complex. They are not an area to try to save money on during the construction phase due to the expensive and potentially hazardous effects of improper electrical system selection or installation. Often the services of electricians and engineers are needed to help with electrical system planning, maintenance, and repair.

Plumbing

Plumbing is a major factor in the design and operation of recreation facilities. Plumbing includes pipes that feed sinks, showers, toilets, water fountains, sprinkler systems, hot and cold water systems, and drains and garbage disposals. All of these areas contribute to the control of water flow. They require engineers and plumbers who can help with use, interpret code, and assist with maintenance.

Finishes

Finishes provide the final appearance of areas. They can be attractive or unattractive depending on the original design and ongoing maintenance. Finishes are usually applied in the final stages of a construction project and sometimes create problems for management if not completed properly. They include

- signs, which help in the circulation of facility users;
- wall coverings, including textures and durability;
- floor coverings, such as tiling, wood, and carpeting;
- keying access and exit control; and
- doors and windows.

Finishes require special attention because they are highly visible and regularly come in contact with users and employees. They can have a positive influence on the appearance of a facility, or they can result in maintenance problems and have a negative influence on the facility.

Acoustics

Acoustics is the science of sound and its impact within an area. In some indoor recreation facilities, the quality of production space can often be judged by how well sound is projected, reflected, and received. Walls and ceilings can be designed to reflect and control sound based on the product and its delivery. Sometimes interior treatment of sound involves the elimination of unwanted noises that travel through ventilation ducts, pipes, walls, and floors.

Climate Control

Management should be concerned with the comfort level of people as they use or work in a recreation facility. User or employee comfort is mostly influenced by a climate-control system, which can require specialists to ensure that environmental conditions are maintained at optimal levels.

Different regions can create unique climate-control concerns in a facility. An efficient indoor climate system is important because it can affect operating costs and user and employee comfort. Other climate-control considerations include noise levels, insulation of hot- and cold-water pipes, exhaust, damp or dry air, air turnover per hour, and thermostat control. The term HVAC refers to heating, ventilation, and air conditioning. Each of these elements is discussed in more detail next.

Heating

Heating an indoor recreation facility to a comfortable temperature requires special mechanical systems. These heating units are unique to each recreation facility based on use and capacity. Generally, a larger and more complex facility requires a more complicated and expensive heating system. Air temperatures should generally be maintained between 64 and 72 degrees Fahrenheit (18 and 22 degrees Celsius). Maintenance of heating equipment is a significant responsibility for facility management. A challenging or potential emergency situation can be created when heating equipment breaks down.

Ventilation

Ventilation circulates air in a facility and balances warm and cool air with outside air. Ventilation ducts and motors, along with the heating and air-conditioning equipment, force air to move throughout a facility. The balancing of airflow is a technical responsibility that requires specialized design, daily attention, and maintenance.

Air Conditioning

Air conditioning, the process of cooling a facility, requires the same responsibility in controlling and maintaining equipment as heating equipment. In certain regions, air conditioning can be essential to maintaining user and employee comfort levels. Air conditioning not only affects the temperature of a facility but also the humidity.

Utilities

All indoor recreation facilities must have electricity, water, and a communication system in order to deliver a product. Natural gas is another utility that may be required in certain facilities. Utilities are essential to a functional recreation facility. Outside sources have the primary responsibility of providing utilities during the construction phase and throughout the life of the facility. Utility costs are usually paid monthly. The following is a brief overview of the various utilities and how they contribute to indoor facilities.

Electricity

Electricity is an energy source that feeds equipment, lighting, comfort systems, communication systems, and security systems. It is provided by an outside source or public utility that charges for the service. Often electrical systems are so important to the production process that facilities have backup generators in the event of an outage. Facilities with extensive lighting or other equipment that requires electricity have a significant energy bill, which can create additional monitoring responsibilities for recreation facility managers.

Sanitation

All structural recreation facilities must comply with laws that require the provision of restrooms. Wastewater or sanitation systems provide for the sanitary removal of contaminated water to the appropriate treatment facility in the community. Wastewater provisions should be planned in the design of any indoor recreation facility.

Water

Water is brought to a facility by an outside source and moves through the plumbing system that feeds water fountains, restrooms, fire hoses, sprinkler systems, showers, fountains, and pools. Water can also be used with hot water or steam heating systems to provide heat. Water temperature for these systems should not exceed 120 degrees Fahrenheit (49 degrees Celsius). Water quality must be acceptable for human consumption and is monitored by local and state agencies. Facility managers are responsible for maintaining the water source so that it is safe and available at all times.

Communication

Indoor recreation facilities are served by local companies that provide communication systems, including telephone service, Internet access, security, and cable or satellite television. These systems are installed and maintained by outside agencies but are also monitored by management. Communication systems can be challenging when a system malfunctions. Facility users and employees are particularly dependent on the conveniences that communication systems provide.

Exterior

Many options are available for the exterior of recreation facilities in terms of the materials used to create the desired appearance and structural soundness. This section describes some of those components and their potential applications.

Structure

One of the most notable aspects of any indoor recreation facility is its exterior or structural appearance. The structural appearance may be designed to help market the product, meet owner or administrative wishes, or create a level of attractiveness that makes a statement to potential users. The details that affect appearance are designed within the height, angles, material, size, windows, doors, rooflines, and siding of facilities. The comparison of different recreation facility structures demonstrates just how diverse and extensive this aspect of indoor facilities can be and reinforces the importance of design and construction as part of facility management.

Landscape

Almost all recreation facilities require landscaping, which may incorporate trees, lawn, plants, shrubbery, rocks, paths, medians, and walls. An attractively designed and maintained exterior can reflect the priority that management places on landscaping. Often, maintenance systems have to be in place with attention paid to growth patterns, temperature, and irrigation. Landscaping can be a time-consuming responsibility for recreation facility managers and is a priority when appearance is a major concern.

Irrigation

Some recreation facilities develop landscape systems that require regular watering or irrigation. Irrigation systems can be aboveground or underground with the capacity to disperse water to help nourish trees, shrubs, grass, and other vegetation. Aboveground irrigation requires addi-

▶Almost all recreation facilities require some type of landscaping, as plant material and walkways are great ways to improve the appearance of a recreation facility.

tional labor hours to apply water, which can have long-term cost consequences for a facility budget. Underground systems are often automated and are programmed to come on at designated times of the day or night. Automated systems cost more to install but require less labor cost in the long term.

Irrigation systems should be adequate for the vegetation present. The cost of irrigation can be significant, particularly in regions where water is a scarce resource. Facility managers are responsible for the proper use of the system to adequately protect landscape environments and maintain appropriate appearance while conserving the use of a potentially expensive resource.

Vehicle Access

Vehicle access is important for all recreation facilities. Roads should not only be considered in terms of normal access but also in terms of how they function in an emergency situation. Roads or access drives are also important for delivery of facility equipment and supplies. In addition, roads should have appropriate signage so that vehicles accessing the facility can do so easily without delay or misdirection.

Walkways

Walkways are essential to provide safe access to the recreation facility. These surfaces can include paths and sidewalks. They should be adequate in size and should be properly lighted. They must be accessible, including the provision of ramps if necessary, according to ADA guidelines. They should be safe without holes or raised areas where users could trip and fall. During inclement weather, sidewalks should be cleared of ice and snow in a timely fashion.

Parking

Adequate parking for users and employees is a consideration for all recreation facilities. The planning agency of each community may have specific requirements for the number of spaces at a particular recreation facility. Parking is usually designed to be close to a facility; however, in some cases it could be at a distance. When parking areas are more remote, transportation in the form of shuttles, monorails, or other options should be considered to conveniently move customers from parking areas to the facility. Parking areas should have proper security and include barriers, trees, and lighting. They must comply with ADA requirements and should be designed with proper signage, making it clear where people should park their vehicles and allowing for easy access to the facility. Parking will be discussed in more detail in chapter 18.

OUTDOOR RECREATION FACILITY CHARACTERISTICS

Outdoor recreation areas can be simple or complex. Outdoor facilities include nature parks, sport complexes, waterfronts, water parks, amusement parks, golf courses, skate parks, ski resorts, lakes, and other areas. Outdoor areas often incorporate landscaping, lighting, irrigation, and walkways. Although some information parallels that of indoor facilities, there are many distinct characteristics. Insight into these characteristics is fundamental for outdoor facility management, especially as it relates to design, construction, utilization, and maintenance.

Site

Depending on the nature of the product, there are a number of factors to consider during the design and construction phases of outdoor recreation facilities. The site can have a significant impact on the daily operations of the facility. This section offers some points of information that are relevant to the site of an outdoor facility.

Size

Before selecting a location for an outdoor recreation facility, the site must be assessed to ensure that it will be appropriate for the delivery of the product. Some products have specific dimensional requirements where length, width, and height must be considered. Adequate space not only for the product but for the support systems, safety zones, landscaping, access, and parking all have to be factored into the size of the outdoor area. Extra land may be desirable because if the product is successful, expansion may occur, and land is rarely less expensive than when first purchased. Often the size of the area acquired for outdoor facilities is insufficient to meet the current or future production needs of the facility because the cost per acre limited the original purchase.

Topography

As with indoor facilities, topography relates to the natural condition of the land. Topography includes elevation, slope, orientation, and any irregularities of the surface. The topography could have a tremendous influence on the construction process, including extensive excavation costs if a significant flat area is required to deliver a product. In most instances, topography plays an important part in the design of natural outdoor areas.

Land

Composition of ground surfaces can be altered by design and then construction. In this fashion a desired surface can be created that contributes to the delivery of the product. Land concerns can affect maintenance, user safety, and landscaping costs. Some outdoor product areas require special surfaces that could include mixtures of topsoil, clay, and sand. Outdoor land areas could also include rock and swampy areas that could be designed as part of the outdoor recreation facility or simply removed. Changes to land areas can drastically increase construction costs and maintenance expenses. The characteristics of the land chosen for an outdoor facility can have short- and long-range implications.

Surrounding Vegetation

Surrounding vegetation refers to the trees, shrubs, and other plants that are already on-site or will be added to the site in the construction phase. Strategically placed vegetation can help reduce surface temperature, retain water, and minimize the effect of wind on the activities provided at the facility. It is wise to be aware of vegetation growth patterns and how they can affect the ecosystem of the area.

Water and Storm Water

Water located at or draining through a site can have an affect on the recreation facility. Natural water sources can aid the growth of vegetation, or they can cause erosion, flooding, and vegetation deterioration. Storm-water management is the process of diverting surface water and draining subsurface water to drainage structures such as curbs, gutters, and detention or retention ponds. Storm-water management is an important factor in the design of any outdoor recreation facility, and when not managed properly, it can have significant cost implications or require extensive rehabilitation to the area.

▶ In most instances, a varied topography plays an important role in outdoor recreation facilities whereas a varied topography at the site of an indoor recreation facility could cause significant increases in construction costs.

Climate

Climate refers to weather conditions such as temperature, rain, wind, humidity, and snow and how each can affect an outdoor recreation facility at various times of the year. Climactic conditions can have a major influence on the success of product delivery. Certain regions experience intense weather conditions such as heavy rainfall or lack of rain, excessive heat or humidity, or extreme wind that can affect the safety of participants and employees. The ability of recreation facility managers to evaluate these climactic conditions and schedule the use of the facility around potentially hazardous weather events can be important to the efficient use of a facility. Managers must evaluate climactic conditions in order to avoid dangerous situations. It is also important to be aware of the long-term effects of climate conditions on ground surface, vegetation, and ultimately the product.

Production Space

Unlike indoor recreation facilities, outdoor areas require a management approach that accounts for the uncontrollable factors involved in the outdoors. This section discusses outdoor characteristics and their relation to production space.

Layout

Layout refers to how areas work together or relate to one another in the overall use pattern of the facility. Whatever the product, the areas of an outdoor recreation facility should be organized to maximize land use with the least amount of wasted space. Product dimensions, standards, and requirements dictate how much space is needed for the proper layout. For example, multi-purpose fields that have dimensions large enough to accommodate football as well as soccer fields are more efficient and provide more flexibility for management than a facility only designed to accommodate football.

Orientation

Facility orientation relates to the angle of the sun and prevailing wind direction and how they affect product delivery. The orientation of an outdoor recreation facility should be given the greatest

▶The proper orientation of an outdoor tennis facility keeps the sun out of the eyes of participants.

attention during the design and construction to avoid an improper orientation. Some products could be seriously affected by orientation to the sun at certain times of the day or prevailing wind direction. For example, baseball and softball fields with home plates in an eastern or western orientation cause players to have the sun in their eyes at sunrise and sunset. Golf-course holes are often designed to incorporate prevailing wind direction. For example, longer holes are designed to be downwind, whereas shorter holes can play into the wind to increase their difficulty.

Drainage

Unexpected or excessive rain can affect the delivery of products at an outdoor recreation facility. Drainage is the removal of unwanted water from a facility in an effective and timely fashion. Some sites have natural drainage, creating few problems. Lack of drainage can seriously affect product delivery by creating delays, inconveniences, and significant maintenance expense, which can result in dissatisfied users and potential loss of user

interest and facility income. Excessive water that does not drain properly can also damage surfaces and vegetation, making areas unattractive and less functional.

Barriers and Fences

In the outdoor production process, barriers and fences can play an important role in segmenting areas as well as controlling use. This can be important for creating secure and isolated use and limiting potential liability. Some facilities require controlled access with specific entrances and exits. Barriers and fences can provide the necessary control methods to limit access. They limit user access to one area and direct users to the entrance for the purposes of tracking attendance and collecting any fees associated with use of the product. They can also help control unwanted noise, sun, and wind.

Landscape

One of the intrinsic benefits of an outdoor recreation facility is users' appreciation of being outdoors. An attractively designed outdoor area that blends into the terrain can create a high level of satisfaction for users. The proper selection and placement of flowers, mounds, trees, shrubs, and walkways that tie together the landscape of an outdoor environment can enhance users' experiences. Proper use of landscape techniques can contribute to the appearance of the facility and assist with drainage, layout, and orientation.

Surfaces

One of the most significant considerations in the delivery of products at an outdoor recreation site is the land surface used for the production process. Outdoor surfaces can influence safety, maintenance, and user satisfaction. Surface qualities to consider include function, appearance, resiliency, longevity, and maintenance costs. Several outdoor surface options are available, and they will be discussed in chapter 6.

Support Systems

Fundamental to most outdoor recreation facilities are the support systems that contribute to product delivery. These systems are usually not noticeable to users, and they can be very specialized depending on the nature of the facility. Listed next are examples of support systems found at outdoor facilities.

© Rhoda Peacher

▶ A barrier fence can be used to control user access and provide security for a facility.

Access

Critical to any outdoor recreation facility is the ability for users to easily access it. Many facilities are located away from populated areas, with external and internal roads, internal sidewalks and paths, and parking areas created to support the facility. The design should facilitate access without hindering users' ability to get to where they desire. Signs and directional indicators should be placed for easy visibility. Pedestrian and vehicle traffic flow should eliminate hazards and congestion, incorporating barriers and fences to help control movement, crowds, emergency vehicles, program registrations, and other activities.

Utilities

Utilities at most outdoor recreation facilities play a significant role in safety, product quality, and maintenance. Most outdoor recreation facilities would be hampered without the availability of water, electricity, and communication capacity. Some outdoor recreation facilities can function without utilities; however, complex outdoor facilities have a greater need for utilities. Water is required for irrigation, drinking, and delivery of food and beverages. Electricity is required for equipment, lighting, security, public-address systems, scoreboards, and food and beverage services. Communication systems may not be necessary for all outdoor facilities; however, they can be extremely important for more diverse operations. Communication systems include telephones, security systems, computers, and televisions.

Lighting

Many outdoor recreation facilities depend on lighting to deliver their product beyond daytime hours. Illumination systems for outdoor recreation facilities can be elaborate and may require certain levels of lighting for television broadcasting. There are various types of lighting for specific facility needs such as safety, specialized product activity, parking areas, and security. The importance of lighting at some facilities may necessitate specific maintenance arrangements to ensure uninterrupted service.

▶Some facilities require just enough lighting to be able to play a game at night, whereas some facilities require lighting at television broadcasting standards for a night game to be shown on television.

Irrigation

An irrigation system is critical for outdoor recreation facilities that emphasize appearance and protection of surfaces and vegetation. Product delivery can cause damage to turf surfaces. Heavy use combined with heat and humidity can destroy turf unless it is maintained properly. An irrigation system can be beneficial to the maintenance and protection of these areas. Irrigation systems can be as simple as handheld hoses and as complicated as computer-controlled irrigation systems. Irrigation, along with chemical applications, is critical for maintaining usable, safe, and attractive outdoor surfaces.

Conveniences

It is common for recreation facility users to stay at a facility from 1 to 3 hours. During this time users may require areas such as restrooms, food and beverage services, public telephones, and water fountains. These conveniences can vary from facility to facility, with the more complex facilities requiring more sophisticated spaces to deliver the conveniences. These areas are usually identified with appropriate signage so they are easily located.

Seating

Spectator viewing areas are a significant element of delivering a product at many outdoor recreation facilities. Depending on the activity, the seating required can vary greatly. Seating areas can range from open space for chairs to permanent stadium seating. Seating options may require the use of ushers, ticket takers, ticket sales, and other considerations. The management of seating areas takes on greater responsibilities as the facility becomes more complex and diverse.

SUMMARY

All facilities are unique, yet they can be categorized in different ways. The most common way is to categorize facilities as indoor or outdoor. Facilities falling in both of these categories have many factors that influence the ability of recreation facility managers to deliver the core product. Details relating to indoor facilities include the site, production space, climate control, utilities, and exterior. Concerns related to outdoor structures include site, production space, and support systems. Many of the topics in this chapter are elaborated in greater detail in the upcoming chapters.

Design and Development of Recreation Facilities

Funding for a facility must be justified in order to move forward with a facility design project. Justification is often established through assessment strategies incorporated by the organization. Information learned through assessment also is important in the planning of a new facility. A planning committee examines facility needs and communicates them to a design team that makes decisions about the function, structure, and aesthetics of a new facility. The design team works with an architect; together they follow building codes and ordinances to develop building blueprints and other construction documents. These documents are then used by the construction manager and contractors in building the project.

Assessment

L E A R N I N G   O B J E C T I V E S

At the completion of this chapter, you should be able to do the following:

1. Understand the influencing factors that should be considered when reviewing facility needs.
2. Recognize and apply the various forms of formal and informal needs assessment.

Assessment is commonly practiced in leisure services. Because recreation agencies strive to provide a product that users desire, it is important to understand user needs. Knowing what users want guides recreation agencies in determining what to provide. Assessment isn't only about understanding user needs, however; it is also about determining if it is feasible for the agency and within the scope of its mission to provide the product. Assessment is an important part of determining what programs a recreation agency will offer. It is also important in facility design and development.

Before a recreation facility development project begins, an assessment must take place. The **assessment** determines the need for a facility and greatly influences the construction. Several methods ranging from very formal to very informal can be used to assess the need for a facility development project. Formal methods can take the form of a needs assessment, **feasibility study,** or **prospectus**. A needs assessment helps an agency understand additional services and facilities that users would like to have provided. A feasibility study is used to determine if a facility design project is financially viable for an agency. A prospectus is a formal summary of a business venture or facility project that may be used to justify funding or attract investors. These assessment tools involve considerable research and are objective in nature. Informal methods used in assessing facility needs are more subjective and may include informally gathering facts that reflect facility needs through observing user behaviors or having casual conversations with facility users.

In the case of constructing a new recreation facility, the assessment process begins with a recognized need either initiated by the recreation service provider or by a **stakeholder.** Once this need has been identified, it is important to assess its importance to the recreation agency and users. Often, consultants are commissioned to help with the assessment of need for a new facility or renovation of an existing facility. Consultants are an important resource that may be required to justify the expense of a recreation facility project. Assessing the need for a facility project can involve many considerations. This chapter discusses factors influencing facility assessment, as well as assessment techniques. In addition, an initial proposal process is suggested that communicates the message of facility needs to administrators and decision makers.

INFLUENCING FACTORS IN FACILITY ASSESSMENT

Influencing factors in facility assessment are the issues that need to be reviewed and documented when observing concerns at an existing facility or recognizing a void that a new facility could fill. The more serious and potentially expansive the project, the greater attention these factors will require in order to influence desired results. The following factors may also be applied to facility equipment limitations: safety, satisfaction, participation, efficiency, comparison, and modernization.

Safety

A fundamental requirement of any recreation facility manager is to provide a safe environment for all users and employees. A safe environment includes a place where risk of harm has been minimized as much as possible. When assessing facility safety, it should be determined if the design or use of the facility creates the potential for injury. Some examples of possible injuries include the following:

- A hardwood basketball court surface may have warped boards or worn surface areas that create a tripping or slipping hazard.
- An outdoor tennis or basketball court may form cracks and create the potential for injury to players.
- An outdoor baseball or softball facility may create the potential for injury to spectators or players from foul or overthrown balls.
- A beach or swimming pool facility creates liability due to the risk of drowning.
- A parking lot at any type of facility will have moving vehicles and people walking in the same area and thus can be dangerous.
- The design of a golf hole may be a problem when drives hit off the tee regularly land in areas of another hole, putting other players at risk of injury.
- The outfield fences of two baseball or softball fields that are too close together create a potential problem when home runs from one field fly into the other field.

Recreation facilities follow national standards recommended by the governing body of a par-

© Human Kinetics/Neil Bernstein

▶ Pools present greater liability concerns for management because of the risk of drowning.

ticular sport. Some tourism facilities follow the requirements established by a franchise hotel chain. Architects may also provide recommendations for facility design that will minimize risk factors. When building a new facility or updating an existing one, it is necessary to be aware of minimum safety requirements and to consult experts to minimize risk. Unsafe facilities become a liability and may necessitate changes to eliminate problems. These changes may require some type of **facility project** that could result in repairs, renovation, or new construction. Safety concerns can play a big role in the need for facility improvements or development.

Satisfaction

Satisfaction is the degree to which the expectations of facility users have been met. The degree of satisfaction among users can be critical to the success of the core product. Facilities only have one chance to make a first impression on users. A perceived lack of quality or a bad experience while using a facility can negatively influence users' satisfaction. Recreation facility managers should attempt to ascertain how users perceive the facility and what additional services they might enjoy. Facility managers can conduct participant satisfaction surveys, establish suggestion boxes, or simply interact with customers to determine their level of satisfaction.

User satisfaction can be affected in a negative way if the facility is perceived to be of substandard quality. For example, golfers may become dissatisfied with the conditions of a golf course if regular maintenance isn't performed, such as fertilizing, overseeding, or controlling weeds. Negative experiences from poor customer service can also contribute to unsatisfied customers. Determining who the users are and their requirements for satisfaction can help recreation facility managers be aware of problems that need to be corrected or facility needs that are unmet.

Participation

In regards to recreation facility management, participation refers to the number of people using a facility. Facilities are designed to accommodate a specific number of users. Even the best architects and consultants have difficulty predicting the usage patterns and capacity of the facilities they design. Some recreation facilities become so popular that they attract more users than

▶ Cracks or worn areas on court surfaces may cause user dissatisfaction.

they were designed to accommodate. Facility managers should recognize when usage creates a sense of overcrowding, which can have a negative impact on the experience of users. For example, an increase in the use of fitness equipment at an indoor facility can lead to participants waiting in line for a particular piece of equipment. Eventually, this condition may cause users to become dissatisfied with management for not providing additional equipment or adding space to accommodate the increased interest in personal fitness equipment. This may lead to users seeking another recreation facility that has sufficient space and equipment.

Efficiency

Efficiency relates to how well management uses a facility and other resources in maximizing revenue opportunities while minimizing expenses. Efficiency also involves allocating space to allow for maximum use without decreasing customer satisfaction. Often the design of a facility can cause problems with the efficient provision of the core product or core product extensions. For instance, if a user wants to access a basketball court, but to access the court they must walk across a running track; this is not efficient design because crossing the track could be problematic for both the basketball and track users. However, recreation facility managers can also influence the delivery of a product with their management practices. By regularly evaluating staff, equipment, and facilities, managers can evaluate whether goals and objectives are being achieved in an efficient way. They should conduct regular assessments to determine whether a better facility improves the efficiency of the product delivery. If so, this is another factor that can help demonstrate the need for facility improvements or a new facility.

For example, the design of an older golf-course clubhouse may have separate areas for the pro shop and concessions. A renovation that combines the two areas into one not only improves the efficiency of the space for users by allowing one-stop shopping for registration and purchasing golf supplies and concession products, it also improves efficiency for management by eliminating the need to staff two separate operations.

Imagine that a recreation facility manager is responsible for an aging ice arena that has outdated and poorly performing compressor (ice-making) equipment. This equipment consistently

▶ This pro shop area in a golf clubhouse also includes a concession area, which allows management to deliver services more efficiently and cost-effectively.

fails, causing regular closure of the facility. As a result, customers are frustrated that they can't access the facility as intended, and over time they begin to find other facilities to pursue their recreational interests. This causes a loss of revenue for the ice arena and creates a poor image of the facility management. Clearly, this inefficiency indicates a need for a facility improvement or renovation.

Comparison

All recreation facility managers, whether in the private or public sector, are involved in comparing their product with those of their competitors. This comparison, often called benchmarking, is initiated so that management can ascertain what products their competitors are providing and how well they are providing them. There are many aspects of facility operations to compare, but the most important is determining how the facility measures up in space functionality and appearance. Most recreation facility managers want to be in a leading position or at least equal with their competition. Benchmarking with comparative information from other facilities can be a valuable

tool in influencing administrators to recognize the need to renovate or construct a facility.

An example of comparison can be found in the development of resorts in Las Vegas. Before designing a new resort, it is common to examine other resort and casino developments in the area. Over the last 20 years, the resort and casino industry has seen tremendous changes in the amenities offered. At one time, resorts simply consisted of hotels with casinos. Now they include entertainment venues, shopping malls, restaurants, amusement parks, water parks, and nightclubs. These developments are a result of benchmarking.

Modernization

Many facilities are constructed with state-of-the-art materials and furnished with the most up-to-date equipment. Over time, however, they become outdated as new technology creates improved options in a variety of facility applications. Recreation facility managers should be attentive to these new options and plan and budget for necessary improvements.

New trends developed by industry manufacturers and interests expressed by users can create

de an existing facility or
'ties can quickly become
mprovements available
ilities can also be less
ke advantage of new
s either updated or
can lose customers
acilities that have been
...ated. Technology advancements
...als and equipment could prevent injury,
create new experiences, improve user satisfaction,
and even improve the appearance of the facility.
Managers of fitness-related facilities frequently
see the introduction of new exercise equipment,
products, and services. Those managers who don't
replace old equipment with the latest updates find
themselves at a competitive disadvantage with
other facilities in their market. This is also true
for tourism-based facilities, including hotels and
resorts. Upgrading rooms, replacing old furniture,
and adding new televisions, video games, and
Internet access can enhance the appeal of such
facilities.

INFLUENCING TECHNIQUES IN FACILITY ASSESSMENT

Sometimes the previously mentioned influencing
factors may not be enough to create awareness
about facility needs. There are additional techniques that recreation facility managers can use
to generate support for the renovation or construction of a facility. These techniques can help
persuade key administrators, board members,
financial officers, and politicians to recognize
the circumstances that warrant attention and
response. They include site visits, surveys, focus
groups, comments and opinions, petitions, and
history.

Site Visits

One of the best ways to bring about support for
facility projects is to take a representative group of
users and administrators to visit existing facilities
with problems or other facilities that may become
a model for a new facility. These site visits are
usually done in the early stages of development or
renovation. They are particularly effective because
personal experience and a visual assessment of
facility problems or of a state-of-the-art facility is
a great way to create insight for what needs to be
accomplished. This personalized experience can
create support among administrators, politicians,
and financial backers.

Surveys

Surveys have traditionally been the most common
method for obtaining information. Several types
of surveys solicit input. An internal survey can be
used to obtain user or employee feedback regarding the facility. An external survey can be used
to obtain comparative information from facilities
with similar products. This type of external comparative survey is often called a benchmark survey
and shows facility managers how their facility
compares with a competitor's facility. External
surveys can also assist in discovering user or
employee habits, interests, attitudes, and opinions. Obtaining objective facts about comparable
facilities resulting from a formal benchmark survey
can be instrumental in persuading administrators
of the need for a facility project. Benchmark surveys should be in written form with appropriate
questions that can be completed within a reasonable time frame. Surveys that compare one facility
with another or written survey information from
users and employees can be used to convince
administrators that a facility has deficiencies.

Focus Groups

A **focus group** consists of people who represent
various segments of users and stakeholders.
These users are simply asked to share their
thoughts on subjects related to facility development. Focus groups generally range in size from 5
to 12 participants. A facilitator guides the group
through questions regarding facility needs. For
example, one focus group may consist of females
and another may consist of males. These groups
could be broken into smaller segments based on
marital status, age, income level, and other characteristics. The value of having different groups
is that each group possesses different opinions
and values. A better understanding of the needs
of different groups can play an important role in
facility design.

Comments and Opinions

The comments and opinions of facility users
and employees are important to consider when
assessing user satisfaction. These pieces of information, both positive and negative, can provide

valuable feedback for management. Both users and employees offer a distinct perspective of a facility that management does not have. User and employee opinions should be solicited in several ways. Comment cards and suggestion or complaint forms should be made available for users and employees to express their concerns, and online options should also be provided as an alternative to written forms. User and employee dissatisfaction should be carefully reviewed and concerns should be addressed in a timely and professional manner. Concerns should be documented in a system that maintains a record of such information. At some point, these records could be an important resource to help convince administrators of the need for a facility project.

Opinions can also be solicited through opinion polls. Opinion polls are designed to obtain user opinions regarding satisfaction with the condition of a facility or the perceived need for a new facility. Such polls are usually conducted via telephone calls or face-to-face interviews. They tend to have fewer than 10 questions and can be completed in a few minutes. For example, users may be asked if they are in favor of the development of a community theater or if they would be interested in attending events put on at a community theater. This is a good technique for getting an initial impression about a project that is under consideration, especially if public support is important.

Petitions

A **petition** is a document stating that people are in agreement on a certain issue. The petition usually has a formal statement that helps demonstrate interest in a project. Petitioning is a common form of creating awareness of the need for a project, especially if the user has an interest or a stake in the facility. The petition should include petitioners' identification information, such as name, address, and telephone number, along with a signature. Sometimes petitions have certain legal requirements. These requirements often pertain to funding sources being considered for a facility project and may vary by location. More information about petitions can be found through government agencies. Recreation facility managers should research these requirements if petitions are being considered.

History and Asset Management

Recreation facility managers should know the history of the facilities for which they are respon-

sible. Important information regarding the age and condition of the structural systems and construction materials are crucial information that affect the need for timely replacement or renovation of infrastructure. Many facility materials have predictable life spans. For example, roofing materials typically need to be replaced on a 20- to 30-year cycle. Paving materials in parking lots typically have a 15- to 20-year life cycle.

Facility managers should document when materials and equipment are installed and then budget accordingly for when the products or materials need to be replaced. Documentation of facility renovation projects and the age and condition of materials and equipment is critical to maintaining the appearance and condition of a facility. The concept of documenting the age and predicted life span of facility components is called **asset management.** The history of a facility can track outdated building materials, design and layout, mechanical systems, and structural equipment including doors, windows, and railings. It is also important to document whether the core product has changed but the facility has not. An example of this would be a facility that was originally designed for physical activity, such as an aerobics room or dance studio, but is now being used for office space or for educational purposes. Visual documentation through pictures is an excellent way to represent changes in physical condition. Sometimes just showing how outdated a facility is creates the necessary support for a facility project.

INITIAL PROPOSAL

An initial proposal is a formal way of communicating the need for a facility improvement or the construction of a new facility. This written proposal is developed by the party creating a case for the facility project, usually a facility manager. The proposal is typically delivered to administrators, owners, investors, governing bodies, or other agencies that control the funding for a facility project. Far too often, assumptions are made, concerns are not communicated, and needed progress is not made if a written statement of need is not developed with as much detail as possible. The initial proposal is not a formal plan but merely the communication of the need for a facility project.

An initial improvement or development proposal is a reasonable and professional way of communicating a facility project need to the entities that must approve such a project, and it can prove to be helpful in gaining initial interest and support for the project. The proposal is usually in written form. Occasionally, a verbal presentation would be effective as well. When drafting an initial proposal, it is necessary to think in terms of the need, limitations, problems, and opportunities and to present the information in written form as outlined here:

- **Need or title:** Assign a specific name or brief description of the project that identifies what is wanted or needed.

- **Recommendation:** Make a formal, short statement of the action or outcome that is wanted or desired. The request should be concise and complete.

- **Introduction:** Express the need by creating awareness of the forthcoming proposal. Provide an overview of what the document will contain and what it is to accomplish.

- **Rationale:** Create a case with logical points of information. Emotional points can also be used to support the proposal. Establish the fundamental reasons for the need.

- **Justification:** Provide real data, background information, and other facts to support the need.

- **Funding:** Summarize the fiscal needs and opportunities of the facility projects. Share the income and expenditure information. Identify estimates or real construction or renovation costs involved. Show how the proposal fits the funding circumstances.

- **Impact:** Share the potential benefits of the project.

- **Conclusion:** Summarize by restating the recommended need.

SUMMARY

In most instances, the need for a facility project must be justified. This can be done by addressing shortcomings of current facilities and by showing user demand for facilities. There are a variety of formal and informal methods for assessing influencing factors in a recreation facility. Surveys, focus groups, comment cards, and petitions are some of the methods that a recreation facility manager may use to understand user needs. It is important that recreation facility managers can apply these assessment strategies as they are essential in making the case for facility development and preparation of initial proposal for facility projects.

Planning

LEARNING OBJECTIVES

At the completion of this chapter, you should be able to do the following:

1. Define the concept of project planning and explain the two approaches in project planning.

2. Recognize the types of individuals who should be included in a project planning committee.

3. Explain the concept of a master plan and understand how it is related to facility planning.

4. Explain the various development options and when each would be appropriate.

5. Understand the purpose of the project statement and the components of it.

It could be said that nothing is more important in the development of a recreation facility than the planning process. This critical stage is where ideas are transformed into details that result in solving problems faced by recreation facility managers. Planning is the foundation for all subsequent steps. It is particularly important to plan ahead and forecast future facility needs as much as is possible. The planning stage is distinct from the earlier assessment process in that it incorporates all information gathered in the assessment phase and transforms that information into the details that result in the construction or renovation of a recreation facility. This chapter will outline the planning process, including planning options, planning committee members, master plans, planning considerations, program or project statements, and development options.

PLANNING OPTIONS

Project planning is the systematic anticipation of information through careful thought and documentation to develop a facility project. The project is planned to meet user and employee needs and to remedy the shortcomings observed during the assessment of an existing facility.

There are generally two ways to accomplish the planning of a recreation facility:

1. Administrative approach
2. Participatory approach

The chosen planning option is usually determined by the nature of the agency, whether it is in the public or private sector, as well as the management philosophy of the agency. Also, the political environment of the agency may influence decisions. For instance, in an agency where employees do not work well together or have a difficult time making group decisions, an administrative approach may be best. In the situation where an administrator is trying to get employee support for an idea or create a stronger bond between employees, a participatory approach may be used. Understanding both of these options should assist recreation administrators in determining which option is best suited for a particular project.

Administrative Approach

The administrative approach to planning a recreation facility is used in the private sector or at agencies where little or no tax dollars are supporting the project. In this approach, although there may be a number of people involved in the process, all technical information, responsibility, and priorities are decided by the administration or executive level. If users, facility staff, consultants, and other specialists are involved, it is only because an administrator sought their input in order to make informed decisions regarding the project. Progress revolves around the administrator or a small team of recreation professionals who are responsible for all planning aspects of the project. The administrative approach often does not appreciate the value of involving others in the planning of a facility project.

Participative Approach

A second type of planning process is the participative approach. This process is typically used in public agencies where tax dollars are the primary funding source for facility projects and input from those who pay taxes is encouraged and sometimes required. The participative process involves a variety of people who have an interest in the project. Input is solicited from users, employees, consultants, and other specialists, and their role in bringing about the project is emphasized. This process assumes that administrators may not possess all the knowledge necessary to determine recreation facility needs. It is a good way to obtain additional information, as well as encourage involvement and gain support. The level of participants' involvement varies during different phases of the planning process based on the need for their contribution. The participative process can be a time-consuming approach, but if carefully managed, it can create a positive team atmosphere and generate support for the project.

PLANNING COMMITTEE MEMBERS

Recreation facility projects can incorporate input from several people, especially when the project is being completed by a public recreation agency with a participative approach. These teams come together because of a vested interest in a facility. Interest from these groups can be strong because of their perceived impressions of existing facility limitations or other problems. Planning committees often consist of user representatives, staff representatives, administrators, consultants, maintenance representatives, and architects.

User Representatives

User representatives are key members of planning committees because they can provide a unique perspective resulting from their hands-on experience with an existing recreation facility. A user representative represents the people who use the facility on a daily basis and actually experience the core product. The user perspective can provide insight to user needs and interests. In a facility with many programs and activities, there may be multiple user representatives.

Staff Representatives

Staff representatives are staff members at a recreation agency. Production representatives are the employees who are specifically involved in making the recreation product available to users. They are responsible for all the details involved in bringing the core product and core product extensions to the users of the facility. They also bring a unique perspective to the planning process. Staff representatives are knowledgeable about the shortcomings of existing facilities and can provide unique

observations because they live the consequences of facility limitations that affect their ability to deliver a product. Their insight can be invaluable in the planning process, and in most instances, multiple staff members are involved.

Administrators

The facility administrator has the ultimate decision-making authority in the process of planning a recreation facility in the public sector. In the private sector, the owner plays this role. Administrators or owners bring a unique perspective to the project because they oversee the master plan for the facility. They have the responsibility for determining priorities and making project budget decisions. Their support and commitment in a facility project must be secured before progress can be made.

Consultants

Often when there are facility limitations, weaknesses, or even the lack of a desired facility, a consultant, or expert, is hired to help with the interpretation and application of what needs to be done to improve or construct the facility. These consultants are usually specialists in the

© iStockphoto/Pamela Moore

▶Architectural consultants aid in the planning process when expert assistance is needed to guide a construction or renovation project.

design, architectural, or engineering fields and bring detailed information, trends, and insight to a project. Consultants assist the committee or administration in developing concepts, ideas, and alternatives while establishing priorities in the building project. Their expertise can guide a project, taking into consideration agency strengths and limitations, construction and equipment needs, cost assessment assistance, comparative data, and other factors that may be involved. Consultants usually have access to comparative information regarding recently constructed recreation facilities similar to the one being planned.

Maintenance Representatives

The maintenance representative, or service specialist, is often forgotten in the planning process. This is an unfortunate oversight that can prove costly to the recreation agency and can contribute to major problems after the construction process is completed. The maintenance representative speaks for those involved in the support functions that include custodial help, equipment setup and takedown, landscaping, storage, equipment repair, waste removal, delivery of equipment and supplies, and daily operations. During the planning process, the maintenance representative can provide insight to the tasks that support the delivery of the core product and core product extensions. Operational maintenance personnel possess details of day-to-day functions that other personnel usually do not. They bring a unique perspective to a project that, if overlooked in the planning process, could create problems in the delivery operations.

Architects

An architect may be hired before the planning phase of a recreation facility project. Almost any level of facility project, whether a minor renovation or new construction, requires the services of an architect. Architects bring expertise and technical knowledge that is invaluable, and the selection of an architect should receive special attention. A request for proposal (RFP) is used to solicit the services of qualified architects for a recreation facility project. This document usually defines the scope of the project and asks respondents to list similar experiences or qualifications that qualify them for this particular project. Selecting the appropriate architect for the project is a crucial step in the planning process. Architects bring together concepts, needs, techni-

cal information, related facts, and interests, creating the documents that guide others to construct the recreation facility. (These documents will be discussed later in this chapter.) Typical fees for an architect range from 8 to 12 percent of the total construction cost.

MASTER PLANS

The work of the planning committee is strongly influenced by the master plan of the agency. This document is vital to any agency and is essential in the planning process. The **master plan** is a formal, comprehensive document that identifies the needs of the facility and prioritizes which construction or renovation will occur. A master plan is usually maintained at the administrative level of an agency. It creates a road map for facility needs in the future. Often, master plans contain an inventory of existing agency facilities, including their current condition and any need for renovation. The master plan goes beyond just facility needs. It outlines demographic details about a community, acknowledges results from needs assessments, and outlines current and future agency practices. In addition, the master plan details an agency's short-term and long-range plans and includes action plans for implementing those goals.

A master plan is the result of considerable research, evaluation, and anticipation of future needs. It is absolutely necessary when there is progressive thinking and concern for ongoing success. The complex master-plan process is greatly affected by the size of the agency, the human and financial resources available, and the planning skills of the people involved in the planning process. In many instances, agencies hire consulting firms to facilitate the process.

The master plan provides details in a logical sequence for the renovation or construction of recreation agency facilities. It takes into account the desires and needs of users and employees and projects those needs in a long-range time frame of 5 to 15 years, providing the big picture for the future. The development and maintenance of the master plan is continuous and is characterized by times of highly active planning. The master plan is constantly updated as new information becomes available and resource allocations change. For example, if funding sources for projects become available, a facility project may become a more immediate priority. Most of the time, however, it is a lack of financial resources that alters facility projects and delays them until adequate resources become available. Recreation facility managers should be aware of the master plan and recognize its importance, especially in facility development.

PLANNING CONSIDERATIONS

No matter what planning option is being applied or the status of the master plan, certain planning considerations must be taken into account. All planning brings together information and ideas that will need to be assembled at a later stage in the design of a facility. In this stage there are preliminary points of information that need to be realized as part of the planning process, including site analysis, assessment information, structure, cost projections, and area impact.

Site Analysis

As a facility project is being considered, the potential location of a new facility should be discussed. This phase of planning is called the **site analysis** and takes into account a variety of factors related to the specific location being considered for a facility. These factors include environmental aspects of the site such as terrain, water, topography, climate, and vegetation. They also include zoning or governmental restrictions as well as any historical significance the site may have. Community planning agencies may have ordinances that limit the amount of land that can be developed in certain areas. Tree and green-space preservation along with storm-water storage often limit the development of certain sites. It is also important to understand the accessibility of utilities to the site, such as electrical, sewage, telephone, and cable, because it could affect development costs. Often projects are delayed or cancelled because of site problems. When preparing a site analysis, it essential that a site visit is conducted where these issues can be identified.

Assessment Information

All information obtained from the assessment stage should be thoroughly reviewed and used in the planning process. This information needs to be considered in an approach that applies human intuition with the facts that have been gathered. The content acquired in the assessment process

▶ The location of this waterway site might possibly influence the development of certain facilities at this site.

leads to the formal architectural design work, or more specifically the project or program statement.

Structure

Ultimately, some type of facility is going to be developed during the planning process. That end product must be depicted in a way that can be shared with others in the process, including those who will provide the funding. Although the final design may not be ready after the site has been analyzed, the potential structure should be conceptually represented. The detail and technical aspects of the facility are not necessary in this step; however, an architect will likely need to create these details at a later stage. The potential structure can be represented in a sketch, rendering, or schematic design and should reflect the information obtained in the assessment. The architect is typically responsible for preparing this representation.

Cost Projections

After a structure has been conceptualized, cost projections are necessary to make progress and create recognition for financial support. All project decisions ultimately are based on the cost to construct and operate the facility. Comparing a new facility with a similar facility already in existence may help provide a ballpark estimate of cost. Architects can also provide a cost estimate based on their knowledge of construction costs in the area where the facility is being constructed. However the informal cost projection is determined, it is a critical component that helps bring a cost reality to the planning process.

Area Impact

Area impact takes into account the impact the area will have on a facility and vice versa. In understanding how an area affects a facility, information such as demographics of the **service area** is important. The service area refers to the people within a certain distance of a facility who will be served by the facility. Distance can be measured in actual geographic distance from a facility, or it can be measured in the amount of time it takes to get to a facility. For instance, many users of a campus recreation facility may be within walking distance. If this is the case, the walking distance from dormitories, classroom buildings, or off-campus student living areas is important. When a facility is being developed where users will have to drive, drive times and access routes play a more important role. With a community center where people may walk and drive, the service area should be understood in walking and drive times. In the instance of a resort or other tourist destination, it is important to consider accessibility of major highways and airports. For a resort to be successful, it must be accessible to users. This has been one of the key reasons why tourist attractions such as Disney World and Las Vegas casinos have been so successful—they are accessible from airports throughout the United States.

Area impact also includes how a facility project will affect the area around the facility. Types of area impact include economic impact, environmental impact, and social impact.

- **Economic impact** refers to money that will be spent by users and employees directly at the facility or indirectly at other businesses in the community. For instance, other businesses in the area may benefit from the addition of a new facility, and the new facility may benefit by being located near other businesses. Having multiple businesses in the same area creates a **gravity effect** where people are drawn to the area by a specific business but end up spending additional money at nearby establishments.

- **Environmental impact** is typically negative and relates to the damage that the facility may have on the environment, such as pollution or overuse of natural resources. As discussed in chapter 2, this is an opportunity for facility planners to thinks in terms of sustainability as they strive to minimize environmental impact.

- Social impact explains how the facility will affect people living nearby or using the facility. It includes understanding the demographics of users and of residents near the facility.

DEVELOPMENT OPTIONS

Various development options must considered when planning to enhance a facility or correct existing problems. The solution could range from a simple repair to a completely new facility. Most facility development projects involve one of the following: repair, renovation, retrofitting, or new construction (including facility expansion). All four options require construction work where specialists or contractors may be necessary to complete the project. Each option has its own application to solving facility limitations.

Repair

Probably the simplest and most common improvement option is the repair of an existing facility. Repair is desirable when a facility simply wears out from overuse or age and needs to be rebuilt or made to function as it was intended. These are usually minor problems where the goal is to revitalize the area to its intended state. Repairing a facility and restoring it to sound condition helps in the production and delivery process. A major concern in repairing a facility is the cost. If the cost to repair a facility is high, it may be more reasonable to build a new facility. In many instances, if the cost to repair a facility is more than half the cost to build a new facility, then building a new facility is a better option.

Renovation

Renovation requires greater planning and supervision than repair. **Renovation** is the rehabilitation of an existing facility with steps taken to rearrange the space within an existing structure. This option usually includes changes that create a more efficient operation or a more attractive facility, make the facility safer, or meet legal requirements. Some structural changes are usually made, but using the original structure is a crucial planning component. Renovation is less expensive than new construction and usually extends the life of the existing facility. The downside is that the facility is often unusable during the renovation. In addition, the old structure may experience other problems in the future. The same guidelines regarding costs for repairs apply to renovation: If the cost to renovate a facility is more than half the cost to build a new facility, then building a new facility is a better option.

Retrofitting

The concept of retrofitting involves updating a facility. More specifically, **retrofitting** is the addition of new technology systems to an existing facility. Retrofitting is used when the space in a facility still has a high degree of functionality but needs to be modernized. New systems can include security systems, computer systems, video, cable, identification-card equipment, and ticketing. Usually the function of the facility sees few changes to activities during retrofitting.

New Construction

New construction of facilities is the most significant and demanding of the development options.

▶While a new facility is under construction, the old facility can still remain in use so no revenue is lost during construction.

New construction involves planning a facility from the establishment of a need for development through the final stages of moving everything in. An advantage of new construction is that it is an opportunity to develop the ideal facility and still maintain the function of the old facility without losing revenue. This option also includes expanding an existing facility. A tremendous number of details are involved in the planning process for a new facility. It is critical for recreation professionals to understand the complexity of constructing a new facility. All information remaining in this part of the book will address detail involved with planning such an undertaking, including design and blueprints, funding, and construction.

PROJECT STATEMENT

Throughout the planning process, it is important to document information and use it in the formal facility design stage discussed in chapter 6. This documentation is called the **project statement** or program statement and will assist in the architect's design of the facility. The information comes from the early assessment and planning efforts, and when approved by administrators, it represents the first formal commitment in the planning process. A project statement is a written report on a variety of subjects providing direction for the architect. It serves as a transitional document between planning and design. This information specifically relates to the facility and its purpose. Often facility managers lack the expertise in accurately bringing this information together. Consultants or architects can provide the necessary assistance in this stage and can play a valuable role. The more detail and clarity the statement has, the easier it will be for the project designer to translate it into a building or facility design. The project statement should include the following: objective, basic assumptions, trends, comparisons, primary space, auxiliary space, service needs, space relationships, environmental impact, and equipment and furniture list.

Objective

The objective describes the specific delivery of the product and how the facility will serve its potential users. It should state the ultimate objectives or anticipated outcomes of the facility, including the primary core product delivery areas of the facility. For example, if an aquatic park is being designed,

one of the primary objectives is to provide a facility that will increase the number of aquatic activities for users.

Basic Assumption

The basic assumption cites how the facility will solve the current problems. This section often identifies current programs and facility offerings. In addition, it identifies desired activities and programs that the agency would like to offer. This statement makes it is easy to identify problems in the current facility and to highlight how the renovated or new facility will address the weaknesses by describing new activities and programs that can be offered.

Trends

Trends reflect how society is changing and how those changes affect demand for the product. Trends may play a major role in driving the project.

▶ Activity pools are a recent trend at water facilities.

They could include technological advancement, legal requirements, population growth in the area, and public interest in the core product.

Comparison

The comparison section compares existing facilities or competition and how they affect the core product and core product extensions of the proposed facility. It also reflects comparisons with recreation facilities in other communities that may be perceived as desirable. This comparison can create political support for a facility. It demonstrates how existence or nonexistence of a potential facility will affect the market in the community and how a new facility might compare with others.

Primary Space

The **primary space** section describes the spaces needed to provide the core products of a facility. The description should include a list of the spaces that are being planned within the facility, along with the size and function of each area.

Auxiliary Space

The **auxiliary space** section lists the name and sizes of the spaces for the core product extension areas. Included in this list should be the requirements of the area and any specialized equipment to be used. This includes food and beverage outlets, equipment rental or checkout space, office space, parking, and reception or lobby areas.

Service Needs

The **service needs** section describes the maintenance functions that the facility will require. This part of the program statement is often poorly addressed by the planning team and is sometimes even omitted. An indoor facility could incorporate areas for custodial service, trash removal, storage, plumbing, mechanical rooms, custodial supplies, and equipment repair. An outdoor facility could incorporate equipment storage for mowers and other equipment, space for lighting systems, and irrigation controls. This category would also include the use of maintenance at the existing facility and how it will contribute to the future success of the facility.

Space Relationships

Space relationships describe how all the areas of a facility will relate to one another, including flow of users and employees throughout the facility. In other words, how do users and employees use the facility, and what spaces should be located in

▶A running track at a track and field facility is an example of a primary space.

proximity to each other? This section summarizes the overall operation of the areas, bringing them together effectively and efficiently. It could include diagrams depicting the functional relationships of all production and delivery areas.

Environmental Impact

The environmental impact section provides a detailed description of the surrounding environment and how the facility may affect it. Typical environmental concerns include water runoff, vegetation impact such as tree loss or other loss of natural vegetation, facility appearance, and effects on habitat. It is important that the architect appreciates the concern of the community about how the facility will influence the environment and takes into account opportunities for sustainable development.

Equipment and Furniture List

The equipment and furniture list is an extensive identification of all moveable and fixed facility items. It includes all the items, mechanical and otherwise, that will be needed for the production and delivery operations of the core product and core product extensions.

SUMMARY

Planning is a key element in the development of a facility. By establishing a diverse planning committee and considering many sources of information in the planning process, agencies can communicate their facility requirements to an architect and a facility can be designed that meets the needs of the agency and its stakeholders.

Designing Recreational Facilities and Reading Blueprints

LEARNING OBJECTIVES

At the completion of this chapter, you should be able to do the following:

1. Explain the roles of the various individuals on a design team.
2. Recognize the design considerations that the design team should be reviewing.
3. Identify the types of surfacing and when each should be used.
4. Identify the types of lighting and when each should be used.
5. Recognize the construction documents used in the design process.

The **design stage** of a facility development project brings together all relevant details of assessment and planning and integrates them into documents that describe what will be constructed. At this stage, the facility starts to take shape. All of the ideas generated during the earlier stages must fit together, similar to a puzzle. The design team usually develops multiple variations of a design that are discussed and reworked to come up with a final design. The final design is a commitment that represents the formal start of a project. At this stage, design documents and blueprints are prepared.

DESIGN TEAM

The **design team,** which usually evolves from the assessment and planning stages, consists of a team leader or architect, administrators from the recreation agency, and the construction manager. This group works together in a cooperative and professional fashion to bring the project to reality.

Team Leader or Architect

Usually the **architect** serves as the team leader. The selection process for an architect has to be thorough, ensuring that the architect has adequate experience in planning and designing facilities. There are several items that should be considered when selecting an architect:

- Check the architect's references and previous work for quality of work.
- Determine if they have done similar jobs.
- Talk to contractors that have worked with the architect to get their feedback on the architect's work.
- Contact the Better Business Bureau (BBB) to see if they have had any reports filed against them.
- Check with the local building and code office to see if they have worked with the architect.

Architectural services can be expensive; fees usually range from 8 to 12 percent of the total construction budget. For just a $100,000 project, that could be $8,000 to $12,000! Because of their expertise, however, architects are an absolute necessity for design teams. The architect is typically responsible for all design documents and drawings associated with the project and understanding legal and technical requirements. In addition, the architect is expected to be knowledgeable about trends in design and materials.

Design documents will ultimately reflect an architect's training, experience, and ability. When additional consultants cannot be afforded, an architect can provide predesign services such as project statement assistance, funding ideas, and site selection. Available funds or projected costs often dictate which architectural firm will be chosen. It is important to hire the best firm based on a balance of qualifications in combination with the fee proposed for services provided. Allowing politics and personalities to affect the selection process can result in less than satisfactory results.

Administrator

Along with the architect, the administrator is an important part of the design team. It is the administrator who will make many, if not all, final decisions. Depending on the project, this could be a demanding role not only during the design stage but also throughout the project. The agency administrator is typically the leader of the organization. Often the facility manager has significant decision-making responsibilities, too, or at the very least assists the administrator.

In developing a design, the design team will be involved in many long meetings. It is often the administrator's role, along with the architect, to organize and plan these meetings. The meetings will require special leadership skills in addition to an understanding of the content involved in developing a recreation facility design. The administrator also plays a key role in keeping the project on schedule. Although the design team as a whole works to put together the schedule for construction, the administrator has the responsibility of seeing that it is adhered to. All projects have a timetable for completion that is determined by factors such as

- desired groundbreaking date,
- seasonality,
- desired opening date,
- changes to the design,
- inclement weather,
- construction material availability,
- subcontractor availability, and financial concerns.

No one has more invested in the project than the administrator, aside from the recreation facility manager. This person is the only member of the design team involved in operation of the facility once it has been completed. The administrator is also the member of the design team most affected by the politics surrounding the project. It is critical for the administrator to commit to the project timetable and keep others focused on the desired completion schedule. The administrator's role is to monitor everything from the perspective of the agency, avoiding undue expense and keeping everything on schedule and reflective of the final design. This can be an enormous responsibility, especially with the many project stages and people involved in the process.

Administrators must be able to recognize, analyze, and discuss the details associated with delivery of the core product because, more than likely, only the administrator has specific knowledge about the core product and will be able to guide a successful design process. Administrators also need to be able to interpret costs for all the product areas and equipment that will be in the new facility, in addition to representing all facets of product and delivery operations. During design, some desired options may need to be eliminated because they are too expensive, do not work in the project plan, or are not as high a priority. It is the administrator's role to keep costs within the project budget by making these difficult decisions, all while ensuring quality control. The administrator functions as a watchdog to make sure that all plans and design information are followed according to design specifications. Sometimes, architects have their own agenda, bias, or interest in a project. It is the administrator's job to make sure the architect adheres to the design goals and represents the interests of the agency.

Construction Manager

During the construction phase, it is desirable to hire a construction management firm to observe the stages of construction. A **construction manager** from the construction management firm ensures that contractors are performing the work as described in the blueprints and specifications for a project. If this option can be afforded, it usually costs 5 to 10 percent of the cost of construction. This service can be well worth it to ensure that contractors adhere to the design specifications and the agency gets what it paid for.

DESIGN CONSIDERATIONS

Before an architect can complete actual design work, certain topics need to be discussed by the design team. Some of these discussion topics include the site, type of structure, materials, lighting, mechanical systems, and aesthetics. Team members should provide insight into and direction on these design considerations because they will help guide the architect.

Site

Where a facility is going to be located is a major design decision. The product will revolve around where it is produced and delivered. A recreation facility can have significant impact on the surrounding area; many facilities are substantial in size and have requirements that can affect the surrounding community. Some sites will not have all the requirements needed to comply with product delivery. By conducting a comprehensive site analysis during the planning stages, as discussed in chapter 5, the design team will have the information necessary to discuss site issues.

Structure

The structure needs to be conceptualized in the design discussions for what it is intended to provide or produce. Much of this information comes from the project statement as discussed in chapter 5. Considerations that should be conceptualized are

- structure size,
- structure shape,
- area impact, and
- square footage.

These factors need to be reviewed thoroughly by the design team. As mentioned, all of the structural details are derived from the information in the project statement. These discussions help to create a mental image of the facility that is important to the architectural work.

Materials

Structural material refers to the materials that are used to construct the facility, including wood, cement, steel, concrete block, fiber cement board, stucco, or a combination of these. There are a variety of factors which may be considered when determining what materials to use. The most important factor is related to the purpose or function of the facility. For example, a facility that will be hosting events such as concerts will want to select materials that will allow for heavy speakers and lighting to be suspended from the roof of the facility. Closely related to function are the design needs established by the architect. The design needs of the architect reflect facility function and aesthetic needs identified by the architect and design team. The environment is also an important factor to consider as some materials may be better to use in certain types of environmental conditions. In addition, local government may have requirements on the types of materials that can be used. A more recent trend related to selecting structural materials is selecting materials that are sustainable. Sustainable, or green, structural materials means that the material is a renewable resource and environmentally friendly. There are numerous sustainable structural materials that include sustainably harvested wood, baked earth, calcium sand stone, and clay, just to name a few. Regardless of the factors that influence structural material selection, materials are a significant part

of the project because they influence all other areas of design in addition to representing a major cost in the total budget for a project.

An important consideration when discussing materials is the type of **surfacing** that will be incorporated in the facility. Surfacing in facilities refers to floors, walls, and ceilings. Walls and ceilings primarily serve as space dividers, but they can be important in program delivery because they have acoustical characteristics and moisture absorbency qualities. Typical materials used in interior walls and ceilings include wood, ceramic tile, plaster, and concrete blocks. Ceramic tiles and concrete blocks are the best materials to have in spaces where there will be moisture, such as in a locker room or aquatic space. In office space and classrooms, plaster and wood is more common because of acoustical characteristics. Walls and ceilings are important to the structure of a facility, but floor surfacing has a greater impact on the types of activities that can take place in a facility. Types of flooring in a facility should be considered based on the purpose of specific areas in the facility. For example, a room that will be used for a dance class is going to have a different surface than a locker room or lobby. Surfacing

▶It is becoming increasingly common for construction teams to use sustainable materials in the building or renovation of a recreation facility.

also varies for outdoor structures such as a playground. Surfaces beneath areas where children will be climbing will be different than other areas of a playground area. Outdoor surfaces will be discussed in greater detail in chapter 16.

Floor Surfaces

The surface used in an indoor area should be selected based on the area function and the cost of the surface. The area function refers to the activities that will take place in the area. Some activities may require a surface that has some **elasticity,** or give, such as basketball or aerobics. Other activities, such as volleyball or dance, may require **slide characteristics,** or how much the surface allows people to slide when participating in activities. In addition, if an area is going to be exposed to water, such as in a pool area, that may also affect the surface that is selected.

In considering costs, it is necessary to calculate initial cost, installation costs, maintenance costs, and life expectancy of the surface. This information can help determine the cost of the surface over its lifetime.

Four types of flooring are commonly used in indoor facilities: carpet, vinyl, synthetic, and hardwood.

• Carpet is typically used in lobby areas, office space, and spaces where no physical activities take place. Carpeting is the least expensive of the surfaces, but it only lasts 7 to 11 years before it needs to be replaced. It is relatively easy to maintain but offers no elasticity and limited slide characteristics. Carpet should not be used in areas that may get wet because it easily stains and hosts mold growth.

• Vinyl surfaces usually involve tiles used in locker rooms or spaces that have limited physical activity, such as office space or classrooms. They are easy to maintain and can last up to 15 years. The slide characteristics vary depending on the type of finish, but vinyl surfaces typically have good slide characteristics. They are not commonly used in areas of physical activity because they have no elasticity.

• Synthetic surfaces, which are also called *poured* or *rolled surfaces,* can have considerable elasticity but typically have limited slide. These surfaces are common to multipurpose rooms and weight rooms, and they are occasionally found in gymnasiums. The life expectancy of a synthetic surface is approximately 20 years, and maintenance is inexpensive.

• Hardwood surfaces are the most expensive type of surface, and they also have higher maintenance costs than the other surfaces. However, a hardwood floor can last up to 50 years. Hardwood surfaces also provide elasticity and slide characteristics. This type of surface is often used in aerobic areas, dance areas, and gymnasiums.

Outdoor Surfaces

Outdoor areas also require various surfaces, including natural stage (existing soil and dirt), turf (sod and grass), masonry, concrete, asphalt, and aggregates (gravel, graded stone, and cinders). Most outdoor spaces take advantage of the natural surface, such as grass or dirt. These types of spaces can include parks, trails, open spaces, or playing fields. The surfaces are typically in areas that are meant to be in a natural state and where **fall protection,** or a safe play experience, is not an issue. Specialized areas such as those designed for playgrounds require surfaces designed for a safe play experience. In other words, usually there are no elevated areas in these spaces where someone can fall. In addition, asphalt and concrete can also be considered outdoor surfaces and are used in parking lots, basketball courts, and skate parks. Such surfaces are typically selected because of functionality and are used in spaces where vehicles may travel or where activities require a hard or smooth surface.

When discussing outdoor surfaces, the major concern is usually the type of surface used in areas where children play and where there is elevated equipment. Because of this, the most important consideration in these areas is fall protection, which is similar to elasticity in indoor surfaces. Some surfaces provide better fall protection than others. Four important considerations in fall protection include the following (see chapter 16 for more details):

1. **Accessibility** to play areas is governed by the ADA. Playgrounds and play structures should be accessible to everyone. Detailed guidelines regarding elevated play structures and the number of play structures that should be accessible are available through the ADA (www.ada.gov).

2. **Adequate use zones** are the areas beneath a structure that should have a surface that provides fall protection. Standard use zones include the space beneath a piece of equipment plus at least 6 feet (2 meters) around. Slides and swing structures have larger use

zones and are governed by the Consumer Product Safety Commission (CPSC). Any new structure should include manufacturer guidelines for use zones.

3. Structure height obviously affects falls, and the greater the height of the structure, the greater the fall protection surfaces should provide. Depth of material is closely related to the height of the structure; however, some materials provide greater fall protection and do not need as much depth to maintain safe fall protection. Detailed information regarding how deep certain materials should be in relation to the height of equipment is available from the CPSC at www.cpsc.gov/.

4. Outdoor surfaces for playgrounds are considered either **loose fill** or **unitary,** and the depth of these materials are major consideration in fall protection. Loose-fill surfaces are the most common and include sand, pea gravel, wood chips, and mulch. These loose-fill surfaces are common, but they are not considered accessible. Acces-

sible loose-fill surfaces include synthetic wood fiber and shredded rubber. These surfaces also provide better fall protection and do not need to be as deep as the other loose-fill surfaces. Loose-fill surfaces need to be added to on a regular basis in order to maintain adequate depth. This is not an issue with the unitary surfaces, which have some of the same characteristics of indoor synthetic surfaces. However, unitary surfaces can be expensive and need to be professionally installed. Unitary surfaces are surfaces that can include a rubber mat or rubberlike materials bound together to give it a consistent depth and shock absorbency qualities.

Lighting

Similar to surfacing, a variety of spaces within a facility require lighting. The most important consideration for lighting is the number of footcandles given off by a light, as discussed in chapter 3. Larger areas or areas where physical activities take place typically require more illumination

▶Loose fill surfaces are very commonly used in playgrounds, but not all loose fill surfaces are accessible. However, unitary surfaces can be very expensive and also need to be professionally installed.

than other spaces. Three types of lighting are used in facilities: incandescent, fluorescent, and high density.

Incandescent Lighting

Incandescent lighting is the type of lighting that many people have in their homes. These lights give off the lowest amount of illumination, require regular replacement, and are the least cost efficient of the three types of lighting. They are inexpensive to purchase, they are easy to install, and there is no delay when they are turned on. Incandescent lighting is usually found in office and administrative areas.

Fluorescent Lighting

Fluorescent lighting has a longer life expectancy than incandescent lighting and is much more cost efficient because it is only slightly more expensive but provides up to four times the illumination. There is a slight delay in turning these lights on and they make a dull sound. Fluorescent lighting is used in offices, small classrooms, storage spaces, and other administrative spaces.

High-Density Lighting

High-density lighting is the most-cost effective and efficient light source because of the high levels of illumination it provides and because it lasts much longer than incandescent and fluorescent lighting. It provides the most illumination of the three types of lighting. There is a delay with most high-density lights, and they usually cannot be turned off and back on quickly. There are three common types of high-density lights:

- Mercury vapor lighting is the least expensive and least efficient of the three.
- Metal halide lighting is the most common high-density lighting used in recreation facilities.
- High-pressure sodium provides the greatest illumination and is the most cost effective of the three.

High-density lighting is used in gymnasiums, large activity spaces, aquatic areas, and outdoor fields.

Mechanical Systems

All facilities have mechanical systems that contribute to facility utilization. These systems can be categorized as indoor or outdoor support systems. Indoor support systems include communication systems; HVAC systems; and plumbing installations. These systems require additional space in a facility, which is especially relevant to indoor facilities. Some outdoor support systems, such as irri-

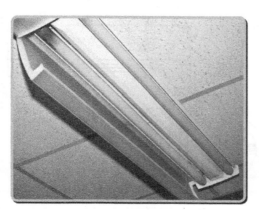

▶The three types of lighting used in recreation facility areas are incandescent (left), fluorescent (center), and high density lighting (right).

gation and lighting systems, also require specific spaces. Usually architects and engineers provide all necessary details for these areas; however, the design team needs knowledge of the mechanical support systems required for the project.

Aesthetics

The appearance, or aesthetics, of the facility is also a discussion topic for the design team. Will the facility appear institutional, or will it be more attractive? The appearance of a structure depends on the style and feel envisioned by the design team. Team feedback provides information for the architect to accomplish the appropriate aesthetics. The nature of the product, in addition to project funding, plays a big part in determining the overall aesthetic design and appeal.

Schematics

One of the design options an architect can present is a preliminary mock-up or schematic of the project. This is accomplished by working with the program statement, site, and related information. The schematic is a graphic or model form that represents the details planned for the project. In this stage, an architect may produce a schematic drawing or model. Both can be helpful for the design team and anyone else interested in the project. A schematic drawing or model allows all interested parties to see a visual representation of the facility (see figure 6.1).

Drawing

Most projects of any significance have a schematic drawing that represents the general design of the facility. This representation shows the core product and core product extensions and may include diagrams of walls, rooms, stairwells, corridors, outside topography, landscaping, and access roads. Drawings represent only a few details of the project; they are simply used to create a feel for the facility. They also provide a footprint, which shows how the facility is laid out as part of the overall site.

Model

Often with large projects, a schematic model is developed so that the actual exterior of the structure or facility can be visualized. A model is a tabletop rendition of the facility that may include landscape, elevations and roads, and a fairly accurate depiction of how the facility will look. This model can prove to be valuable when trying to influence project funding. Models can also be drawn using computer generated graphics.

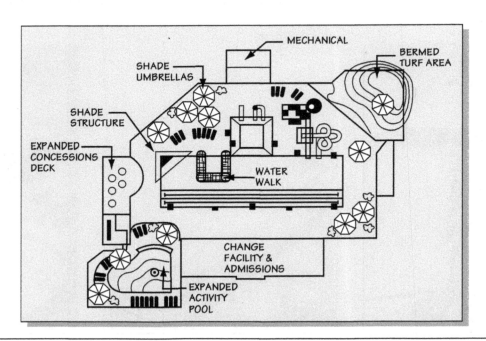

Figure 6.1   A schematic depicts what a renovated or new facility will look like when completed.

Adapted by permission of Water Technology, Inc. (www.wtiworld.com).

▶A schematic model helps to visualize the actual exterior of the facility on the site where it will be located.

© iStockphoto/Chlorophylle

BLUEPRINTS AND DESIGN DOCUMENTS

As with all facility projects, design documents that are completed by the architect represent a great deal of general and specific information that is communicated to the contractor. At various times during design, the administrator and the rest of the design team review these design documents to make sure everything is going as planned. These documents are called blueprints. They can be a drawing of a particular part of the project or can be integrated and overlap with other sections of the blueprints. Blueprints become more individualized as the size of the project increases. Larger projects also require more pages and detailed sections that depict all the elements of the facility. Design documents cover all areas of a project, including the demolition or preparation, site, structural, mechanical, electrical, landscape, and other design documents.

Demolition or Preparation Blueprints

Most projects require some degree of land preparation for construction. The demolition or preparation blueprint represents the design that will lead to removal of existing material and vegetation from the site. In addition, the preparation component may include changing the elevation of the site by removing or adding dirt to level some areas and raise others. This phase may also include moving utilities as well as the demolition of existing structures, roads, sidewalks, and trees. Some planned facilities may be in a flood zone or may require leveling, which could necessitate filling in the area with extra dirt or other material to support the structure. Some sites may have too much elevation that requires removal of dirt or other materials. The demolition or preparation documents show exactly what is expected to prepare the site for construction.

Site Blueprints

The site blueprints show how the facility is situated in relation to the entire area where it will be built. Site blueprints include information about utilities, environmental concerns, zoning ordinances, and land requirements. They also identify where all aspects of the facility will be placed on the site, including existing structures, access roads, sidewalks, landscaping, utility lines, and drainage.

Structural Blueprints

The first blueprints to be prepared are the structural prints. They are usually extensive drawings that diagram all rooms, corridors, stairwells, entries, exits, floors, and ceilings, as well as other details. The structural section of blueprints may require many pages to capture the necessary information. It shows the areas that will house the core product and its extensions with appropriate details that indicate exactly what needs to be developed structurally. Structural blueprints not only reflect the overall facility layout but also the foundation plans. The foundation is what supports the structure. In an outdoor facility, structural blueprints represent the different areas and their layout with separate blueprints of any buildings that may be required.

▶Demolition is not just removal of an existing building; it may also include removal of existing vegetation, roads, sidewalks, trees, dirt, or other materials from a site.

Mechanical Blueprints

Mechanical blueprints have separate design information but are almost always integrated with the structural blueprints. Anything that is mechanical in the facility is drawn in detail, including plumbing, heating, air conditioning, ventilation, lighting, and drainage. Mechanical drawings require special knowledge that administrators and architects usually do not have, so engineers often help the architect with the detailed interpretation and application of the technical requirements.

Electrical Blueprints

Another section also integrated with the structural blueprints is the electrical blueprints. No utility requires greater knowledge and adherence to technical standards to ensure safety than electricity. This section of blueprints is often too complicated for the design team, so the project engineer provides the technical expertise required. Everything that requires electricity in order to operate and support the administrative and delivery operations is represented in these blueprints. All detailed wiring is shown with diagrams identifying exactly where and how everything is located, sized, and connected. The project engineer must define the degree and level of all systems such as communication, lighting, and security, as well as HVAC systems. The actual locations for all electrical outlets are shown (including hookups) for cash registers, public-address systems, junction boxes, computers, alarms, security cameras, lights, and other electrical devices.

Landscape Blueprints

Landscape blueprints diagram the details of exterior aspects, such as trees, shrubs, mounding, fences, grass, flowers, and irrigation systems. Details include the type and number of plants, grasses, trees, and other vegetation in addition to how to plant and where to locate these materials. Other information includes maintenance of plant materials. The landscape blueprint is a significant element of outdoor facilities that include many types of vegetation, such as parks.

Other Design Documents

There are other design documents that are not in the form of a blueprint but may be vital to the design of the facility. These documents include information regarding the structural equipment, finishing plan, specifications, and laws, codes, ordinances, and standards.

Structural Equipment

Often the structure of a facility requires certain equipment to be attached to the facility. This equipment, such as a sound system or scoreboard, is necessary for the production of the product and is usually integrated into the structural blueprints showing designed locations, hookups, and installation requirements. Structural equipment is considered part of the facility and in some cases the facility could not be what it is designed to be without it. Other equipment and furnishings are purchased later with the input of the administrator and architect. Additional equipment needs do not require as much detail in the blueprints as other components.

Finish Plan

Although not an actual blueprint, the finish plan, or schedule, is a design document that cites information for the finishes for all facility areas, including paint colors, types of doors and hardware, floor coverings, ceiling types, light fixtures, sinks, toilets, partitions, and windows. During design, the administrator provides input about finish details. It can be difficult for the design team to understand and interpret all of the options associated with a finish plan. An architect can provide assistance in interpreting the information. The layout and organizational scheme is a condensed way to present information to the contractor, subcontractors, and vendors.

Specifications

The **specification book,** also called the *spec book,* describes the blueprints in a narrative, descriptive format. Although not always used, these documents provide detailed directions on each item to be used in the project. Spec books contain a greater number of pages and details as the scope of a project increases. They provide information for contractors, subcontractors, and vendors and are written so that every page is coded in reference to the appropriate blueprint. This cross-referencing assists users in interpreting what they are to do so that there can be no mistakes from the intended design.

Laws, Codes, Ordinances, and Standards

Laws, codes, ordinances, and standards exist that all architects must follow in the design stage of any project. This information must be incorporated in both blueprints and spec books. Failure to adhere to laws, codes, and local ordinances can cause delays with the timeline or even substantial monetary losses for the agency if discovered after construction has been completed. Common requirements governing facility design and accessibility are included in the ADA guidelines (www.ada.gov) for all types of building construction. In designing a playground, requirements and guidelines established by the Department of Children and Family Services (DCFS) and Consumer Product Safety Commission (CPSC) need to be considered. Other examples of requirements include municipal building codes, fire and life safety codes, National Register of Historic Places (NRHP) requirements, and environmental ordinances. The details regarding electrical, security, plumbing, access and exit areas, and building capacities all have to conform to local or state codes and laws.

This information should always be drawn in the blueprints and stated clearly in the spec book. Requirements may be missed or ignored by contractors and subcontractors if their work is not monitored. Architects and engineers are fully aware of these requirements and are required to meet them by law or they will be penalized by their professional associations. These requirements do not end with the design phase but are also prevalent throughout the construction stage of a project and use of the facility. This is one of the primary reasons why an architect should remain on contract with a project through implementation of the design and the conclusion of the construction. For a small construction or renovation project where the services of an architect may not be necessary, the builder or contractor may be responsible for adherence to requirements. Recreation agencies can hire construction managers or rely on local inspectors to monitor this kind of work.

READING BLUEPRINTS

All design projects require blueprints, whether they involve rehabilitating a building or designing a park. A critical role in designing a recreation facility is reading and interpreting blueprints. It is important for recreation professionals to be able to visualize what has been drawn, no matter how complex it may appear at first. Blueprints are a road map that offers formal information about all aspects of the project, diagramming how everything should be developed.

The architect is responsible for the majority of the blueprint content. The engineer is also involved in preparing the blueprints. An administrator or designated representative, often the facility manager, may be required to interpret the blueprints in order to assist with the project. This responsibility can require technical knowledge and an understanding of terminology used in design and construction documents. With study and practice, reading and interpreting blueprints will become second nature.

To gain a clearer perspective, recreation professionals must imagine themselves in the area that is detailed in the blueprint, orient themselves to the view and direction of the drawing, and visualize the finished project. Most importantly, evaluating the blueprints is the last chance to represent, correct, or change what will ultimately be developed for the core product and core product extensions. Mistakes in the design that are not caught and corrected will cost more later in the process to correct. If mistakes are not corrected before construction or renovation begins, facility managers will be forced to work with the facility as it is designed in the final, approved blueprints.

To better understand how to read blueprints, we will use an outdoor skate park as an example. The components of the skate-park blueprints included in this chapter are not difficult to read. The blueprints are integrated and include overlapping aspects of the construction project because it is a single-purpose project and not large or complex. The skate-park blueprints consist of two sections of drawings. All blueprints include specific sections of important information to assist in understanding the document. These sections include the title block, direction indicator, drawing index, scale, drawing title, drawing area, notes, legend, schedules, symbols, keys, and cross section.

Title Block

The title block contains standardized information about the drawing. It is usually in the lower right corner of each page of the blueprints. The title block contains significant information about the overall project as well as specific identification for the drawing being viewed (see figure 6.2). Some of the details include the administrative seal, project

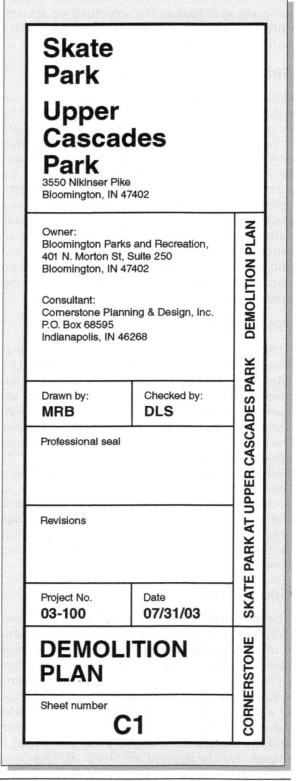

Figure 6.2 This is a title block for a skate park project. It lists the name of the project, architectural firm, and other pertinent project information.

Adapted by permission of Lawrence R. Moss and Associates (www. lrmassoc.com).

number, drawing title, architectural company, project sponsor, date of drawing, engineer's name, drawing identification number, and client's name or company. This area also has space for the architect's authorization of approval, allowing for a signature and date for each page of the blueprints.

Direction Indicator

The directional indicator shows the facility in relation to north with an arrow pointing in that direction as it would if a compass were part of the blueprint (see figure 6.3). When reading blueprints, it is important to be aware of the direction being

viewed. A directional indicator simply helps the reader realize north, south, east and west and provides an orientation to identify the particular area being viewed.

Drawing Index

The drawing index is a coded list of the drawings similar to the table of contents of a book that lists the various blueprints that are involved with the project (see figure 6.4). These corresponding letters and numbers are located in the title block on each page, telling readers what blueprint page or section they are reading or searching for.

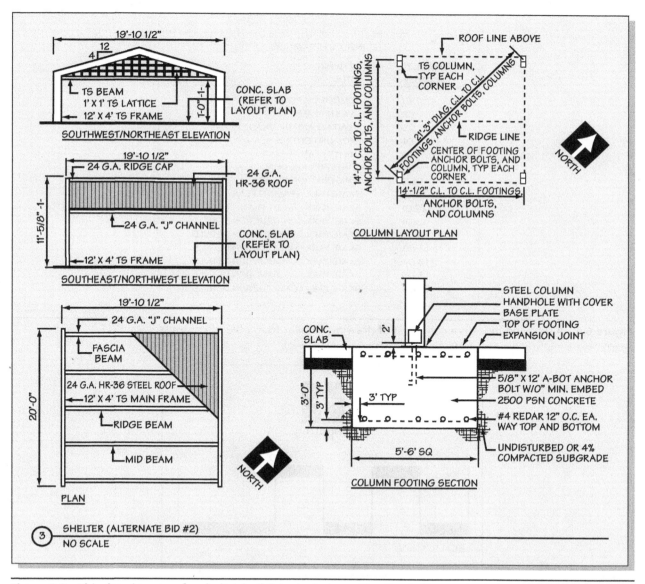

Figure 6.3 This drawing area for shelter buildings includes a direction indicator depicting where the shelter is in relation to north.

Adapted by permission of Lawrence R. Moss and Associates (www.lrmassoc.com).

Scale

The scale of a blueprint is a ratio of the drawing measurements (in inches) to the actual size of the facility (in feet). This represents the size of the structure, which makes the blueprint an accurate representation of the facility. In blueprints, the following symbols or abbreviations are used to indicate inches and feet: inches = " and feet = ' (see figure 6.5). In the skate-park example, 1 inch (2.5 centimeters) = 10 feet (3 meters), or 1" = 10'.

Drawing Title

Sometimes there can be more than one drawing providing details of a section within the same blueprint. The drawing title indicates the area being viewed (see figure 6.6). In this case, it also includes a scale for the drawing.

Drawing Area

The drawing title includes detail that reflects more specific information about the drawing, with the subtitle of a particular drawing area. In this case, it is part of the total area or view, providing a specific descriptive title that names the area (see figure 6.6). In general, the drawing area gives the reader a closer look at a certain area, showing details from a top view. It can include electrical outlets, fixtures, cabinet work, walls, dimensions, telephone jacks, and doors. In the skate-park

INDEX TO DRAWINGS	
DRAWING NUMBER	DRAWING TITLE
C1	DEMOLITION PLAN
C2	LAYOUT PLAN
C3	GRADING AND DRAINAGE PLAN
C4	EROSION CONTROL PLAN
C5	UTILITY PLAN
C6.1	CONSTRUCTION DETAILS
C6.2	CONSTRUCTION DETAILS
L1.01	SKATE PARK GRADING PLAN
L2.01	SKATE PARK LAYOUT PLAN
L3.01	SKATE PARK CONSTRUCTION PLAN
L3.02	SKATE PARK CONSTRUCTION DETAILS
L3.03	SKATE PARK CONSTRUCTION DETAILS
L3.04	SKATE PARK CONSTRUCTION DETAILS
L3.05	SKATE PARK CONSTRUCTION DETAILS
L3.06	SKATE PARK CONSTRUCTION DETAILS

Figure 6.4   A drawing index is a coded list of drawings similar to a table of contents.
Adapted by permission of Lawrence R. Moss and Associates (www.lrmassoc.com).

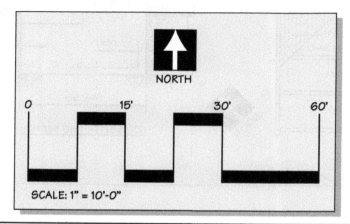

Figure 6.5   This is a scale for measuring various elements of a particular page of the blueprint. Here 1" = 10'.
Adapted by permission of Lawrence R. Moss and Associates (www.lrmassoc.com).

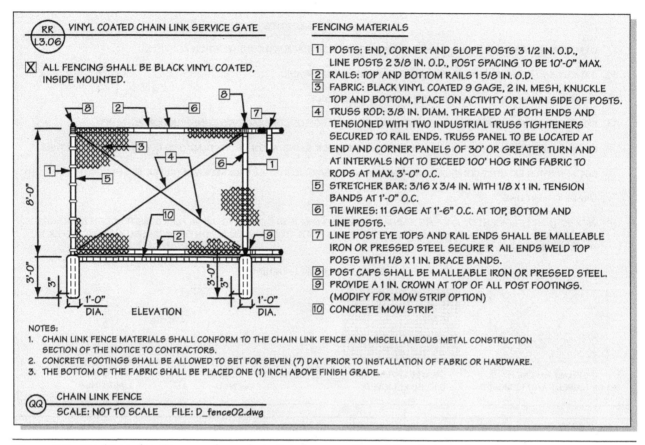

Figure 6.6 Depicts a drawing area for a chain link fence section of the skate park.

Adapted by permission of Lawrence R. Moss and Associates (www.lrmassoc.com).

example in figure 6.6, the drawing area represents a wall section with the drawing title "Vinyl Coated Chain Link Service Gate" and details on how to construct this particular area.

Notes

Some blueprints can have notes that provide special information for the contractors or subcontractors. This area is labeled with the title *Notes,* as seen in figure 6.6.

Legend

The legend indicates how each surface is labeled on the drawing and what to do with the surface. By looking at the legend in figure 6.7 and looking for the similar pattern on the corresponding blueprints, readers can find out what areas are to be removed from the site and what surfaces will remain.

Schedule

There can be a number of construction schedules in blueprints. They are usually charts that coincide with the blueprints and provide detailed information for the contractor. The schedule depicted for the skate-park project in figure 6.8 shows the electrical components that are part of the project and includes details on the parking-lot lighting, sump pump, and power receptacle circuits. Although not included in these blueprints, often there is a facility finish schedule that maps the details of lights, doors and hinges, windows, paint colors, floor surfaces, and so on.

Symbols and Keys

Symbols are pictures that represent certain items in the blueprints that need to show location as well as detailed descriptive information (see fencing materials section in figure 6.6). They diagram

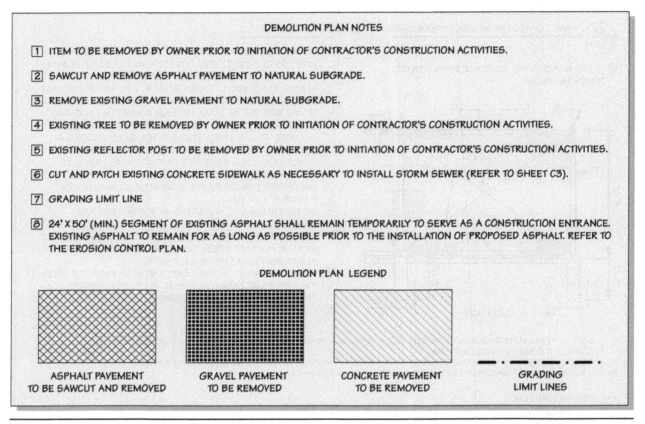

DEMOLITION PLAN NOTES

1. ITEM TO BE REMOVED BY OWNER PRIOR TO INITIATION OF CONTRACTOR'S CONSTRUCTION ACTIVITIES.

2. SAWCUT AND REMOVE ASPHALT PAVEMENT TO NATURAL SUBGRADE.

3. REMOVE EXISTING GRAVEL PAVEMENT TO NATURAL SUBGRADE.

4. EXISTING TREE TO BE REMOVED BY OWNER PRIOR TO INITIATION OF CONTRACTOR'S CONSTRUCTION ACTIVITIES.

5. EXISTING REFLECTOR POST TO BE REMOVED BY OWNER PRIOR TO INITIATION OF CONTRACTOR'S CONSTRUCTION ACTIVITIES.

6. CUT AND PATCH EXISTING CONCRETE SIDEWALK AS NECESSARY TO INSTALL STORM SEWER (REFER TO SHEET C3).

7. GRADING LIMIT LINE

8. 24' X 50' (MIN.) SEGMENT OF EXISTING ASPHALT SHALL REMAIN TEMPORARILY TO SERVE AS A CONSTRUCTION ENTRANCE. EXISTING ASPHALT TO REMAIN FOR AS LONG AS POSSIBLE PRIOR TO THE INSTALLATION OF PROPOSED ASPHALT. REFER TO THE EROSION CONTROL PLAN.

DEMOLITION PLAN LEGEND

ASPHALT PAVEMENT TO BE SAWCUT AND REMOVED

GRAVEL PAVEMENT TO BE REMOVED

CONCRETE PAVEMENT TO BE REMOVED

GRADING LIMIT LINES

Figure 6.7 Notes provide the contractor with additional details about a particular element of a blueprint.

Adapted by permission of Lawrence R. Moss and Associates (www.lrmassoc.com).

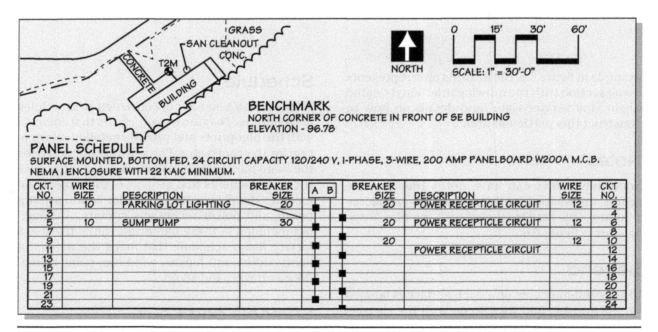

Figure 6.8 This schedule shows electrical components that are part of the skate park project.

Adapted by permission of Lawrence R. Moss and Associates (www.lrmassoc.com).

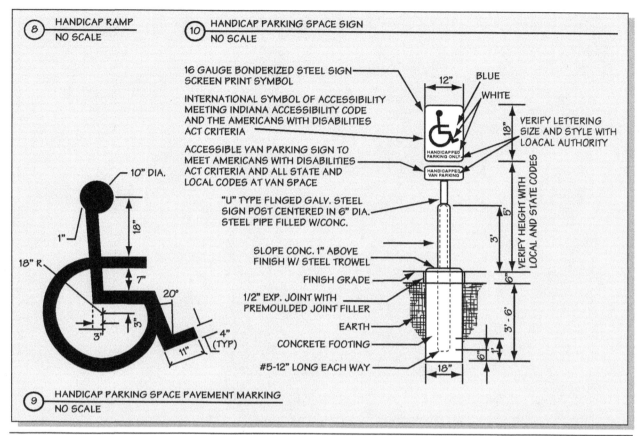

Figure 6.9 A cross-section view of the details for a handicapped parking sign.

Adapted by permission of Lawrence R. Moss and Associates (www.lrmassoc.com).

and describe specific design considerations such as name, size, type, and model number for lights, switches, and telephones.

Keys present detailed information that otherwise cannot be shown in the blueprints. A key describes elements in a certain area so that contractors know exactly what they are expected to do.

Cross Section

A cross section is a dissected or side view of some part of a blueprint, usually a wall, foundation, roof, tree planting, or signpost, that helps show the details involved (see figure 6.9). A cross section demonstrates the importance of details in helping contractors to understand what is expected of them.

SUMMARY

The design team must consider many types of information in the development phase of a project. In addition, they are required to make many decisions about the structure, its function, and how it will look. All of these decisions must be made considering the guidelines and laws, codes, ordinances, and standards of various agencies. The design team must ultimately come up with a final design that can be used to develop the final blueprints to be followed in construction. The blueprints and other design documents, provided by the architect, include a great deal of information for the contractor. It is important that the design team regularly review these documents to make sure the project is proceeding as planned.

Funding and the Bid Process

LEARNING OBJECTIVES

At the completion of this chapter, you should be able to do the following:

1. Recognize the various hard and soft costs associated with a design project.

2. Understand the construction options that can be used in completing a facility project.

3. Explain the bidding processes that are used for public and private agencies.

4. Explain the various funding options in facility design.

A facility development project is going to have a price tag attached to it. Whether it is a smaller project such as retrofitting an aerobics room or a large project such as building a water park, it cannot be done without adequate funding. Funding is perhaps the most important part of starting a design project. Numerous funding methods are available for recreation facility projects that are based on the type of project, the cost of the project, and the type of agency responsible for the project. Regardless of these variables, a design project is more likely to be funded if the design team researches the funding options available. This chapter addresses details associated with locating funding for a recreation facility project by examining project costs, construction options, the bid process, contract arrangements, and funding options.

Before looking at costs and funding, it is important to establish the need for the project during the assessment stage. It is also necessary for the design team to have administrative support for the project. The ultimate success of a facility development project will depend on the support given and interest generated for funding the project.

PROJECT COSTS

Funding for a design project is closely associated to the cost of the project. By understanding how much a project will cost, recreation administrators can then examine funding options. Early in the development of a project, projections are made to help estimate cost in order to give planners an idea of what they are creating and at what cost. The eventual construction costs result from the design, bid process, negotiations, and signing of a final contract for construction. Throughout the design stage, costs are assessed by calculating the hard costs and soft costs of the project. Hard and soft costs are the two detailed budget aspects associated with the design and construction process for facilities.

Hard Costs

Hard costs are the elements of a project that are fixed, meaning they are a permanent part of the facility, and include all that directly relates to the construction process. Hard costs stay with the project barring any unforeseen circumstances

▶A construction manager's fee is generally a percentage of the total construction cost.

© iStockphoto/Imad Birkholz

▶ Equipment, such as a lawn mower, is part of the owner-purchased equipment for a facility and factors into the hard costs for a facility.

or change orders. They can be changed early in the planning or predesign discussions by using different construction materials. A number of categories make up the hard costs that affect the construction of the facility, including construction, construction management, furniture, equipment, and signage.

Construction

Estimating the cost of a construction project can be challenging considering all of the steps required to complete a project. Typical construction elements include the demolition, site-work, structural, electrical, mechanical, and landscaping stages. A basic formula to establish the construction cost of a facility follows:

$$\text{Quantity of material} \times \text{cost of material} + \text{labor}$$
$$= \text{construction cost}$$

Another way of looking at the cost is a monetary amount per square foot of the facility. A square foot is 1 foot by 1 foot (30 centimeters by 30 centimeters). Square-foot costs vary by the type of facility, region, and climate. The monetary amount per square foot generically applies to all areas of a facility. However, it also allows for variations in cost for the different areas planned for the facility. The design team and contractors assess what it will cost to develop the facility using gross square footage and assignable square footage.

Gross square footage (GSF) is the total square feet of a facility. GSF is established by measuring the perimeter of a facility and multiplying the result by the number of levels. Multiplying the length times the width times the number of levels will provide the total number of square feet, establishing the total area of a structure. GSF includes space that is not necessarily useable or directly related to delivering the core product and its extensions.

All facility designs take into consideration the number of square feet needed to deliver the core product and its extensions. **Assignable square footage (ASF)** is the total number of square feet that can be assigned for actual use or that is required for product delivery.

Understanding GSF and ASF will help to establish tear space in the facility. **Tear space** is the difference between the GSF and ASF. Tear space can be used for other purposes, such as corridors, stairwells, hallways, mechanical rooms, and storage. It is space that is absolutely necessary in all facilities but is not usually recognized by owners and administrators because they are most concerned with the product and its delivery space or ASF. Architects and engineers who understand the need for tear space in a facility can assist with identifying and including it in a facility project.

Construction Management

When owners or administrators cannot or do not want to oversee the construction phase of a project, they can hire a construction management firm. These firms are usually hired for large projects or when the facility owner or administrator does not have the experience to oversee the project. A construction management company has the expertise to make sure the contracted work is done safely, properly, and according to the plans for the project. The specification books and blueprints guide construction managers through completion of a project. Construction management firms charge a fee for their service that is generally a percentage of the total construction cost. This fee is in addition to the contractor's construction costs and is included in the hard costs for a facility. Additional details about construction management are covered in chapter 8.

Furniture

All facility projects require furniture. Typically, there is a cost allowance that allows the administrator to select furnishings up to the amount allocated in the budget. Furniture includes all the items to be placed in the facility, such as desks, chairs, sofas, lamps, conference tables, filing cabinets, and bookcases. Often, the amount allocated for furniture is less than sufficient to furnish a facility. Any furniture not funded by the budget may require additional funds provided by the owner to meet this expense.

Recreation facility managers could take a sustainable approach to furniture by recycling old furniture from a former facility, if possible, rather than buying all new furniture. This also keeps costs down and reduces waste.

Equipment

The **equipment** for a facility generally includes structural equipment and owner-purchased equipment. Both are included in the hard costs of a facility. **Structural equipment** is permanent and is critical to the core product and extensions. Common examples include HVAC systems and scoreboards. Owner-purchased equipment includes anything that is not permanent but is critical to product delivery. Examples of owner-purchased equipment may include lawn mowers, golf carts, and ice groomers. Often the owner includes an allowance for equipment as part of the hard costs. Equipment can be expensive, and as with furniture, the budget may not allow enough funds to fully equip a facility.

Signage

Signage is a hard cost that encompasses the attached signs throughout a facility. All facilities have a directional system that helps users get to where they want to go. Typical facility signs include directories, wall signs, posted areas, regulatory signs, and informational signs. Signage also includes signs required by the ADA. A significant number of signs may be necessary depending on the size and complexity of a facility. The recreation facility manager is responsible for identifying what kind and how many signs should be located at a facility and should view the need for signage from the perspective of a user who has never visited the facility.

Soft Costs

Soft costs are expenses that are necessary to get a project started and to meet extended or unexpected costs. These costs include architectural fees, engineering fees, consultant fees, permit fees, reimbursable costs, and contingencies. Soft costs can be one-time expenses as well as ongoing throughout the project and do not relate directly to the construction process.

Architectural Fees

In most facility projects, an architect is hired to design and oversee the development process. Architects have great influence on the entire project. Their fee is generally a percentage of the total estimated construction cost of a project and ranges from 8 to 12 percent of the project budget. Sometimes a flat fee is negotiated with an architectural firm. However architectural costs are determined, they are included in the soft costs of a facility project.

Engineering Fees

Most facilities require help with the design of certain areas and equipment. Engineers with technical backgrounds and expert capacities in specialized areas such as heating and cooling, aquatics, and structural design are hired to review the design detail to make sure there are no problems. Their services are invaluable and complement the architectural effort. Often an engineering firm partners with an architectural firm on a facility project. It is common for the engineer's fees to be included in the 8 to 12 percent associated with the architect's fees.

Consultant Fees

Consultants have extensive experience in a field and can bring unique knowledge to the project. They are usually part of the planning and design team, providing advice on everything from product design and feasibility studies to mechanical and equipment needs. Their role is most common in the early phases of a facility project, and they often assist recreation agencies in establishing a need and support for the project.

Permit Fees

All construction projects are required by law to obtain certain permits. Each locality has regula-

▶An architect is necessary for most projects to plan, design, and oversee the entire facility development project from assessment to completion of construction.

tions regarding permits. Typically, grading, building, and environmental permits are required. Often, it is the administrator's role to determine what permits are needed, apply for them, and obtain permission to proceed. This responsibility can also be performed by others associated with the project, including architects, engineers, contractors, and construction management firms. Permits should be obtained once a design has been agreed upon but before construction begins. A fine may result for working without a permit. A building permit could stipulate requirements that must be met before a construction project is approved, such as the development of roads, sidewalks, access, and parking. These requirements are designed and presented as part of the project and are depicted in the blueprints and specification books.

Reimbursable Costs

Another part of soft costs is reimbursable costs, which repay the architects, consultants, and engineers for any costs outside the direct project cost. This line allows for expenses beyond contract costs, such as travel, lodging, meals, supplies, or phone services, that are not accounted for in the design or construction management fees.

Contingencies

A contingency is money set aside in the overall project cost to take care of unexpected developments that come up during construction. Contingency funds allow for correction of design flaws or mistakes or substitution of different construction materials or equipment. The amount usually allowed for a contingency fund is 10 to 20 percent of the construction cost. Omission of a contingency fund in the project budget can prove to be unfortunate. Inevitably, unanticipated situations occur that can negatively affect the funding plan if a contingency fund is not in place.

Other Costs

It is important to be aware of the construction cost, but in some respects it is even more important to be aware of the potential cost of operating the completed facility. An awareness of **operational costs** can affect the design and construction process. Architects and engineers can incorporate certain elements in the design that can reduce operational costs. For example, a sustainable approach to operating a facility may result in building materials that are more energy efficient, which in turn will reduce utility costs. Consideration of operational expenses in the design phase is wise in order to avoid building or renovating a facility that cannot be properly maintained or kept operational because of unexpected, avoidable expenses.

CONSTRUCTION OPTIONS

Part of the funding analysis is determining which of the available construction options is most appropriate for the project. These options are greatly influenced by the cost of the project, the setting (public or private), and what the owner is willing to pay. In selecting a construction option, it is important to consider available funding and the time frame for completion of a project. The construction options include conventional, design-build, fast track, and turnkey. They provide recreation professionals with options to save money, time, or both during the construction process. Each option will vary based on the setting and expertise of the company bidding the project. When companies bid a project, they are essentially informing the recreation agency what it will cost to complete the project.

Conventional Option

The most common construction method is the conventional method. This process takes the completed design for the project and formally bids out the project to interested contractors. Bids are generally submitted in a lump sum or fixed amount for the entire project. They are reviewed by the recreation agency and the lowest and most responsive bidder is usually awarded the contract. The contractor then develops the facility according to the blueprints and specifications completed by the architect and engineers during the design process. The conventional method is most often used for recreation projects in the public sector.

Design-Build Option

Under the design-build option, one company is responsible for both the design and the construction of the facility. This option results in design cost savings because a price for both the design and construction of the project is established early in the design process. This construction option may also accelerate completion of the project. As the plans for each segment are completed, that stage can begin rather than waiting for the total project design and bid process to be completed. Additional expenses can be added to a project

▶ Public sector recreation facilities are often funded using the conventional option.

if owners or administrators are not sure of what they want as a finished product. This option is often used in the private sector. In many areas, this option is not available to the public sector based on laws regulating the bid process.

Fast-Track Option

The fast-track process compresses the time between the start of design and the completion of construction. Time is saved by starting construction on selected parts of the project before the completion of the total design effort. The fast-track process requires careful cost allocation to ensure sufficient funds for the entire project. This time-saving process also restricts the designer's ability to incorporate desired changes into the project after the initial construction contracts are

▶Private sector facilities are often funded with the fast track option.

awarded. This option is often used in the private sector and may not be available for public-sector projects based on laws regulating the bid process.

Turnkey Option

In a turnkey project, the contractor bids a lump sum for all aspects of the project; obtains all necessary design work, financing, and permits; and then develops the facility. Once the project is complete, the contractor exchanges the title of the facility for the full payment or an agreement for future payments. The turnkey approach saves money because many details, negotiations, and communications are controlled by the contractor. The turnkey process can be used in either the private or public sector.

BIDDING THE PROJECT

Part of funding a facility project is making the transition from planning and design to obtaining financial quotes or bids from potential contractors who will commit to build the facility. In the facility construction, owners, architects, and contractors come together as a team to build the facility. Before that can happen, contractors need the opportunity to bid on the project. The owner and architect agree on what is to be developed (through the design) and then potential contractors submit a price or bid based on their estimated costs to construct the facility and their margin for profit. This process usually takes 3 to 5 weeks. It requires that all pricing information submitted by contractors be kept confidential, allowing contractors to work independently of one another. Most of the time, the bidding process can be competitive, with pricing (total package) the only variable under consideration. The bid process does have some variations, however, for public and private projects.

Public- Versus Private-Sector Projects

Not all facility projects must go out for bid. Private agencies can do whatever they want in finding a contractor to complete construction work for a project. If an owner feels comfortable with a contractor who has a good reputation, it is not uncommon for that contractor to be awarded the contract without going through a bid process, which can be long and costly. Some private agencies use the bid process to save money because many contractors will lower their quote when they are put in a competitive situation. The bid process can be applied to private projects if judged necessary or advantageous.

On the other hand, public-sector projects must go out for bid to find the lowest price and the best contractor. Public projects go out for bid because they use taxpayer money and are required by law to create fair competition for all interested contractors. In this situation, all contractors and vendors should have an equal and objective opportunity to bid on the project. Because the bidding process for public agencies is more involved and can be more complicated, bid information must be made available to all interested firms.

Quotations

Whether used in the public or private sector, the bid process results in a quotation submitted by a potential contractor to the agency bidding out the work. A quotation indicates the contractor's cost for a facility project. It represents the contractor's cost analysis and calculation that incorporates all aspects of the project. In the bidding process, contractors and owners can choose one of two quotation options. One option is the **lump sum** or **fixed-priced bid.** With this option, all designs and specifications for the project are awarded to one general contractor to complete all the work. A lump sum results in a single sum of money paid for all work to be accomplished. The general contractor is responsible for making all arrangements and paying all subcontractors.

Another quotation method is **separate bid pricing,** where quotes are solicited from different general contractors for separate elements of the construction process. These separate elements include excavation, plumbing, landscaping, electrical work, structural work, and mechanical work. The separate bid process may save money by eliminating the general contractor's markup for overhead or profit. However, it places greater responsibility on the recreation agency to make sure that subcontractors get things done in a timely fashion, requiring the administrator to work closely with the various contractors.

© iStockphoto/Andrew Howe

▶In separate bid pricing, a recreation facility owner decides to solicit quotes from different contractors for different elements of the construction process, such as installing the plumbing system.

Alternates

Often agencies bidding a project are not sure whether the amount they have budgeted for the project will cover all components. To ensure that they don't have to throw out all bids and start over, agencies often include alternates in the bid documents. Alternates are parts of the project that are bid on outside of the original bid package. They may be identified as extra or not as necessary to the project because they may be expensive or beyond the anticipated budget. However, alternates may be important project components. They do not affect the original bid price, but if the original bid comes in under the budgeted amount, it may be possible to include the alternate bid components in the construction project. Often, alternates are left for later inclusion when funds are available or decisions are made to put an alternate into the project. Using an alternate bid process helps keep costs manageable. It is the discretion of the agency administrator or owner and the architect to decide if the alternates should be included, with the decision being dictated by the funds available.

Bonds

Along with the bid, contractors submit a **bond,** usually a large percentage of the project cost, which guarantees their quote as a commitment to complete the project. The bond is returned to all other contractors that do not get the business or contract, but it stays with the winning bidder and is applied to the project or returned at the completion of the project.

Bid Process

Although quotation options and alternates are mentioned, the bid process can take on varying degrees of formality, and requirements are often determined by the recreation agency as well as the government. Sensitivity to this process is important, especially when working in the public sector.

The bid process begins with making the design documents (blueprints and specification books) available to all interested parties after a public announcement is made that the bid is available to all who are interested. A formal timetable is established with deadlines for when the bids are due to allow all potential contractors a fair and impartial chance to submit their bid. The bid requires that every monetary cost be accounted for as related to every detail in the blueprints and specification books.

At the end of the timetable, there is a public opening of the bids where all contractors are invited to see how their bid compared with those of competing contractors. At this formal bid opening, each bid is opened and read aloud for the benefit of all in attendance. The agency may then take the information received before a public or private board before awarding a contract, taking the bids under advisement until all details can be examined by the project design team. Generally, the most responsive contractor with the lowest bid is awarded the contract after bids have been reviewed for accuracy. Bidders may withdraw their bid for any reason before awarding of the contract. Once a contractor is awarded the project, contract arrangements can be finalized.

CONTRACT ARRANGEMENTS

At the end of the bidding process, the administrator or owner, architect, and contractor come together to work on the project as a team. A contract commits the contractor to many obligations, but because the entire process can be so involved, formal conversations are held to make sure everything about the process is clearly understood. During the contract arrangements, both parties move toward a written document that ties everything together in the form of a detailed understanding. Agreements and guarantees must be established to protect the administrator and the contractor from any misunderstanding. The following are various considerations as the owner and contractor move toward a formal agreement.

Value Engineering and Assessment

With the lowest bid received and the contract being awarded, the contractor and owner work together on the bid details to make sure everything is designed and interpreted properly. A number of elements in the project could require detailed assessment and interpretation. At this stage, the administrator and the contractor may seek assistance from architects, engineers, and specialists to make sure the bid prices accurately reflect the details in the specifications. This process of looking at prices and specifications is referred to as

value engineering. This team looks at the blueprints and reviews the pricing to make sure the owner does not pay too much and the contractor receives fair compensation for work performed. The team works toward solving problems that the administrator or contractor may not have been aware of during the design and bidding process. This can lead to negotiations to ensure that both parties are in agreement and that all details are understood and correct. No one wants to learn during construction, when it will cost much more to correct, that a mistake was made. Both sides benefit from value engineering because facility projects can be complicated and details can be missed during the planning, design, and bid processes.

Insurance Coverage

In the final stages of contract arrangements, contractors have to demonstrate that they have appropriate insurance covering all aspects of the project during the construction stage. The insurance package should protect against any situation that could occur at the construction site, including workers' compensation and property and casualty loss. Insurance coverage is important because the owner should not be responsible for anything that goes on at the construction site. The contractor is at great risk because construction sites can be dangerous. Every precaution should be taken to protect against claims of injury, with insurance established in case something does occur.

© iStockphoto/Joe Gough

▶Contractors must show facility owners or administrators that they have insurance to cover any possible accidents that may occur at a construction work site.

Financing Plans

Just as contractors are held responsible for their work with a bonding and insurance plan, recreation agencies are responsible for providing an adequate amount of money to pay for the project and a system for distributing payment as the project progresses. Every project should have a financial plan and an established system for the contractor to request payment for work completed. It is appropriate for the contractor be aware of the financial system that the administrator has arranged to pay for the facility.

In making these financial arrangements, the recreation agency will have to justify the cost of the facility to the mortgaging or loaning entity. Sometimes financial arrangements can influence the viability of a project. Without adequate financial planning, it's possible that a decision could be made regarding whether the project can be funded or not. Recreation administrators must justify the cost of a facility and assess the highest potential for reward and the lowest financial risk. The construction cost of a facility is usually the greatest financial concern that administrators must consider. Lending agencies expect there to be a way to ensure that the loan will be repaid. Specific calculations can be done to determine the net amount of investment required for the project, the return expected for the investment, and what rate of interest will be charged. When the amount of the loan is determined, financial assistance may be sought by going to a financial institution or private lender.

When recreation agencies are looking for loans to finance projects, they must carefully look at the terms of the loan. Loan terms include interest that will be charged on the loan, the length of the loan, the closing costs, the penalty fee or charge for a late payment, and any financial consultant fees required to complete financing details. Although most of these are administration concerns, it is information that contractors should be aware of because they are entering into a contract with the agency.

Controlling Costs

A contract arrangement is designed to protect the facility owner and the contractor from unexpected construction costs. No matter what plans are made to move the project along, facility owners should be aware of unexpected costs that could occur during construction. The contract can establish a maximum price for completion of the facility. Owners can offer financial incentives for contractors if they can reduce the construction cost. Owners can also pay the actual cost of all materials and labor plus a fixed percentage or fee to the contractor to help keep the final cost of the project from rising. These two contract concepts can contribute to the overall effort in getting a facility developed and keeping costs under control.

Signing the Contract

After all the discussions, meetings, engineering assessment, and other arrangements have been determined and the formal blueprint and specification books have been finalized by the architect and authorized by the administrator and contractor, then a contract or formal arrangement can be completed. Both parties, recognizing and accepting all responsibilities as documented in the blueprints and specification books, sign the formal contract at an established time and place. Once the finalized contracts are signed, the price cannot be changed unless both sides agree with an appropriate cost-adjustment agreement. The formal contract signed by the contractor and the owner binds the price and establishes the work to be completed.

FUNDING OPTIONS

There are many possible sources for funding a recreation facility project. Some facilities can receive funding from a single source, whereas others can receive funding from a combination of sources. Some sources may apply to certain facility projects only. This section provides a sampling of funding options.

Mandatory Fees

An agency can establish a fee requiring payment from users of the product. This fee, often called a mandatory fee, can be designated to pay for new construction, renovation, or repair. Mandatory fees are most often associated with public agencies and are usually established by a governing body, trustees, or representative administrative system. Often this fee can be designated to pay for an expensive project over an extended length of time, from 5 to 30 years. These fees can be attached to other ongoing user fees or payment obligations such as memberships, monthly dues, payments, or school tuition. Often, mandatory fees are designed to meet operational expenses as well as construction or renovation costs.

Another type of mandatory fee that can be used for less expensive projects is an **assessment fee.** Assessments are usually collected for a short duration not exceeding two or three payments or perhaps a half or full year. Usually members, customers, or patrons make monthly payments for an improvement to a facility. Private golf courses often use assessment fees to pay for facility improvements. Mandatory fees or assessments can be unpopular with those who must pay. Attention should be given to opposition to make sure everyone understands and appreciates the need for the facility project.

Tax Levy

A **tax levy** occurs in the public sector and earmarks a portion of local taxes for a recreation facility project. Usually, this type of funding requires a great deal of community support and can take years to evolve. A number of public boards, commissions, and elected officials may have to authorize this type of funding. A tax levy is limited to a certain amount based on the conditions imposed by governing bodies. It is often used for community projects such as schools, fire stations, and recreation centers, as well as state facilities such as universities and government buildings.

User Fees

User fees come from people who pay to use the core product of a facility. The amounts charged for services usually equate to the type of use, the user's ability to afford the services, and what others in the market are charging. User fees often come in the form of memberships, monthly dues, payments, or school tuition. They differ from mandatory fees in that mandatory fees are additional fees related to facility construction and operation whereas user fees are not related to facility development. The agency provides a competitively priced product that users will benefit from in the hope that there will be repeated use and satisfaction. Income and expense analysis should be conducted to make sure the fee is fair and users will not be discouraged by the amount. Accurate projections of income from user fees are critical in the planning stage. User fees can be a primary source of revenue for private agencies that depend

▶User fees come directly from people who pay to use the facility's core product.

on this type of income to meet facility expenses. Public facilities can also institute user fees to help offset expenses. In the public setting, user fees are usually lower and may be less critical to the support of the facility because of funding generated through taxes.

Bond Issue

A bond issue is a method of raising funds for public facilities. It is often the primary source of funds for local or state facility construction projects. The process offers tax-exempt bonds for the general public to buy with a return of the principal amount plus interest after a certain amount of time. The state bonding authority controls the process and has the authority to allow or deny such an option. Prior to final approval by the state bonding authority, local boards and elected officials will be required to authorize the sale of the bonds. Citizens in a community can object in writing to a bond issue if they do not want their taxes to be used for a particular project. Requirements for the approval of bond issues vary from community to community. Financial consultants are generally hired to assist with projects funded by bond issues. Bonds of this nature are sound investments because they are supported by tax income, which

is safe and regular income that can be counted on to pay off the loan on a facility mortgage.

Revenue Bond

A revenue bond is for a public project and relies on projected revenue that will be generated by the facility for repayment of a loan. A revenue bond is backed up or supported by property taxes in the event that the revenue collected is less than projected. This type of funding is used only when a facility project is able to generate substantial revenue from its core product. Examples of public facilities funded by revenue bonds include water parks and golf courses.

Donations and Contributions

Additional sources of funding for facility projects include gifts, donations, and contributions from interested individuals and groups. These sources come from supportive people or businesses that usually have a vested interest, possibly from past involvement with the receiving agency. Contributors may have the financial ability and benefit from making donations of this nature for tax purposes. Sometimes there can be a campaign to raise funds of this nature. Such campaigns often use

▶Depending on the size of the donation, some contributors may require a facility to use their name when naming a facility area or the entire facility.

fund-raisers who have expertise in raising money for causes. Some contributors can have requirements that the agency must meet, such as using the contributor's name in recognition of a particular area of the facility or in naming the facility.

In-Kind Gifts

Another source of outside assistance in funding a project is **in-kind gifts.** They represent a unique approach that can get some aspects of a facility project completed that otherwise may not be possible. With an in-kind gift, a contractor or other interested party provides labor or materials to a facility at no cost in exchange for a tax deduction for the amount that is donated. The recreation environment provides opportunities to solicit a potential contractor or vendor for an in-kind gift by targeting people or businesses that use the facility. Often, the emotional tie to a program offered at a recreation facility creates the appeal for a business or individual to donate an in-kind gift. In-kind gifts are a good way to get minor repairs, renovations, and small parts of a new project completed at a lower cost.

Grants

There are many granting institutions that can be approached about helping with the funding for a facility project. Grants are an excellent option for public projects, especially if the requesting agency has a similar mission, interest, or purpose as the granting agency. Grant funds can be provided by the government, private institutions, or public or private foundations. These sources usually require a formal grant proposal before the grant is awarded. Generally, the directions for writing a grant are straightforward. However, a recreation professional seeking grant dollars may want to participate in grant-writing workshops provided by professional recreation organizations and grant-writing agencies. Granting sources may have certain conditions that must be met for the grant to be awarded. In some cases, there may be no restrictions on how the grant funds can be used. The grant process can be very involved and competitive. Larger recreation agencies often have a full-time staff member designated to research and apply for grants. Funds from grants can vary from several thousand to several million dollars. Grants can provide a significant funding source for a project if the criteria for the grant match the mission of the agency applying for the grant.

Sponsorships

The construction of a new facility often provides an opportunity for outside entities to provide funds so that their business receives recognition of some type at the facility. This relationship is usually established through a contractual arrangement before construction with detailed understanding regarding the level of funding support to the project in return for recognition at the facility. It is common to see professional sport facilities named after a business in exchange for a significant amount of money. These arrangements may become more prevalent in the recreation environment as agencies attempt to raise funds for projects. In such cases, matching facilities with businesses that may benefit from exposing their name to the users may be a winning combination. Common examples of sponsorship opportunities include exposure of sponsor names on scoreboards, sport field fences, and golf-course hole

▶Some businesses may decide to sponsor part of or an entire facility in exchange for having their name prominently displayed at the facility.

signs. Sponsorship opportunities are available for both public and private recreation facilities.

Combination Funding

Usually private entities do not have access to the same sources of funding as public agencies. Private facilities generally rely on mandatory fees, user fees, and private investors as their primary sources of facility funds. The public sector has greater latitude in seeking funds for a project, often resulting in a combination of the funding sources mentioned. In addition to fees and charges, public-sector agencies are funded through tax dollars and are often eligible for grant dollars. Public-sector agencies also occasionally benefit from individual and corporate donations. Recreation professionals should be aware of all funding options and be creative in considering the mix that may work best in accomplishing the project.

Campaign Funding

Often facility development projects require significant persuasion of administrators, investors, the general public, and politicians in order to create the necessary progress to fund a project. This is especially the case with a large project that requires extensive financial support. The effort to create awareness among the parties mentioned could be viewed as a campaign that helps people to realize the need for a facility project. The ability for facility advocates to influence people and create an interest in funding support is instrumental to the success of a project. The two primary methods used to influence attitudes toward funding a project are individual selling and specialty firms.

Individual Selling

Often, the person responsible for initiating the support for funding a facility and taking on the task of individual selling is the recreation agency administrator or facility manager. Raising support for a facility project means extra hours on the job outside the daily routine. Typical duties include speaking on behalf of the project by attending functions where knowledge and enthusiasm for the project can be shared. In the individual selling effort, the important thing is to disseminate accurate information about the project to all interested and influential parties. This can be done through direct conversations, telephone calls, petitions, special presentations, fliers, press releases, and press conferences that focus on the benefits of the facility. The ability to network or interact with others who can sell the vision and assist in obtaining the necessary funding for a project can play a huge role in gaining financial support.

Specialty Firms

Firms with fund-raising expertise can be hired to help lead a funding campaign for a facility project. Hiring a specialty firm as a consultant to assist with a project comes at a cost that will vary depending on the size of the project. These firms retain professionals who know how to reach target audiences that recreation agencies may not normally consider. They also possess the knowledge and skills to present the appropriate message or pitch that leads to a successful fund-raising campaign. Such firms are typically hired when a project is expansive and affects a large number of people, when it has conflicting interests or complicated funding requirements, or when recreation administrators or facility managers recognize that their help is needed. Specialty firms may be brought in on a project when an independent perspective of the need for a project may help to assuage public and political dissension. Often, these firms specialize in damage control, and when a project is very large, they may devise methods to soothe public and political concerns and ultimately influence the funding process.

SUMMARY

Funding a facility development project is a serious consideration in the evolution of any facility. Funding could be described as the process for acquiring money to support a project and allow it to become a reality. Without funding, a facility simply remains a plan with a design. The funding of a facility project can be complicated and involves consideration of funding options, project costs, construction options, the bid process, and contract arrangements.

Constructing Recreation Facilities

The construction stage of a facility development project is an exciting time, because all the work to this point starts to take shape into an actual structure. It is often a time of celebration and ceremony, especially with larger projects. Design project construction frequently begins with a groundbreaking ceremony and concludes with an opening ceremony.

Before the construction begins, a ceremony is often held to recognize the official start of the project. This step, called a **groundbreaking,** recognizes the project as having gained the necessary support to become a reality and initiates the construction process. To get to this stage takes a tremendous effort, often involving many people. The groundbreaking is a time to recognize the people and groups that helped bring the project to this stage. The ceremony can range from an informal gathering to an elaborate program involving speakers and a literal groundbreaking (or shoveling) activity. A newspaper article, photos, and media coverage can also be part of the groundbreaking ceremony, communicating the event to a greater audience.

CONSTRUCTION DOCUMENTS

After design documents or blueprints have been reviewed during the value assessment and engineering step, the architect creates final drawings reflecting adjustments decided on by the owner or administrator, architect, contractor, and construction manager. These revised documents are called construction documents. As mentioned in the design chapter, as the size of the project increases, so does the number of blueprint pages. Each design area within the facility (structural, mechanical, electrical, landscaping) has its own layers of blueprints with specific details. With smaller projects, these design areas could be incorporated into fewer pages with some of the blueprint areas overlapping each other. The following documents are generally understood to be the construction documents that are provided to the contractor. They represent the project in detail and are the formal communication among owner or administrator, architect, construction manager, and contractor.

© G. Newman Lowrance/MLS/Getty Images

▶A groundbreaking symbolizes the beginning of the construction phase for a project as well as recognizes garnering the necessary support to see the project come to this stage.

Final Blueprints

The **final blueprints** are the design documents that communicate the details of what is to be constructed. The final blueprints indicate how each component of the project is to be completed by the contractor. These documents are also copied and given to subcontractors and craftspeople to serve as their guide for how to construct their part of the project. They are carried to the construction site where they will be referred to frequently throughout the project. Every detail must be followed as drawn because the contractor is financially responsible for all errors. Mistakes can be costly, time consuming to correct, and compromise the safety of the facility. It is crucial that the final blueprints be accurate to ensure accurate construction of the facility.

Specification Book

The specification book, or spec book, is an important part of communicating the details of a project to the contractors. It provides written detailed references to the blueprints. When there are problems and misunderstandings, the spec book can clear up the differences. As the project increases in size, so does the amount of detail in the spec book. Small projects may not even require a spec book if the blueprints provide enough detail. Spec books are an extension of the contract and final blueprints and include design information, as well as requirements for the design, including codes, laws, and standards that need to be conveyed accurately to the contractor and subcontractors.

Shop Drawings

Shop drawings support blueprints and spec books. They are another step in the construction process that assists contractors with design expectations. Shop drawings are interpretations of the blueprints by the contractor or subcontractor that are approved by the architect. A shop drawing can be drawn by the architect or contractor and can be simple and informal or complex and formal. Whatever is included in the shop drawing is subject to final approval by the owner or administrator. Shop drawings help ensure that details in blueprints are understood and accurate as they relate to specific items, customized areas, or unique design elements. This can be a time-consuming component of facility projects. With the extent of details that many projects require, shop drawings help clarify the design expectations and avoid problems in the long run.

Change Orders

No construction project proceeds exactly as planned. Problems are discovered by contractors, architects, and administrators. Change orders occur for the following reasons: errors or an omission in the design, a change in the method or construction material, or contractors recognizing a problem from their experience with the project. When these situations occur, a change order is initiated to create the communication and authorization for what needs to be corrected. The **change order** is a written design order that authorizes the contractor to make the proposed changes in the work at the construction site. These changes can have serious cost implications that all parties want to avoid. However, it is usually understood that if the change can be made during construction, it will be less expensive than correcting it later. Change orders should be approved by administrators, architects, and contractors.

Project Schedule

One of the most interesting and comprehensive construction documents is the project schedule. The project schedule could be in the form of a book or a poster displayed on a wall. The content or layout represents all aspects of the project, including site preparation, demolition, architectural developments, electrical work, mechanical installation, landscaping, and when each stage is to be accomplished, including the day, month, and year. This schedule is usually set up with all construction functions, tasks, and responsibilities listed down the left side and proposed dates for completion across the top. Bars or lines depict when each stage is estimated to be completed. At first glance, a project schedule appears difficult to comprehend. Once studied, it presents the entire picture of a project from beginning to end.

CONSTRUCTION MANAGEMENT

More often than not, owners do not have the capacity to supervise a construction project, especially if it is large and complicated. As noted in chapter 6, companies exist that can bring expertise to overseeing all aspects of a construction project. These firms provide construction management expertise and can contractually assume the role of the owner and work with the architect to ensure that all project requirements are accomplished in a timely and suitable fashion. Construction managers are responsible for all phases of a construction project. They have the knowledge, insight, and ability to supervise all phases of the project. This arrangement should be formalized in writing between the facility owner and the construction management company. The following are functions that are usually fulfilled by the construction management team, whether this team includes a construction management company or not.

Progress Meetings

The construction management team schedules and conducts regular **progress meetings** with key people in the project. Attendees include the owner

© iStockphoto/Mel Stoutsenberger

▶Weather is just one type of delay that can occur and lead to greater problems, which are discussed at construction progress meetings.

or administrator, user representative, architect, vendors, contractors, subcontractors, and when necessary, engineers and consultants. At these meetings, all aspects of the project are discussed in detail. Any existing or potential problems should be resolved to avoid project delays that can lead to greater problems. Some problems that can affect construction include weather, worker productivity, material imperfections, materials delivery, timetables, accidents, changes, conflict, quality concerns, and coordination challenges. At each meeting, verbal and written progress reports are made by the construction management team leader detailing everything since the previous meeting. Progress expectations and timetable details are also addressed and confirmed in progress reports.

Coordination

The many facets associated with the construction of a recreation facility require attention to ensure that conflicts are avoided and work is progressing as planned. Coordinating the various aspects of a project can be challenging because of the number of workers, subcontractors, vendors, timetable requirements, unexpected problems, inspections, and weather delays that often occur. Coordination of a project is a critical role for the construction manager because delays can cost money, create tension, and negatively affect the completion schedule of a project.

Project Schedule

Many phases transpire from groundbreaking to occupancy during a construction project. It is the construction manager's responsibility, along with the administrator and architect, to establish the detailed schedule of the project. Work functions are identified for each part of the construction team, and timetables are established with each function to be monitored by the construction management firm. The **project schedule** is a conceptual plan that reflects every phase of the project. It is the construction manager's responsibility to keep construction progressing according to the project schedule.

Quality Check

One of the most important functions of a construction manager is to review the work of contractors and subcontractors. Occasionally, contractors do not have the same commitment to a project as the architect or administrator. Contractors may try to find cost savings through workmanship and material substitutions in order to enhance their profit margin, and some contractors may attempt to hide worker mistakes and oversights to avoid additional costs. It is the construction manager's responsibility to monitor contractors' work and identify problems and then take the necessary steps to rectify the situation. A construction manager is the agency representative and must ensure that the agency receives what is outlined in the blueprints and specification book.

Interpreting Legal Requirements

Administrators or owners often do not initially realize how many local and state codes are involved in the construction of a recreation facility. Construction managers serve a valuable role in interpreting these codes that must be observed during construction. Specific codes are available through local government agencies and state gov-

ernments and can usually be found on the Internet. Construction managers make sure everything is done accurately and meets specific design requirements. The watchdog role of the construction manager comes into play with electrical, mechanical, plumbing, and structural details and the legal codes that must be applied to each phase of the project. Failure to follow certain requirements can result in the owner or contractor being held responsible and can result in lawsuits that affect all those involved with the project.

Inspection

Construction managers are also involved in scheduling and overseeing inspections that are conducted by local governing agencies. Inspections are a required part of a construction project. An inspector's role is to act in the best interest of the future employees and users of the facility by ensuring that the construction process does not create inconveniences or dangerous situations.

Inspectors can examine any number of elements at a construction site. Throughout construction, specific situations, items, or areas will

© iStockphoto/Justin Horrocks

▶One part of a construction manager's job is to schedule inspections during the construction process to ensure that the construction does not create hazards, inconveniences, or dangerous situations.

be inspected by outside agencies to assess the workmanship and ensure that contractors are in compliance with all codes. It is the construction manager's responsibility to work with the inspectors to help them do their job and to recognize that they could show up unannounced. Some of the items that inspectors scrutinize in detail are electrical work, plumbing, accessibility, and structural requirements.

Changes

No construction or renovation project progresses from beginning to end without changes. Changes are expensive; therefore, the construction manager needs to make sure the change is necessary and that it is best for the project. Construction managers must coordinate any changes with contractors, architects, and administrators.

Once changes are agreed upon by administrators and the construction manager initiates change orders, they are forwarded to the architect, who reviews and forwards the changes to the administrator for approval. After the administrator authorizes the change, it is then returned to the contractors for correction. Construction managers keep track of all change orders and coordinate when the work is to be completed.

Site Safety and Security

Every construction site is a potentially hazardous area. Contractors cannot have people visiting the site without authorization because they could be seriously injured. Contractors are legally liable for keeping people out of a construction site. Typically, barricades or fences are put up to control access. Construction managers play a key role with this responsibility, using techniques that include monitoring access, posting signs, installing tape warning barriers, and hiring guards and watchdogs to monitor the site. Efforts to secure a site at night may require additional security measures, such as hiring security guards or using surveillance equipment, to keep people away. These security efforts must be taken seriously due to the potential

© iStockphoto/Darren Wise

▶When a visitation from people with a vested interest in the construction project occurs, assuring the safety of the visitors is a top priority of the construction manager.

danger for and cost of any accidents that might occur.

Visitation

Those invested in a facility construction project enjoy experiencing the progress of a project. Construction managers have the responsibility to control this interest through a process called *visitation*. Traffic at the construction site is controlled with strict rules for all visitors, including the facility administrator or owner and architect. A well-planned visitation system can help significantly with public relations while at the same time ensuring the safety of the visitors. Every precaution is taken to avoid dangerous areas during visits. All visitors are required to wear hard hats, and visitors are usually required to sign in, be supervised by the construction manager throughout the tour, and then sign out at the end of the visit.

FINAL STAGES

Late in any construction project, after all the structural, mechanical, and electrical work is done, steps are taken to complete the facility. This fine-tuning brings to the facility those things that make the core product and core product extensions function as they were intended. As with the other phases of the project, the construction manager plays a key role in directing all aspects of this final stage by seeing that everything is done in a timely and proper fashion. Following are the final-stage activities that occur before the facility is occupied.

Owner or Operator Training

Toward the end of a project, certain aspects of a facility, including the use of equipment, needs to be explained and its proper use demonstrated. Training is usually provided for operators of technical equipment that requires special knowledge to operate or maintain. It may also be important for facility managers to participate in training in order to train future staff and assist in operation and maintenance of equipment and systems. Examples of this vendor transfer of information include HVAC systems, security equipment, lighting, public-address systems, and all core product and core product extension areas and equipment. These training sessions are organized and scheduled by the construction manager, making sure the appropriate people are in attendance. This may be the only time the administration or its representatives will learn what is necessary to know about specialized equipment or systems.

Maintenance Manuals

Many facility areas and equipment require specific maintenance attention. Maintenance details about the care of product equipment, utilities, mechanical systems, electrical systems, and landscape areas must be conveyed to the administrator or owner. If maintenance requirements are not fulfilled properly, areas and equipment will not meet expectations and at some point, a vendor, contractor, or administrator will be responsible if equipment fails. Maintenance manuals provide instructions for taking care of these areas and systems. This transfer of maintenance responsibility is an important role that is organized by the construction manager.

Finishing Stage

One of the most significant aspects of construction is the **finishing stage.** The finishing stage includes work done by the contractors that includes painting walls, installing light fixtures, hanging doors, and installing windows and floor coverings. The finishing stage is the fine-tuning of aesthetics, acoustical considerations, and other appearance details and also includes moving in equipment and furniture. Usually a finish schedule or design chart or system guides the contractor through every aspect of this phase.

Key System

All facilities will eventually need to be secured from inappropriate access. The extensiveness of a project will dictate just how complicated a key system will need to be. From the beginning, key access should be planned, designed, and controlled with a number or coding system to identify the specific key with an area or piece of equipment. Key systems can be divided into the following categories: masters (open all doors), submasters (open interior locks), and individual keys for each area.

In recent years, new key systems have become available for recreation facilities. New options include combination locks, magnetic-strip cards, and bar-code cards. Each facility has its own key requirements. The construction manager's role is to help administrators interpret the details and

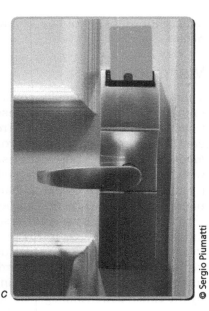

▶Some more recent types of key systems include *(a)* a card reading system; *(b)* a keypad system, and *(c)* a magnetic strip card system.

responsibilities involved that will result in the appropriate keying system for their facility.

Signage

Directional signs are necessary to inform users of facility locations. A common mistake made by facility administrators is not providing adequate signage to direct users to appropriate areas. Planning and designing signage requires the capacity to visualize the total use of a facility. The perspective of a first-time user should be considered when designing signage that links all areas into a logical flow that gets people to where they want to be. Signs communicate directional information that includes entrances and exits, area identification, directories, and information about facility policies and procedures. The same type, style, size, and color schemes should be followed throughout the facility so that signage is uniform and visible and also matches the aesthetics of the facility.

Punch List

Near the conclusion of a facility construction project, a system of assessing and recording everything that is to be finalized is compiled into a **punch list**. During a final walk-through of the completed facility, there are usually a handful of items or areas that do not meet design expecta-

tions, are incomplete, or are completed below acceptable standards. The construction manager plays a critical role in influencing the contractor to recognize these conditions and ensuring that the necessary adjustments are completed. It is generally accepted that all identified items on the punch list will be fixed, completed, or installed by the contractor before the owner will accept the facility. As items are corrected to meet design expectations, they are removed from the punch list. The owner should not provide final payment to the contractor until the entire punch list has been completed.

Furniture and Equipment

Planning, designing, purchasing, and coordinating the installation of furniture and equipment can be one of the most demanding aspects of a facility project. Many detailed decisions on furniture size, quantity, and layout will have to be addressed. Depending on the facility, the same equipment decisions regarding functionality, quality, and quantity must also be discussed. The selection and placement of furniture and equipment requires a great deal of planning and leads to a purchasing process. The administrator or owner ultimately makes many decisions regarding what the contractor will be responsible for as part of the project and what the owner will provide with separate funds.

During this stage, all items that are brought to the facility by the facility owner and project vendors are coordinated by the construction manager in the most cooperative and effective way possible. Vendor responsibilities can include shipping, delivery, receiving, and installation and can be difficult to schedule without complications and communication problems. Sometimes items are delivered outside planned times, requiring patience and cooperation between the contractors still on site and the facility employees who are anxious to occupy their new facility. Every effort should be made to avoid inconveniences and the extra labor costs associated with the move-in process by planning ahead and budgeting extra time for this stage.

Acceptance and Occupancy

As noted in the previous two sections, the final stage of a facility project involves moving in the furniture and equipment in addition to finalizing all items on the punch list. The final stage is coordinated by the construction manager and concludes with owner acceptance and occupancy.

Often there is a need for facility employees to take over or move in while a few minor aspects of the construction process are still being completed. This may be necessary for facility employees to prepare for the delivery of the core product or product extensions. The construction manager should consult with contractors to allow for this transition unless there are serious problems that need to be resolved. Facility management employees may not move in without contractor approval. Sometimes items on the punch list are allowed to linger, but it is agreed that they will be completed by a certain date after occupancy.

With the acceptance of the project, the owner formally acknowledges that the facility is complete. Final steps including key and maintenance-manual exchanges, employee training, and final payment to contractors culminate with employees being allowed to occupy the facility. Once acceptance of the project has occurred and the owner has occupancy, the opening ceremony occurs.

The opening ceremony is a culminating event or celebration that may be similar to the ground-breaking ceremony. This ceremony creates an opportunity to publicly thank everyone involved

▶ Opening ceremonies, which often include a ribbon cutting, are an opportunity to recognize that a facility project goal has been achieved as well as to thank those associated with the project.

with the project as well as promote the official opening of the facility. It can incorporate a ceremony including speakers and a ribbon cutting, as well as photographs, tours, and commemorative gifts to those who played a significant role in the project.

The ceremonial activities involved in the construction phase are just a small part of actual construction. The construction stage of the design process is when plans have come together; design documents have been put out for bid, reviewed, and accepted; value assessment has been finalized; and all contractual arrangements have been made and signed. Depending on the size or type of project, the construction process can involve many details, and recreation facility managers should be aware of these variables. The responsibilities associated with any construction project can involve diverse interpretations and applications, and much of this information is included in the construction documents.

SUMMARY

The construction phase is where all of the planning and hard work starts to take shape. It is important that construction documents have been properly prepared so the construction manager can facilitate the construction process and oversee the many responsibilities included in that position. Once construction is finished and the owner or administrator is satisfied that all work has been completed to specifications, the project is deemed complete. At this point, the agency is prepared to start using the facility.

Resources for Recreation Facility Management

The recreation facility manager must manage resources in order to deliver the core product. Most recreation facilities have three basic resources: equipment, financial resources, and people. Equipment includes many objects that must be purchased, distributed, used, and maintained so that users can enjoy them while at a facility. Financial resources are vital to the operation of a facility, although they are not directly used by the consumer. Fiscal responsibility and understanding financial practices are part of everyday life for a recreation facility manager. People (the employees at a recreation facility) are also a vital resource for a recreation facility manager. Great care must be taken in hiring, training, and developing employees.

Managing Equipment

Few recreation facilities can function without equipment. **Recreation facility equipment** could be described as items that enhance, make functional, and complete the administrative and delivery operations of a recreation product. In basic terms, anything in a facility that contributes to the administrative and delivery operations can be considered equipment. Managing and understanding equipment initially seems simple, but it can be logistically and technologically demanding. Specialized knowledge and procedures may be involved to purchase and maintain equipment. It would be virtually impossible to describe in one chapter all the unique equipment that exists in recreation facilities. This chapter gives an overview of the basics of facility equipment, including purchasing equipment, receiving and distributing equipment, renting and leasing equipment, using equipment, and general information on types of equipment.

BASICS OF RECREATION FACILITY EQUIPMENT

Any person in a management role should have a basic understanding of equipment in order to realize its potential. This section outlines the key concepts of equipment diversity, complexity, use, and status to illustrate the scope of equipment in facilities.

Equipment Diversity

Every recreation facility has equipment that contributes to its core product and core product extensions. Each piece of equipment has a unique role within the delivery of the product. Equipment may serve a maintenance, protective, decorative, or administrative function. **Equipment diversity** simply means that there are a variety of purposes that can be served by equipment designed to help deliver a specific product. Recreation facility managers should seek out this information and be knowledgeable of the many equipment options that exist.

Equipment Complexity

Some recreation facility equipment is easy to use and requires little instruction or preparation before use. However, some equipment can be complicated and create greater responsibility for management. Complexity factors include

- special instructions;
- warranty concerns;
- start, operation, and shutdown procedures;
- maintenance requirements;
- storage;
- employee training; and
- safety.

Laws and standards could also influence equipment management. For example, an ice arena that uses an ammonia system requires a piece of equipment called a *compressor*. A compressor is so critical to the function of an ice arena that if it fails to operate, the facility will not be useable. Laws and codes related to the safe operation of an ammonia-based compressor system may require detection and alarm devices to warn customers and employees of unsafe conditions that may result from the compressor.

In addition, equipment delivery, distribution, installation, inventory, and maintenance all have to be monitored properly. When more complex equipment is used in a recreation facility, it requires recreation facility managers to be educated about potential problems or costs associated with use of that equipment.

Equipment Use

Each piece of equipment has a unique application toward enhancing product success. Use of certain recreation equipment could require training ranging from basic to extensive. Some equipment even requires certification before use. For example, chemical-application equipment for outdoor facilities may require an employee to obtain a certification to apply the chemicals. Management must be sensitive to all facets of these requirements. Any equipment use can have potentially hazardous consequences for users and employees. Examples of equipment that can have harmful consequences for employees include mowing equipment, chainsaws, and bucket trucks used to repair lights or other items off the ground. Every precaution should be taken to warn users and employees of the potential dangers of and detailed instructions for using equipment. Some pieces of equipment have user manuals that provide instructions, descriptions, precautions, and safety measures. More technical equipment requires greater user awareness of use and protection. Management must be aware of the use requirements of all facil-

▶A compressor used at an ice arena is a complex piece of facility equipment that is regulated by laws and codes so that people are warned if there are unsafe conditions.

ity equipment and make sure that proper training takes place and appropriate supervision is available at all times.

Equipment Status

Equipment status refers to the condition and availability of equipment for users. In determining the status of equipment, recreation facility managers must consider

- product warranties,
- preventive maintenance,
- projected life span,
- replacement schedules, and
- repair factors.

Equipment that is not functioning affects the ability to properly provide services to recreation facility users. Malfunctioning equipment could create inconveniences, as well as unnecessary expenses. Management should have a system in place that

provides information regarding the status and condition of equipment. Appropriate equipment management practices, which are discussed in more detail in chapter 14, include

- assessing the status of equipment,
- scheduling equipment for and providing funding for preventive maintenance, and
- scheduling appropriate repair or replacement.

This concept is known as *asset management.*

TYPES OF EQUIPMENT

As mentioned in the introduction to this chapter, equipment is anything in a facility that contributes to administrative and delivery operations. Equipment can be broken down in greater detail by considering the cost of the equipment and how it is used. Recreation equipment can be categorized as permanent, expendable, and fixed.

- **Permanent equipment** is not affixed to the facility but is necessary in order for the facility to fulfill its intended purpose. It usually costs more than $500 and has a life expectancy of 2 years or more. This type of equipment usually receives special maintenance consideration and is managed carefully because of its initial cost to purchase and ongoing operational expenses. Permanent equipment includes specialty mowers, vehicles, golf carts, and scoreboards.

- **Expendable equipment** generally costs less than $500 and has a life expectancy of less than 2 years. Expendable equipment mostly relates to the delivery process and is used with the expectation that it may get lost, broken, or worn out. By some definitions, this equipment might also be called **supplies** and includes items such as basketballs, softballs, and netting for sports or furnishings such as beds, desks, tables, and chairs at tourism facilities.

- **Fixed equipment** is firmly attached as part of the facility structure and is usually installed during construction. Removal has a negative impact on the appearance and functionality of the facility. Fixed equipment includes efficiency systems (HVAC); fencing, football, basketball, and soccer goals; playground apparatuses; and restroom fixtures.

Equipment can also be classified in a more specialized manner. It can be categorized as part of efficiency systems, structural equipment, administrative equipment, delivery equipment, or maintenance equipment. These descriptions define equipment as it relates to its function within each type of equipment and recreation operations.

- **Efficiency systems** are the electrical and mechanical systems of equipment that support the overall use of the facility. Efficiency equipment includes HVAC, irrigation, and lighting systems. It maintains comfort, efficiency, and security for users and employees. It is installed during construction and requires technical ability to operate and maintain.

- **Structural equipment** is a permanent, attached part of the facility structure. It is usually installed during construction and is

▶Maintaining permanent equipment, such as this scoreboard, is a top priority for a recreation facility manager because of its high cost and impact on the facility's budget.

included in the construction cost. It is not movable, and if eliminated it would negatively affect facility design and functionality. This category of equipment includes doors, windows, railings, permanent barriers, and permanent seating.

- Every recreation facility has space and **administrative equipment** that supports the administrative and executive operation of the facility. Recreation facility users typically do not use administrative equipment unless they interact with the administration. Often this equipment takes on a sense of ownership among employees even though it belongs to the facility. It includes all computers, scanners, and printers; telephones; file cabinets; cash registers; calculators; fax machines; dictation equipment; copy machines; and typewriters.

- Each recreation facility has **product delivery equipment** that relates specifically to the delivery of the product for which the facility was designed. Employees use this equipment when providing services to customers and users may operate it when using the recreation facility. Some examples of product delivery equipment include the following:

  - A fitness facility may provide weightlifting or cardiorespiratory equipment for users.

  - A golf course may provide golf carts, pull carts, rental clubs, or range balls for users.

  - A white-water rafting company often provides rafts or canoes for participants.

- A variety of maintenance equipment helps keep both recreation facilities and equipment in proper working condition. Many types of maintenance equipment require qualified, capable personnel. Training may be provided in-house and is necessary for safe and proper use. Maintenance equipment includes lawn mowers, vehicles, chemical sprayers, fertilizer spreaders, floor cleaning equipment, and custodial equipment.

There are a few other equipment items that should be incorporated into the management process because they assist with the delivery of the core product and core product extensions. They include all forms of equipment that are planned, designed, and purchased to be used in the management of a recreation facility, such

▶ Rafts are product delivery equipment for a white water rafting company.

as supplies, keys, furniture, security equipment, fire protection equipment, decorative equipment, and signage.

- Supplies are expendable items that are consumed during the production process. Examples include office supplies (e.g., paper, pencils, staples, paperclips, pens), cleaning products (e.g., toilet paper, paper towels, soap, trash bags), and similar items. They are generally used in administrative and delivery responsibilities to help present or support the delivery of a product but are not as costly as other forms of administrative equipment. Supplies require processes similar to other equipment when it comes to storage, inventory, stocking, and replacement.

- Although keys and locking systems are not often thought of as equipment, they involve similar responsibilities as part of recreation facility management. All recreation facilities need to be secured or locked outside of business hours.

It is also important that recreation facilities have key and locking systems in place during business hours to keep unwanted people out. The process or system for securing a facility can be very involved. A variety of options in key styles, systems, and sizes will be discussed in detail in chapter 12. New technology for securing recreation facilities include bar-coded cards and even fingerprint or other technical access options. Keys or cards require a system of control for distribution and inventory. They are distributed in a process similar to that for other equipment, including recording the person the key is assigned to, the date assigned, and the date returned (see figure 9.1). Keys should be subjected to regular inventory checks. Locking systems can also vary from those built into doors and gates to padlocks that are externally attached.

- Furniture is another recreation facility item that generally involves the same planning and purchasing process as equipment. Furniture is permanent and is purchased, inventoried, and distributed in a similar manner as all other equipment. It includes office desks and chairs, credenzas, conference tables and chairs, lounge chairs, sofas, coffee tables, end tables, and televi-

sion equipment. Furniture often requires repair because of abuse, overuse, or parts that no longer work as intended.

- Facility security requires **security equipment** that is in place to protect the employees and users as well as the facility and its equipment. Some examples include turnstiles, barriers, identification readers, video cameras and monitors, alarms, specialized exit doors, and metal-detection devices. Security equipment can be permanent or expendable.

- All recreation facilities must be designed, constructed, and maintained to protect users and employees in the event of a fire by being equipped with fire protection equipment. Fire is the most common form of serious emergency or disruption, and there are legal codes in place specifically for fire protection that must be followed. Fire protection equipment includes smoke sensors, exit signs, sprinkler systems, fire hoses, fire extinguishers, and fire alarms. This protective equipment is assessed regularly and repaired or replaced as needed.

- Decorative items make the recreation facility more aesthetically pleasing, adding to the appear-

▶ It is crucial for all staff to be trained on how to use a fire extinguisher because fire is the most common form of serious emergency or disruption.

Staff Key Checkout and Return Agreement

Checkout

Date_____

Staff checking out key _____
Print   Signature

Staff receiving key _____
Print   Signature

Check-in

Date_____

Staff checking in key _____
Print   Signature

Staff returning key _____
Print   Signature

From R. Mull, B. Beggs, and M. Renneisen, 2009, *Recreation Facility Management* (Champaign, IL: Human Kinetics).

Figure 9.1 Key check-in and check-out form.

ance and pleasantness to help users and employees feel comfortable. These items can include window coverings, pictures, sculptures, displays, plants, and floral arrangements. Recreation facility managers should make these items a priority and maintain them as they do other expensive equipment.

• Signage is another type of item not commonly recognized as equipment in a recreation facility. Items of this nature are planned, designed, purchased, and usually installed at the time of construction. Some examples of signage include facility directories, directional signs, arrows, floor and wall guides, individual area signs, and emergency signs. The signage style and content can be changed or replaced as facility areas take on new functions.

PURCHASING EQUIPMENT

Appropriate equipment has to be purchased and placed in the recreation facility in order for the facility to fulfill its purpose. The timeline for purchasing equipment varies based on the type of equipment being purchased and the timeline for construction. Recreation facility managers should refer to the construction schedule, research how long it takes to get a piece of equipment delivered, and determine an appropriate timeline for purchasing the equipment. This section contains a detailed series of steps to follow when purchasing equipment for a facility:

1. Research
2. Purchase requisition
3. Bid process

4. Purchase orders
5. Invoicing and payment
6. Warranty purchasing

Research

Equipment purchasing usually begins with a recreation facility manager providing a written description of need and interest that is based on sound rationale, or research. Research is a prepurchase action, and it is necessary to identify the most appropriate equipment for the desired function and the best price. This process involves reviewing available options in terms of quality, durability, price, and payment. It also involves understanding the amount of time required for obtaining a piece of equipment.

Purchase Requisitions

Once a piece of equipment has been identified through the research process, recreation facility managers must make a request to purchase the equipment. The preliminary request for obtaining equipment is called the **purchase requisition,** which is a written request to administration indicating a need for a particular piece of equipment. Usually there is a standard form to be completed by employees that allows space for justification for the purchase (see figure 9.2). The form also allows for specifications that include type, size, model, cost, quality, and delivery timetable. A recommended vendor may be listed who has provided assistance with the details of the purchase or has already submitted the most competitive price.

Bid Process

In some instances, a bid process is involved before a purchase can be made. The bid process allows vendors an equal opportunity to obtain the business of a recreation facility. The bid process entails the solicitation of price quotes, either formally or informally, from two or more vendors. A bid process is not required in all recreation facilities; some recreation facility managers can purchase items directly without having to solicit prices from vendors. A formal bidding process is usually required by public agencies, especially as the cost of equipment increases. Different agencies have different guidelines for when the formal bidding process must take place. There are also occasions when private businesses use this process in order to obtain the best price. It's best for recreation

Purchase Requisition

Location, facility, and program _____

Requested by _____ Date requested _____

Purchase justification _____

Vendor _____ Address _____

City, state _____ Zip code _____

Phone _____ Fax _____

Quantity	Unit	Description (type, size, model)	Unit price	Amount
			$	$
			$	$
			$	$
			$	$
			$	$
			$	$
			$	$
			Shipping/freight	$
			Total	$

Delivery to _____

_____

_____

_____

Approved by _____ Date _____

Other _____

From R. Mull, B. Beggs, and M. Renneisen, 2009, *Recreation Facility Management* (Champaign, IL: Human Kinetics).

Figure 9.2 Purchase requisition form.

facility managers to follow agency guidelines for the bid process.

Once all the details, or specifications, are established, the request for bids is made available to prospective bidders and the bid process begins. All information submitted by vendors remains confidential until the deadline for submittal. This process ensures fairness, eliminates favoritism, and stimulates competition to reduce pricing. A deadline is set and a bid opening announced so that all vendors may attend the bid opening to hear the outcome. The equipment order usually is awarded to the lowest and most responsive bidder. See chapter 7 for more details on the bid process for contractors.

Purchase Orders

Once a vendor is selected, a formal written request is initiated to order the equipment and arrange for delivery. This form is called a *purchase order* and can include quantity, size, color, model number, warranty information, delivery information and timetable, price, and method of shipping. It is a contract with the vendor that states the intent

and understanding of the purchase. The vendor receives this purchase order and is expected to meet the specifications as presented and deliver the equipment in a timely fashion. The equipment should be ordered well in advance, allowing ample time for shipping and receiving.

Shipping

Shipping and delivery should be included in the bid process. Time and place of delivery are important because equipment arriving at the wrong location can create additional work for delivery personnel and may delay access to the equipment or even delay the opening of a new facility. Equipment could require special arrangements for handling and installation, particularly large or costly equipment, such as playground equipment or picnic tables.

Invoicing and Payment

Shortly after delivery, the vendor usually sends an invoice requesting payment. A payment process follows after the equipment is assessed to determine whether it has arrived undamaged and performs as intended. The payment process can be as simple as writing a check or paying in cash to a more elaborate process that may take several weeks before a vendor receives full payment. Sometimes a percentage of the payment is withheld until the equipment is known to fulfill its intended use and performance requirements are met. Holding a percentage of payment under these terms is referred to as *retainage*. Each recreation facility has its own process for completing a purchase transaction based on the accounting controls established by the administration.

Warranty Purchase

Another way to ensure that the equipment performs as it should is to purchase equipment that comes with a warranty. A warranty includes a length of time after the purchase where the vendor is responsible for replacing or repairing the equipment should it not function properly. In such instances, the equipment must be repaired or replaced by the manufacturer or a third party. Warranty arrangements are usually built into the purchasing arrangement, especially with expensive equipment. Other factors to consider when purchasing a dealer or manufacturer's warranty include whether installation and training are provided, access to any parts that may be needed,

▶It is especially important to make advance arrangements for delivery and installation of larger equipment, such as this playground equipment.

and service or maintenance expectations until the expiration of the warranty.

RECEIVING AND DISTRIBUTING EQUIPMENT

Whereas shipping and delivery is the vendor's responsibility, receiving and distributing equipment is the responsibility of management. At the point of delivery, the owner accepts the equipment knowing from that point on it will be difficult to return, a process known as *receiving*. Before receiving equipment, facility owners or managers must be sure they are receiving what they ordered both in quality as well as in quantity. Vendors can make mistakes in the shipping process, and the order should meet expectations as stated in the purchase order. Equipment orders also should be inspected for damage that may have occurred during shipping and handling. Equipment can be rejected and returned to the vendor at no cost if equipment was damaged during delivery or shipping. Management should not accept equipment that cannot be used or does not meet expectations.

Once a piece of equipment has been received, it must be documented and temporarily stored before it can be distributed. Inventory is the process of recording the receipt and ownership of equipment. Through an inventory system, equipment arrival, condition, and status can be recorded and maintained. An inventory system should also include the following equipment information:

- date received,
- cost,
- condition,
- quantity, and
- identification number.

Once it has been inventoried, the equipment will either be immediately distributed or temporarily stored. Sometimes equipment, particularly specialty items, requires arrangements for storing and protecting it until it is needed for use. All security measures should be taken under consideration when storing equipment, including proper lighting, locks, and inventory controls. Also, the storage environment could affect the equipment, so temperature and humidity should be considered.

Size and shape of equipment could also affect where items may be stored. Finally, accessibility should be considered so that equipment can be easily distributed.

Equipment storage areas are critical, but unfortunately, these areas are often the first to be eliminated when designing a recreation facility or when additional space is needed. Management should recognize the importance of adequate storage space for equipment. The reality in most facilities is that there rarely seems to be enough storage space.

Distribution of equipment to the appropriate employee or area should be linked to the inventory records and tracked annually or semiannually. Usually, some type of arrangement is made so that the user or employee accepts responsibility for proper use and care of the equipment. Management also may require training, experience, or certification before certain equipment is made available for use, such as in the instance of climbing equipment, certain aerobic and strength equipment, and equipment used for specialized maintenance.

RENTING AND LEASING EQUIPMENT

Sometimes facilities require equipment that the agency does not own or desire to purchase. In other situations, certain equipment may only be necessary for a short duration or to meet a specific need. The purchase of extremely specialized equipment may not be justifiable because of the expense involved. In this case, two options to consider are renting or leasing. Renting equipment is common for small recreation facilities because it requires few arrangements and usually minimal expense. Renting generally requires some paperwork, valid identification, a deposit (which is returned when the item is returned undamaged), and a rental fee.

Leasing equipment is an option to consider when equipment may be needed that is not available for rent or when the cost of the equipment is too great to consider purchasing in one payment. Usually, an equipment lease is for a designated length of time with a signed contract that stipulates the leasing agreement between parties. Some advantages to leasing equipment are that it can be less expensive than a new purchase and maintenance and insurance costs are usually covered. Types of equipment that are commonly rented or leased include

- tables and chairs,
- sound systems,
- specialty cleaning and maintenance equipment,
- temporary or portable playground equipment, and
- concession equipment.

USING EQUIPMENT

The purpose of equipment is to make it available to employees to assist in delivering the product or to make it available to users. Most equipment is available for open use such as fitness equipment or play structures. It is the responsibility of facility employees to ensure that equipment is used properly and in good operating condition. Recreation facility managers should have systems in place for employees to supervise equipment use and monitor its condition.

Sometimes a fee is charged for use of the equipment for a certain amount of time, and this is called a rental. Equipment rental systems should record the condition of the equipment at the time of checkout and when it is returned. Depending on the original cost of the equipment, a deposit could also be required, which is then returned when the equipment is returned undamaged. Checkout systems can have many rules, including advance reservations, use experience or training, damage responsibility, and proof of age or insurance. A master file can be kept as a record for equipment that has been checked out that includes the user's address, phone, and e-mail, and depending on the complexity of the system, computer software could be used to keep track of everything. In this system, the facility is responsible for providing equipment that functions as intended, and the user is responsible for using it properly. Both parties are responsible for meeting expectations established at distribution.

SUMMARY

Equipment plays an important role for recreation facility managers in delivering the product in a recreation facility. Equipment includes many objects and is unique to each recreation facility. Great care must be taken by management to understand the types of equipment needed for a facility and proper ways to purchase, distribute, use, and maintain that equipment to create optimal experiences for staff and users.

Managing Finances

In recent years, greater emphasis has been placed on the fiscal responsibilities related to recreation facility functions. Chapter 7 discussed fiscal responsibility in terms of funding and the bid process for construction. This chapter will address fiscal responsibility in regards to managing a facility. Although the basic principles that influence funding for private and public recreation facilities are different, as discussed in chapter 7, many of the concepts are similar. Increased expenses, including inflation, wages, and utilities, in addition to higher expectations from users have made fiscal responsibilities more involved for recreation facility managers. Also, recreation facility managers need to be able to minimize the expenses associated with the deterioration of recreation facilities and equipment. Recreation administrators play a role in preparation, implementation, review, and control of all related funding sources as part of managing finances.

Expenses associated with recreation facilities fall into the categories of construction expenses and management expenses. Construction expenses for a recreation facility can be extensive and vary greatly. The planning, design, and construction expenses are overhead expenses that will exist for management as long as the facility exists. Planning and design costs are considered a part of the construction costs of a facility, and although categorized as soft costs, typically are included on part of the long term financing package of a facility. Management-related expenses are ongoing costs to operate, maintain, program, supervise, promote, and renovate a facility and include salaries, supplies, equipment, marketing costs, and so on.

It is not uncommon for users, and to some extent, employees, to have little appreciation for the expenses associated with recreation facility construction, maintenance, and management. The expenses associated with product delivery in a recreation facility are much more involved than most people realize.

EXPENSES

Numerous expenses have an impact on recreation facility management. These expenses can be extensive, and they are greatly influenced by the success of the product in generating the income necessary to support management responsibilities. A large percentage of all recreation agency expenses revolve around facilities and their employees, maintenance, utilities, repair, and renovation expenses. Typical recreation facility expense categories can be broken down into two broad categories: structural expenses and support expenses.

Structural Expenses

The presence of a recreation facility as a structure creates **structural expenses.** These are expenses associated with maintaining or improving the physical structure of the facility and can include repair, renovation, and retrofitting. In addition, structural expenses can include loan or mortgage, depreciation, taxes, reserve, and insurance expenses.

Repairing, Renovating, and Retrofitting

Over time, facilities and equipment deteriorate, no longer fulfilling their original purpose. When this occurs, expenses are incurred to keep them functional. Typical repairs to recreation facilities include repairing broken doors, windows, locks, and other equipment or spaces. Sometimes facilities undergo a complete renovation that modifies the original layout and design purpose. Some renovation projects include expanding existing facilities, creating greater recreation production space, and expanding administrative areas or other spaces in demand. Retrofitting also modifies a structure by adding new or more modern systems to a facility. An example might include adding new plumbing or retrofitting the facility with a new security system. All of these situations require proper planning and budgeting, as discussed in chapter 5.

Loan or Mortgage

One of the greatest ongoing expenses for recreation facilities is the monthly or quarterly loan or mortgage payments for construction or purchase of a facility. This arrangement can be in the form of a bank loan or bond payment and commits management to repay the debt for the purchase or construction of a recreation facility over a predetermined length of time. The payment includes the cost of purchase or construction plus interest, which varies depending on market conditions. The predetermined length of time for satisfying the obligations of the loan is usually between 10 and 30 years. Part of the responsibility for recreation facility managers is generating enough income to meet this expense.

▶Renovating any part of an existing facility is considered to be a structural expense.

Depreciation

As soon as a recreation facility or piece of equipment is purchased, it begins to lose value. The decrease in value of recreation facilities and equipment by a certain percentage each year is called **depreciation.** The amount depreciated can be recorded as an expense for tax purposes.

Taxes

One of the big differences between public and private agencies is that public recreation facilities may receive tax support for construction or operation. Another significant difference is that public recreation facilities may be exempt from paying certain taxes on income generated from a product or from paying property taxes. Private facilities can be at a serious disadvantage when they are in direct competition with a public recreation facility that has tax support as income in addition to not paying taxes due to its public status. In the private sector, paying taxes is a responsibility that must be factored into operational expenses. Recreation professionals, particularly in the private sector,

are encouraged to seek advice from accountants or financial planners in order to maximize tax deductions and correctly prepare facility tax returns.

Reserve Fund

In order to protect against having to spend funds from the daily operational cash flow, a reserve is created as an expense management category. A reserve fund is a sound fiscal practice of setting aside money for potential facility problems. Unexpected situations can include vandalism, weather damage, fire, and equipment breakdowns. These situations vary greatly from facility to facility, and they are often unpredictable and sometimes unavoidable.

Insurance

Competent recreation administrators or facility managers budget for adequate insurance coverage. Insurance should cover potential losses for management with a policy that defines the conditions for coverage. Several categories of insurance may be necessary at any given recreation facility.

Typically,

- liability insurance,
- accident insurance,
- workers' compensation, and
- property damage or theft insurance coverage

all may be needed. Not all problems can be anticipated, and having insurance coverage is the key to being able to pay for these unexpected problems. Examples of unexpected problems include user or employee injuries or fatalities, equipment damage, or destruction of facilities. Management should purchase adequate insurance to cover these and other potential problems.

Support Expenses

The second general expense category includes costs that support operations. It includes expenses associated with employees, maintenance, equipment, utilities, and contractual services.

Employees

One of the greatest recreation facility expenses is labor costs. Several expenses are created by the people who keep facilities and equipment functional, including

- salary,
- hourly wages,
- payroll taxes,
- benefits,
- training, and
- professional development.

Employee compensation is important to understand and manage because it can easily account for 50 to 80 percent of the budget. Employees will be discussed in more detail in chapter 11.

Maintenance

Allocating adequate funds to support maintenance is paramount. Some recreation agencies consider facility maintenance as one of the most important aspects of presenting their product. Proper maintenance of recreation facilities and equipment is not only a serious consideration to the comfort and efficiency of product delivery, but it also contributes to facility and equipment longevity by preventing unnecessary wear and tear. Maintenance expenditures should be analyzed, including

▶Snow removal is just one example of the numerous maintenance costs involved in managing a recreation facility.

routine, nonroutine, and preventive maintenance. These categories will be discussed in more detail in chapter 14. Maintenance costs include both building and ground maintenance tasks, such as performing custodial services, lubricating machines, painting, fixing broken equipment, repairing fencing, repairing lighting, maintaining turf, removing snow and leaves, and so on.

Equipment

A primary responsibility of recreation administrators is budgeting funds for the purchase and care of all equipment. There is an extensive array of items, objects, and equipment within a recreation facility that can vary greatly in cost. There is not only the initial equipment purchase expense, but also ongoing costs to keep equipment functioning as intended. Some equipment can be extremely expensive. An ice-resurfacing machine, commonly known as a Zamboni, may cost $65,000 to $80,000. Certain types of mowing equipment for golf courses may cost between $25,000 and $50,000. Annual maintenance-related costs associated with the type of equipment can be 5-10% of the original purchase price. It can be frustrating for facility users and employees if equipment is not functioning. As with maintenance costs, recreation administrators and facility managers must allocate adequate funds to keep equipment functioning properly.

Utilities

Virtually no recreation facility can function without access to water and electricity, or utilities. Each utility represents an expense category that usually has to be paid for on a monthly basis. Recreation facility managers must maximize the use of a facility and scrutinize the utilities to minimize their cost where possible. Recreation facility managers can compare past usage information to help monitor costs and identify savings through more efficient use. Computer software can assist in minimizing the costs associated with utilities by analyzing usage and determining the most efficient way to operate.

Additional utility expenses include provisions for communication devices commonly used at recreation facilities. This equipment can come in many forms, including telephones (both land lines and cellular phones), two-way radios, computers, and cable or satellite television. Monitoring expenses so that employees do not abuse these services and create unnecessary expenses presents an additional challenge for managers.

Contractual Services

Another facility expense category is outside **contractual services** that assist with facets of the facility that cannot be managed internally. Typical contractual services include repairs to HVAC systems, janitorial services, garbage removal, landscaping, design assistance, consultant assistance, and snow removal. Usually these arrangements are made with interested vendors who bid for the job, with the contract going to the lowest and most responsive bidder. Outside contractual services, also called **outsourcing,** can be an important means of meeting recreation facility needs. Contractual service expenses should be planned, negotiated, and agreed upon with careful attention to the need for outside assistance and the costs of providing the service.

INCOME

Sources of income for recreation facilities can also be complex and difficult to fully understand. In order for a facility to be viable, income must be generated by the facility. Income generation is critical to the success of recreation facility managers in delivering the core product to the user. Many decisions regarding the delivery of a recreation product revolve around pricing the core product and core product extensions and the ability for those products to generate income. This income is categorized, classified, applied, and analyzed carefully to meet monthly, quarterly, and annual expenses.

Income generated can be viewed in two categories: **gross income,** which is the total amount of money generated over a specified amount of time, and **net income,** which is the remaining funds after all expenses, including taxes, have been paid. Net income is also known as profit, which is the primary source of revenue for private recreation entities.

A number of income sources exist for facilities depending on their classification as profit or not for profit. Sources of income can include fees and charges, rentals, donations, investors, investments, sponsorship, and tax support.

Fees and Charges

Many ways of collecting income through fees and charges relate to the purpose of the recreation facility and the desire for users to access a product. Fees and charges can come from

- ticket sales,
- user fees,
- membership fees,
- activity fees, or retail outlets.

The amount of the fee is based on expenses that can include overhead, construction, mortgage, personnel, supplies, maintenance, and utilities costs. These are all direct expenses resulting from the delivery of the product in the recreation facility.

Market factors also influence fees and charges. The simple business principle of supply and demand affects the ability of recreation facilities to charge more for certain products. If the existence, appearance, and service quality of a recreation facility are in demand, higher fees can be charged and thus generate greater income. The condition of a recreation facility in relation to its ability to generate income should never be underestimated. The amount of income deemed adequate is based on the mission of the agency in addition to its status as a profit or not-for-profit facility.

Rentals

Some recreation facilities may present the opportunity for income generation by renting space or equipment. Renting is an option when interest exists to use space or equipment and customers are willing to pay a rental fee. Recreation facilities that often provide rental opportunities include park pavilions, public pools, community-center meeting rooms, banquet halls, and athletic facilities. The rental amount that the customer pays varies on what is being rented, the going rate for such a rental, and whether an agency is public, private, or nonprofit.

Donations

Many recreation agencies create an interest in and image of their facility that results in an opportunity for donations. If a recreation agency appeals to a community, particularly if it provides services for young people, financial support through donations may be an option. This is especially the case in public or nonprofit settings such as local schools, park and recreation departments, and other organizations where the public interests are primary to the mission of the agency rather than making a profit. Donations can also offer tax advantages to the donor, which presents an even better opportunity for those who can afford it to extend their financial support.

Arrangements can also be made for receiving in-kind gifts for recreation facility projects. As dis-

▶User fees and charges are a major source of income for recreation facilities.

cussed in chapter 7, an in-kind gift is when an interested party places a monetary value on a donated asset; intangible item, labor, or service supplied for a recreation facility project and receives a tax advantage in exchange. Some facility programs and equipment needs can depend partially or entirely on donations for support.

Investors

An individual or group of individuals with adequate financial resources, or **investors,** can provide funds for a recreation facility project in the hope of eventually receiving a dividend on their investment. Investors have a percentage interest in a for-profit recreation facility. For example, private golf courses, particularly high-end courses, may have one or more investors who provide financial resources for the construction and continuing management of the facility. A return on the investment greatly depends upon the profitability of the facility.

Investments

Recreation administrators can invest excess cash in marketable securities to generate income.

Certain recreation facilities may generate excess income beyond expenses during a fiscal year. In these cases, it may be possible to invest the excess cash instead of letting it sit idle in a checking or savings account. Investments can be short term or long term in the form of interest on bonds and notes or dividends on shares of stock. Investment strategies should be investigated thoroughly before implementation. Financial consultants may be an important resource to consult before choosing to invest funds to produce additional income.

Sponsorships

In recent years there has been an increase in recreation agencies supporting their financial responsibilities through **sponsorships.** This form of fiscal support usually results from cooperative interests between two agencies, both looking to gain something from the sponsorship. Usually a sponsor offers financial resources to help with expenses in exchange for access to advertising space or promotional exposure. Income from sponsorships can be used to defray operational expenses, complete facility projects, satisfy equipment needs, or pay for employee expenses. Sponsorship income

▶Usually a sponsor will offer financial resources to help with facility expenses in exchange for advertising space at the sponsored facility.

is not usually part of the annual budget unless it is a long-term arrangement that can be counted on year after year. Many professional sport facilities generate significant income from sponsorship arrangements. In these cases, a facility may give naming rights to the sponsor in exchange for a long-term (often 10 years or more) commitment. Recreational facilities have also been successful on a smaller scale, recruiting sponsors for items such as scoreboards or wall space in ice arenas or indoor soccer facilities.

Tax Support

Most public recreation agencies depend on some type of income from local, state, or federal taxes. The general funding philosophy of tax-supported facilities is that the facility serves the needs of the community. These needs are extensive and can be observed in public schools, correctional settings, military bases, colleges and universities, and other municipal settings. Although most local public recreation agencies would be unable to operate without tax support, even professional sport venues are relying more and more on tax support to finance construction. Tax support is not only important in construction, but for public recreation agencies, it is also essential for programming and daily operations. Tax support is highly political and evolves from political leadership that can persuade government entities to fund a public need. In most instances, increasing income through taxes is decided by residents of a taxing jurisdiction by voting on **referendums** in elections.

FISCAL PRACTICES

Managing facility finances involves many more details and responsibilities than what has been presented in this material. In addition to having an understanding of expenses and sources of income in delivering the product, recreation facility managers must also organize and present systems for managing finances. The most common fiscal practices for managing finances include budgeting, accounting, and cost analysis. Although these are complex tools that should be understood in great detail before starting a career in leisure services, this section offers a brief overview of what is taught in classes for managing recreation finances.

Budgeting

Budgeting can be described as a systematic effort to project all income and expenses for a given length of time. Most recreation agencies budget in yearly cycles, submitting budget projections to the administration 3 to 6 months before a new fiscal year. The fiscal year is a 12-month cycle, which does not necessarily correspond with a calendar year, during which a recreation agency determines and monitors its financial condition. A financial forecast, or budget, is critical because it allows for financial planning and anticipation of income and expenses for a fiscal year. Reviewing historical expense and income information when preparing budget requests, calculating inflation or other cost increases, and projecting anticipated revenue for the coming fiscal year is a common budgeting practice. Each facility has its own way of administering its budget. Recreation professionals must understand their role in the budgeting process.

Accounting

Recreation professionals must be aware of their accountability for funds generated at their facilities. Part of the budget process requires ongoing record keeping of income and expenditures, or accounting. Accounting practices are usually done by an accountant or fiscal officer in the organization and involve generating reports on a monthly, quarterly, and annual basis. These reports reflect specific income and expense categories and are often compared with data from the previous year, other time frames within the year, or a predetermined budget that outlines management expectations. Administrators should regularly review these records from the accounting system or accountant and strive to keep facility expenditures within budget and maintain income levels.

Cost Analysis

Cost analysis is the process of comparing and analyzing costs associated with delivering a recreation product in an effort to determine the true costs of delivering the product and applying ways to save money. Expenses have a direct correlation to the profitability of a recreation operation. Facility managers use the accounting systems and budget to see what costs are, but cost analysis goes beyond this. It involves comparing data from previous years, finding trends, benchmarking income and expenses against similar recreation operations, reviewing internal and external influences, comparing vendors, and analyzing dramatic changes to thoroughly evaluate the costs of an operation. Ultimately the cost analysis results in recommendations to reduce operational costs and provide savings.

SUMMARY

Recreation facility managers must be aware of a wide variety of details in relation to managing finances. These responsibilities are integral to the viability of a recreation facility and can ultimately determine its success or failure. Competent recreation professionals will acquaint themselves with their fiscal responsibilities and attend to these responsibilities on a daily basis.

Managing Employees

LEARNING OBJECTIVES

At the completion of this chapter, you should be able to do the following:

1. Define the concept of staffing.

2. Explain what job classification is.

3. Understand the difference between the job description and the job announcement.

4. Explain the steps involved in the hiring process.

5. Recognize what a recreation administrator can do to create a good work environment.

The most important aspect of recreation facility management is selecting and assigning the appropriate people to perform the functions associated with delivering a product to users. The work environment often leads to relationships between the employee and employer that can last for many years. Recreation facilities require a diverse array of employees to fulfill their various responsibilities. The nature of recreation facility work can vary greatly from supervising facilities, training users on new activities, and marketing programs and services to performing simple maintenance tasks, coordinating space and equipment, and managing finances. Finding people to fulfill all of these tasks makes the process of recruiting, hiring, and training recreation facility employees extremely important.

The process of recruiting and hiring employees to fulfill job obligations associated with the delivery of a product at a recreation agency is called staffing. It is vital to have employees with appropriate skills assigned to positions that maximize their expertise in performing the functions of the position. Recruiting and hiring employees is a detailed process that requires a considerable amount of planning. Before recreation facility managers can actively recruit employees, however, they must determine precisely what type of position they need to hire for and where that position fits within the organization. This process is called *job classification.*

JOB CLASSIFICATION

The process of **job classification** places a value on each job that is required to fulfill the mission and goals of a recreation agency. This value determines the compensation and responsibilities associated with each position. Collectively, this process results in a hierarchical compilation of the job title and responsibilities of each job necessary to deliver the products of a specific recreation organization.

Recreation organizations vary in complexity and diversity. Some may not require a great deal of attention to managing the various jobs required for operations. However, all jobs in the facility need to be thoroughly analyzed, and that content needs to be organized into a meaningful structure. Some jobs will require many technical skills whereas other positions will require few if any such skills. As noted earlier, the first step in managing employees is to realize all the job responsibilities needed for operating the recreation agency and to classify all jobs. Job classifications result in all positions having a title that demonstrates the classification of each position within the organization. An organizational chart is a common way to classify and organize positions (see figure 11.1).

Job classification also should reflect compensation for performing the job. It is important that all employees be compensated fairly according to their responsibilities. Benefits such as health insurance, vacation and sick leave, and retirement benefits are usually part of the compensation package and are critical to recruiting and retaining qualified staff. Compensation packages are usually established by human resources management professionals. However, recreation administrators bring expertise regarding the unique personnel requirements of the agency that can influence the compensation offered to potential employees.

▶ Vacation leave may be one part of a benefit package that recreation facility managers offer their employees.

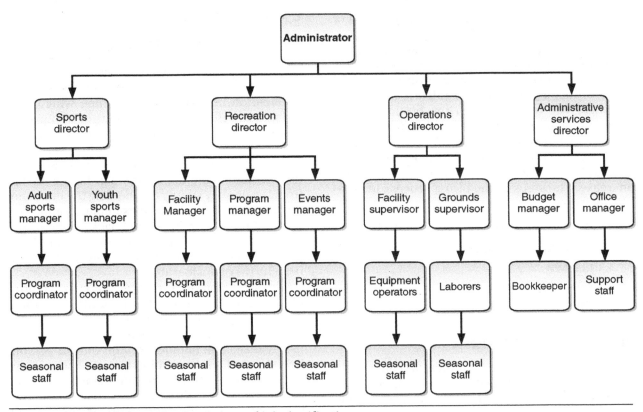

Figure 11.1 Sample organizational chart of job classifications.

JOB DESCRIPTION

Once the job classification has been determined, the next step is to prepare a job description. The **job description** is a detailed document that includes all the responsibilities of the position. This information must be present to get the attention of prospective employees and also to eliminate unqualified applicants. A job description includes the specific job area, its placement in the organization, and its responsibilities. This formal way of communicating job responsibilities to potential employees should be given detailed attention. Job descriptions also should be reviewed and updated regularly to reflect the addition or subtraction of responsibilities. Ultimately, the job description can serve as a contract between management and the employee. The job description could include the following:

- Summary of the position
- Primary functions
- General and specific responsibilities
- Selection criteria
- Details on whom the employee reports to

In addition, the job description is used during the performance evaluation described later in this chapter.

HIRING PROCEDURES

Once the job has been classified and the job description has been written, the hiring process can take place. At this point, recreation administrators and recreation facility managers should be aware of the regulations that affect the selection of prospective employees. Human resources departments and legal counsel for agencies can provide information regarding hiring practices. There are also a number of handbooks and Web resources available, such as Web site found at http://employment-law.freeadvice.com/hiring/. Recreation administrators must base hiring decisions on the competency of the person applying for the position while also taking into consideration laws, ethics, and practicalities. For example, it is illegal to discriminate against an applicant based on race, sex, or age. Human resources professionals can advise managers on the various laws and regulations that apply to the hiring procedures of the organization.

The responsibilities of many positions require recreation facility managers to make difficult choices in hiring applicants. Applicants will have to display a variety of talents, skills, and abilities. The basic steps of the hiring process should remain the same for every position in the organization. However, the challenge of selecting the best candidate for the position becomes more demanding as the responsibilities of the position increase. The steps in the hiring process include the following:

1. Job announcement
2. Application screening
3. Interview
4. Assessment exercises
5. Job offer

Job Announcement

The first step in recruiting potential candidates for recreation facility positions is to make a formal **job announcement,** also called a *job posting,* that can be used to create candidate awareness of the opportunity. This announcement could be advertised in local newspapers, in professional journals, on job-search Web sites, and on facility bulletin boards where potential candidates might look for job opportunities. Another resource for promoting employment opportunities is referrals from existing employees. Some organizations even provide referral bonuses to employees, especially for high-level positions that are more difficult to fill. Often, current employees have friends or other professional contacts who may be interested in a job opportunity. If a position is at a higher level in an organization, it is common to make the job announcement available to a larger pool of candidates. Lower- and entry-level positions tend to be advertised on a regional or local scale but can also be posted to a national audience.

One important component of the job announcement is the deadline for applications to be submitted. This information should be included in all job announcements along with the person and address to where the application should be sent. The job announcement should also specify what documents should be included in the application. Some agencies require that a résumé be sent with a formal application letter. It is also common for agencies to require letters of reference or an application form, which can be obtained from the hiring agency.

Screening of Application Materials

Once the application deadline has passed, recreation facility managers must review the submitted application materials to determine which candidates to interview. Assessment of application materials should be as objective as possible and should be based on the selection criteria and specific screening requirements listed in the job description. Some applicants can be eliminated from the pool by simply not meeting the minimum requirements of the job. For example, an applicant may not have the educational background or the years of experience required for a higher-level position. These applicants should be removed from further consideration.

It's not uncommon to receive a large number of applications for some recreation positions. Depending on the position, a multistep process may be necessary to narrow the field of applicants to a manageable number to interview in person. Recreation facility administrators and managers may choose to conduct phone interviews to narrow the field. This process also eliminates travel expenses for candidates or the agency. Ideally, the initial screening process should lead to a ranking of the top three to five candidates for the position. These candidates should be advanced to the next step in the hiring process, the interview.

Interview

A common practice for interviewing the top three to five candidates is a face-to-face interview with the supervising staff member. Occasionally, a team of staff members including the supervisor, potential coworkers, a subordinate, and possibly a member of the board or administration may participate in a group interview. Another potential member of the interview team is a representative of facility users. Whatever process is chosen for the interview, it is critical that the interview questions be carefully prepared in advance. The questions should be crafted to determine if the candidates possess the most important competencies required of the position. In determining questions to ask, it is necessary to avoid questions that are illegal. It is not legal to ask personal questions that are not related to the position, such as questions about religion, marital status, and family status.

Each candidate should be asked the same questions, and the responses to each question should be noted and later compared when selecting the most qualified candidate. This ensures that each candidate is given a fair and equal opportunity to earn the position.

Assessment Exercises

Assessment exercises may also be included in the interview process depending on the complexity of the position. If the position requires the applicant to be competent in writing, it would be appropriate to include a writing exercise. Positions that require certain maintenance skills, such as operating heavy equipment, may include a field exercise to have the applicants display that particular maintenance skill. Positions that require extensive use of certain computer software may include an exercise that tests the use of that software. These exercises complement the face-to-face interview in an effort to fully assess the competencies of each candidate.

Following the conclusion of the interview and assessment exercises, candidates should be ranked in sequential order based on how they meet the competencies of the position. In a situation where two or more candidates are ranked closely, the recreation facility manager may wish to conduct another round of interviews. At the conclusion of the interview process, the appropriate agency representative should make a job offer to the candidate and negotiate the details of the offer. The job offer should provide the potential employee with an offer of a starting salary and benefit package. The benefit package could include medical and dental benefits, vacation days, personal days, and any other work-related benefits such as the use of a vehicle, compensation time, or an expense account. The prospective employee may wish to negotiate the salary and benefit package. Once it has been agreed upon, the agency may require that the prospective employee sign a contract verifying the agreed amount.

ON-THE-JOB TRAINING

The final stage of the staffing process involves conveying the job responsibilities directly to the new employee. The employee may have a certain level of experience and education that influences the orientation required. The orientation process may include giving the new employee a tour of the facility, meeting a variety of agency staff members, training on the use of computers and other equipment, and reviewing personnel manuals to acquaint the employee with the benefits and policies of the agency. Even if an employee has been hired from within the organization, it is still important to provide a complete orientation for the new position.

Every recreation agency has unique training circumstances and conditions that need to be brought to the employee's attention. This is accomplished from meeting with various agency staff, including the administration, supervisors, and coworkers. In addition, workshops and retreats may be offered where both general and specific job responsibilities are reviewed. It is important for recreation administrators to convey the specific responsibilities of a job and ensure that the employee understands them. Training is especially important in technical areas of recreation facilities, including the operation of recreation equipment, such as weight machines or machinery; maintenance; and facility scheduling practices, including software programs.

A genuine commitment from the trainers and all levels of management is essential if a training program is to be successful. This requires the active participation of recreation facility managers throughout the entire training program. It is important for managers to motivate the trainees, to understand the trainees' knowledge and experience, and to set goals so they have something to reach for. Managers and supervisors need to be involved in training in case any misinformation is provided or the new employee does not interpret information or responsibilities correctly. Managers closely involved in the training of a new employee can make corrections right away before further problems arise. The goal of any training program should be to provide new employees with every opportunity possible to succeed in their new position.

PERFORMANCE APPRAISAL

Recreation facility managers must monitor, assess, motivate, and offer constructive input to employees. In essence, they have to assess employee performance and correct the areas where expectations are not being met. One of the ways to correct or compliment employee performance is through a performance appraisal. A **performance appraisal** (see figure 11.2) is a formal process resulting from the observation and evaluation of an employee in an effort to assess how the employee is meeting expectations.

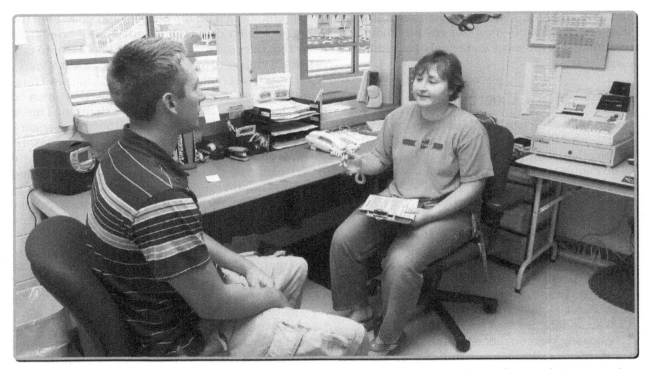

▶Performance appraisals are important because supervisors and employees are able to discuss what a supervisor's expectations are and whether or not the employee is meeting these expectations.

Professional Performance Appraisal

Employee Name _____ Title _____

Supervisor Name _____ Title _____

Department _____ Review Period _____

Ratings

Consistently outstanding: Consistently exceeds expectations and demonstrates high performance on this responsibility.
Excellent: Exceeds expectations; work is typically above required performance on this responsibility.
Good: Meets expectations; satisfactory performance on this responsibility with some room for improvement.
Improvement required: Below expectations; needs significant improvement on this responsibility.
Not applicable: Too new in position to demonstrate competence or category not applicable to this position *(rarely relevant)*.

BEHAVIOR RATINGS		
Behavior	Rating	Examples of observed behaviors
Teamwork		
Customer service		
Judgment and decisiveness		
Planning and prioritizing		
Initiative		
Open-mindedness and adaptability		
Communicating effectively		

Supporting comments _____
_____
_____
_____
_____
_____

From R. Mull, B. Beggs, and M. Renneisen, 2009, *Recreation Facility Management* (Champaign, IL: Human Kinetics).

_____
_____
_____

JOB-SPECIFIC RATINGS		
Responsibility or goal	Rating	Examples of observed behaviors

Supporting comments _____
_____
_____
_____
_____
_____
_____
_____

From R. Mull, B. Beggs, and M. Renneisen, 2009, *Recreation Facility Management* (Champaign, IL: Human Kinetics).

Figure 11.2 Professional performance appraisal. *(continued)*

Recreation facility managers should reinforce positive job performance when an employee is performing job responsibilities as expected or exceeding expectations. When expectations are not being met, managers should provide direction and help to keep employees focused on their responsibilities. When employee performance consistently fails to meet expectations, termination may be necessary. Certain procedures should be followed when considering termination of an employee. Procedures may include

- written or verbal evaluations,
- counseling,
- written assessment, and
- written warnings.

These procedures should be followed until the situation leaves no alternative but to terminate the employee. The termination of an employee is a difficult process for both the supervisor and employee, which reinforces the importance of a thorough and well-thought-out hiring process that results in selecting the best candidate for

a particular position. The termination of an employee often indicates that the hiring process was flawed.

An employee grievance procedure also should be in place to allow employees to express their concerns. This process provides for external review of the employee's performance and also a review of the employee's supervisor. Specific personnel and human resource management training is provided to managers in order to address these types of concerns.

TYPES OF EMPLOYEES

Often, recreation facility managers underestimate how much is involved in keeping a facility at its optimal level of operation. Recreation facility managers have to supervise a wide variety of employees in order to keep a facility operating efficiently. In general, employees can be described as either internal or external.

Internal Employees

Certain roles and responsibilities can be fulfilled as part of the in-house or internal staffing operation. In these cases, the job function is directly influenced by administrative operations. Internal employees can be identified in four general categories: administrative, supervisory, specialized, and maintenance.

Administrative Employees

Administrative employees represent the executive level of an organization. The highest level person may be the chief executive officer (CEO) in the private sector or the administrator or director in the public and nonprofit sectors. This person's role is to make all decisions that affect the mission and vision of the organization. This person may or may not be involved in the day-to-day operational decisions of a recreation facility, depending on its complexity and size. All other employees ultimately report to this person.

Usually a representative of the owner or administration is in charge of daily facility operations. Typically, this person is referred to as a recreation facility manager. Recreation facility managers may need years of experience and specific certifications or degrees in order to perform their responsibilities. They are in charge of employees, budgeting, office management, and all other responsibilities that support the administration of the facility. These professionals should be trained,

Figure 11.2 *(continued)*

SUMMARY

Areas of strength | Areas for development

Overall rating

Supporting comments

Employee comments

Employee signature _____ Date _____ (to acknowledge receipt)

Supervisor signature _____ Date _____

Second level signature _____ Date _____

From R. Mull, B. Beggs, and M. Renneisen, 2009, *Recreation Facility Management* (Champaign, IL: Human Kinetics).

experienced, and capable of overseeing all facets of recreation facility management. In more complex facilities, there may be additional managers of certain areas. For example, in a resort hotel there may be a front-desk operations manager, a food-service manager, a housekeeping manager, a retail manager, and a concierge manager.

Supervisory Employees

The person responsible for reviewing the work of one or more subordinate employees is called a **supervisor.** In some organizations, this person may also be called a *coordinator* or *foreman.* Supervisors have full responsibility for the employees in their area and accept the responsibility for accomplishing the tasks assigned to them by recreation administrators. Supervisors are representatives of the administration and are often held responsible for their employees' performance. They have an important influence on control, motivation, and quality of the job performed.

Specialists

A variety of job functions in recreation facilities require specialized employees, or specialists, who have received training to assist in delivery of the recreation product. In terms of recreation and leisure activities, specialists may be skilled in aquatics, therapeutic recreation, or fitness, just to name a few. Specialized recreation certifications may include the Certified Parks and Recreation Professional (CPRP), Certified Therapeutic Recreation Specialist (CTRS), Certified Pool Operator (CPO), Certified Playground Safety Inspector (CPSI), American College of Sports Medicine (ACSM) Exercise Specialist, and the American Council on Exercise (ACE) Group Exercise Instructor, just to name a few. Certifications usually have specific requirements that an individual must meet before they can even take a certification exam. For example, a person may be able to sit for the CPRP if meet the following requirements found at NRPA.org:

- They have just received, or they are about to receive a bachelor's degree from a program accredited by the NRPA Council on Accreditation.
- They have a bachelor's degree from any institution in recreation, park resources, or leisure services, and they also have no less than one year of full-time experience in the field.

- They have a bachelor's degree in a major other than recreation, park resources, or leisure services, and they also have no less than three years of full-time experience in the field.
- They have a high school diploma or equivalent, and they have five years of full-time experience in the field.

A specialist can also be an employee with training who assists in keeping the facility operational. Areas of responsibility that require this type of specialist include plumbing, electrical systems, mechanical systems, horticulture, motorized equipment maintenance, graphic design, and event planning. These positions may be full time and have a designated physical location within the agency that houses their particular function. Separate physical areas for these functions are

© Bill Crump/Brand X Pictures

▶A therapeutic recreation specialist will require extensive training in their field before they can become certified to do their job.

especially prevalent for hotels, resorts, convention centers, and other large recreational facilities.

Maintenance or Operations Employees

Maintenance employees consist of skilled, semiskilled, and nonskilled employees. The maintenance process may only include regular cleaning, upkeep, and minor repairs that can be done by nonskilled or semiskilled employees. Specialized tasks such as plumbing or welding require the expertise of a skilled employee. The size and classification system of the agency dictate the number of maintenance employees. As the agency increases in size, maintenance responsibilities become greater and more specialized.

In addition, the more a facility is used, the greater the maintenance responsibility becomes. Imagine an indoor sport facility where a basketball game is played one day, followed by a concert the next night, followed by a convention or ice hockey game the next day. This type of multiuse recreation facility may require leadership for coordinating maintenance-related functions in a timely fashion to facilitate the numerous uses of the facility. Janitorial services, minor repairs, event setup and takedown, and leaf and snow removal can be so extensive that maintenance efforts at some recreation facilities can be very demanding for just one person to handle. Maintenance responsibilities can require several types of employees, including janitors as well the types of maintenance employees mentioned earlier.

Today's recreation facility users place a high value on pleasant, comfortable, and properly functioning environments. Facility maintenance employees have a tremendous impact on creating this environment. The work of these employees helps create the image of a recreation facility.

External Employees

Many functions in the recreation environment are accomplished by external or outside companies or people. The use of external resources to accomplish a task is called **outsourcing.** This option is

▶A larger facility may require an entire maintenance team to keep everything at the facility running smoothly for users.

often exercised when a recreation organization is relatively small. Outsourcing can be a viable option when the agency cannot afford to have a full-time staff person for a particular facility need. It provides an effective, cost efficient means of addressing a specific and sometimes infrequent organization responsibility. External employees can include maintenance experts, vendors, and volunteers.

When recreation facility managers decide to outsource a job, they often use a formal contract agreement. A contract or written agreement can protect both parties and ensure that the recreation administrator's expectations are met. These contractual relationships may be specific to each job assigned to an outside source. For example, an ice arena may have a contractual arrangement with a vendor who specializes in cooling repairs. This agreement should stipulate how to contact the vendor's maintenance representative during or after hours, how soon the vendor will respond to a call from the recreation facility manager, how much the vendor charges per hour, and when the contract expires.

Management Professionals

Other types of management professionals may be required to be part of the administration and delivery of a product. Many revenue-producing facilities have large budgets and generate significant revenue. Examples of these recreation facilities include water parks, professional sport stadiums, and hotels and resorts with recreation amenities. Even smaller organizations may generate enough revenue to warrant consideration of assistance by outside accountants and other financial consultants.

The inherent risk for accidents, injuries, or other legal concerns in most recreation facilities creates the possibility of lawsuits. In addition, contracts with employees or vendors often need to be professionally and legally prepared. These situations would necessitate professional assistance from a lawyer.

Some recreation production efforts may require the availability of a member of the medical profession. A large special event, such as a fireworks show, national track and field meet, softball tournament, or aquatic event may warrant on-site medical staff. These types of outside resources could include trainers, nurses, emergency medical technicians (EMTs), and doctors.

Some outdoor recreation facilities require the assistance of horticulturists or landscape architects. Horticulturists or landscape architects are often important resources for park and recreation agencies, colleges and universities, and hotels and resorts where the outside appearance and natural landscape of the facility needs to be presented in an appealing fashion.

Finally, in almost every recreation facility development project, consultants are necessary to conduct feasibility studies. In addition, as discussed in chapter 6, the design of a recreation facility almost always requires a professional architect. In some cases, these professionals could be placed on a retainer and paid an annual fee so that they are available as needed.

Field Experts

Much like the specialists who are hired and trained within an agency, external field experts can be necessary to respond to certain problems. Field experts may have a trade that is necessary to keep the facility operational. Plumbers, electricians, tree surgeons, general contractors, and laborers may all be hired to provide expert assistance for specific tasks.

It is important to research the expertise or certification of outside specialists to make sure they are qualified to complete the necessary task. In some instances, their fees may be higher if they have attained a certain level of education or certification. Outside experts who are insured to protect themselves and the work they do may also charge a higher fee. Recreation administrators should make sure that any work done by an outside expert is clearly specified and documented.

Vendors

Outside companies usually provide a product, such as fertilizer, concessions, or sport supplies, or a service, such as mowing, snow removal, or uniform laundering. These outside companies, or **vendors,** endeavor to create an ongoing relationship with recreation facility managers. A vendor may or may not have a warranty responsibility for the product or service they provide. However, it is in the best interest of the vendor to provide a quality product or service in order to maintain a positive relationship and generate continued business with the recreation agency. This ongoing relationship can result in the vendor providing assistance to the organization in the form of advertising or sponsorships or offering accelerated delivery or discounts on products in an effort to maintain a good working relationship with the recreation facility manager. Vendors can be a

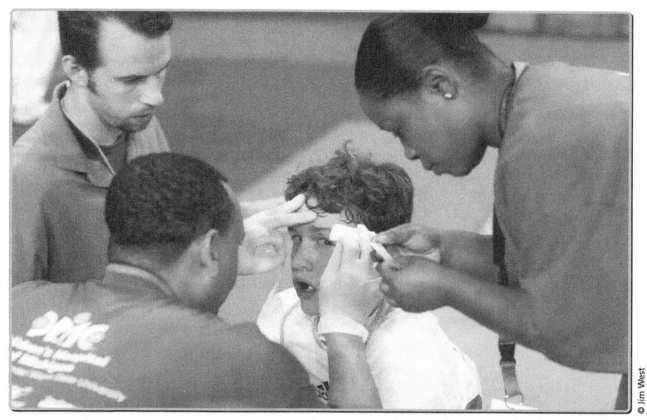

▶Most large special events, such as this sporting event, require a medical team from an outside source to be on-site.

valuable resource, and the relationship between management and vendors should be nurtured to benefit agency operations.

Volunteers

Although not technically an agency employee, another external workforce that is beneficial to the delivery of services at a recreation agency is volunteers. Many municipal or not-for-profit recreation organizations use volunteers to meet a variety of needs. The role of volunteers can be sophisticated or basic. In either case, volunteers help fulfill production responsibilities as well as facility needs. Typical functions or roles filled by volunteers include

- planting trees,
- mowing grass,
- painting rooms,
- controlling crowds,
- serving food,
- coaching youth sport teams,

- ushering art events,
- serving as docents in a museum,
- administering youth sport leagues, and
- helping out backstage for theatrical productions.

Volunteers can be cultivated to offset the cost and supplement the work of employees and to create a positive impression of the organization. If volunteers are an important component of an organization, their recruitment, training, and retention is a critical management task. Volunteers can be recruited from a broad cross section of any community. University and college communities can attract student volunteers to encourage service learning and to fulfill class requirements. Schools may encourage students to volunteer for the benefit of the community and to teach long-term volunteerism. Recreation facility users are also a good volunteer resource. In addition, retirees are often interested in volunteering for a variety of recreation-related needs and have the time and experience to manage numerous responsibilities.

▶Recreation facility managers have many opportunities to use volunteers to supplement the work of their paid employees.

WORK ENVIRONMENT

Employees perform best when they are in a comfortable and safe work environment. It is the responsibility of recreation administrators to create a safe and appropriate environment for employees to meet their obligations without stress resulting from the workplace condition. Work assignments should be thought out, organized, and presented to employees with full understanding of the conditions of the environment to which they are assigned. Employees in an unpleasant work environment are not as productive as those who are comfortable. However, some work environments cannot always be absolutely comfortable and safe because of the nature of the work:

• Many outdoor maintenance tasks expose employees to extreme weather. Providing appropriate clothing and other safety items such as goggles, gloves, steel-toed shoes, and high-visibility uniforms can decrease employee injuries and increase productivity.

• Employees who lead fitness or dance classes are at risk for injury because of the physical nature of the position. Providing surfacing materials that minimize injury and efficiency systems that adequately cool classroom space can reduce risk. Providing opportunities for these employees to become certified and improve technique can also create a safer environment.

• Employees who work in outdoor recreation leading outdoor excursions are in positions where safety is vital. Providing the proper gear in terms of footwear, ropes, and helmets as well as spending the time to make sure the outdoor space has as few as risks as possible will help create a working environment where the employees feel safe.

© Jim West

▶Outfitting outdoor recreation employees with the proper safety equipment to perform their job is crucial for providing them with a safe environment to work in.

Even office employees should be provided with conditions conducive to increased productivity and decreased risk of injury. Appropriate lighting, comfortable and ergonomically engineered office chairs and computer accessories, and hands-free phone accessories can minimize eye strain, neck strain, carpel tunnel syndrome, and other common office-related injuries. Recreation facility managers must do everything they can to protect and make the employees comfortable as they fulfill their responsibilities.

EMPLOYEE RELATIONS

Employee relations can be one of the most important and challenging considerations in the recreation work environment. Fair and consistent treatment is critical in relating to employees. Policies, procedures, rules, and regulations should be clearly communicated in employee handbooks that all employees receive during job training. In addition, the ability to interact and negotiate with employees can be instrumental in maintaining employee morale and support. Various activities can be incorporated into the work environment to create a positive atmosphere. Some recreation agencies have social functions, staff retreats, and other activities that encourage a team environment. Recognizing employees for outstanding achieve-ment or for years of service are other ways to enhance employee relations. Maintaining a professional and enjoyable work environment contributes to increased productivity and job satisfaction.

As discussed earlier in the chapter, a well-thought-out and thorough job description establishes a framework of responsibility that can help greatly with employee relations. However, problems may arise that can lead to disagreements, sometimes known as *grievances,* that must be formally addressed in a process that ensures a fair and objective review of the situation. Having a peaceful resolution to a grievance can help maintain a productive and efficient work environment.

SUMMARY

It is of great importance that jobs are properly classified within the organization and specific requirements are detailed in a job description. This will help ensure that qualified employees are hired. Once an employee has been hired, job training and performance appraisals must be conducted. In addition, it is the responsibility of the organization to provide a work environment that allows employees to be productive and helps the organization efficiently and effectively deliver the core product to facility users.

PART IV

Utilization of Recreation Facilities

The recreation facility manager must coordinate all of the activities that take place in a facility. Facility procedures and policies allow for effective and efficient use of the core product, ancillary spaces, and core product extensions in a facility in order to ensure a positive experience for users. By maintaining equipment, being aware of risks, and being prepared for disruptions, the recreation facility manager ensures that the facility is properly maintained and secure for users.

12

Circulation, Safety, Control, and Security

Recreation facility managers must be aware of issues associated with user and employee behavior. Employees are much easier than users to influence from a management perspective. Users create the greatest challenge for management because they can exhibit such a wide variety of behaviors while using a facility. In an effort to control user behavior, recreation facility managers must have systems in place to direct and monitor users in the facility. These systems include facility circulation, safety, control, and security.

USER CIRCULATION

In the early stages of any facility development project, especially the design phase, a great deal of attention focuses on the circulation of users throughout the facility. Whether it is an indoor or outdoor recreation facility, the ability for users to get from one place to another easily and safely is critical to the efficient utilization of a facility. In creating good facility circulation, the following concepts must be taken into consideration: area relationship, signage, and comfort.

Circulation Areas

A recreation facility is a comprehensive space that management must coordinate in terms of how users access various areas of the facility. In addition, each area of a facility relates to others in design and function, which affects facility management practices. Within every indoor or outdoor recreation facility, certain areas have the specific purpose of circulating users throughout the facility. These spaces commonly include hallways, stairways, landings, corridors, and pathways. Entrances, including atriums or lobbies, are additional areas that facilitate user access to a facility. Exterior circulation areas could include

- roads,
- sidewalks,
- trails, and
- paths

that provide access to parking or other auxiliary components of a facility.

Some facilities have commodity and food-service outlets, whose success can depend greatly on patterns of user circulation. Probably the most important area of any facility is its production space, or where the core product and core product extensions are delivered. All of the previously

▶Some facilities may be so large in size that more than one level of hallways, landing, sidewalks, and stairways, may be necessary to accommodate the user circulation in facility.

mentioned areas should facilitate access to the primary product area in a smooth and functional fashion.

Signage

Fundamental to efficient circulation patterns in a recreation facility is a signage system to communicate information that allows ease of movement throughout the facility. As discussed in chapters 8 and 9, this is most often accomplished with facility signs of varying colors, shapes, and other information that create visibility of various destinations. Signage should be consistent throughout the facility by using the same colors, fonts, and sizes. The location of signs in the facility is also important. Larger facilities should have large signs and maps to assist users in moving though the facility.

Other circulation enhancements include color-coded lines on floors or walls that assist users in locating specific areas. Reception areas should also be appropriately located to provide information to users on how to find desired areas. Additionally, facility employees facilitate circulation by assisting users as they travel from place to place. Sometimes, barriers and fences are strategically placed to influence direction and control access to areas.

▶A facility directory plays an important role in the circulation of users and employees throughout a facility and helps people new to the facility to locate where they want to go.

Comfort for Efficiency and Aesthetics

A large part of circulation is creating a sense of comfort or satisfaction for people as they move around a recreation facility. Certain applications can maximize this effort, such as configurations or systems that incorporate designated lines to make waiting time more pleasant for users. Entertainment, including videos or television, murals, paintings, music, and landscaping, can be provided for users' enjoyment or distraction while they are moving or waiting. Where appropriate, seats should be made available, especially if extensive waiting or delays are likely. These provisions are particularly important for elderly users. Some facilities may require coverings or awnings in order to shelter people from inclement weather or intense sun. Entrances and exits for a single area may need to be located in completely different areas to avoid congestion.

© Inger Helene Boasson/Nordic Photos/age fotostock

▶Facilities with a high number of users may have some areas where users must wait in line, so they install television monitors to entertain users while they wait.

The best use of these elements can be seen in major theme parks and the techniques they use to enhance customer comfort. Lines for attractions are often intentionally configured to limit views of the line length. Television monitors are placed in many waiting areas or lines to entertain customers while they wait. Background music is also used to enhance the experience as users wait in lines. Additional comfort features include water misters, air conditioning or heating, and structures intended to shelter users from inclement weather.

SAFETY

Recreation facility managers must ensure a safe environment for employees and users. This care involves sensitivity toward the well-being of facility users and employees. Managers must consider many factors in providing a safe environment, including the product, equipment, weather, design, and user attitudes and behavior. Managers should consider five general points as they provide a safe environment:

1. User age
2. Activity participation
3. Experience level
4. User behavior
5. Environmental conditions in specific areas

User Age

The age of facility users requires specific safety management practices. Ages may vary widely depending on the core product, and facility managers will have different degrees of responsibility depending on the age of the users. If the average facility user is between the ages of 18 and 65, users are expected to be responsible for their actions. However, management practices require a heightened alertness when users are below age 18 or when parental supervision is not expected. Young people have limited life experience and cannot be expected to be fully responsible for their actions. They could behave inappropriately, be distracted, or simply do something that a mature person would not. On the other end of the spectrum, elderly users, although more mature, may have reduced physical capacity and require assistance. Recreation facility managers must be aware of the ages of the people using the facility and take appropriate action.

Activity Participation

Activity participation must be observed because a degree of risk is inherent in recreation facilities. Depending on the core product, activity levels can vary greatly from nonstrenuous and casual to highly physical and competitive. These extreme levels of activity can create a dangerous environment by leading to significant fatigue, altercations between participants, and other actions that could result in potential injury to facility users and employees. Recreation facility managers have the responsibility to care for users and employees and to be aware of their activity. Managers may require that employees be certified to administer first aid and cardiopulmonary resuscitation (CPR). They may also need to take action to modify any activity that may result in potential injury or jeopardize users' safety and well-being.

Experience Level

All users and employees come to a facility with unique skills and abilities. Similar to age, experience can also influence management practices. The use of certain equipment or the delivery of

© Photodisc/Getty Images

▶ For extremely difficult activities that require a higher experience level, such as scuba diving, an elevated level of supervision will be required by the facility manager.

certain products may require instruction before use. For example, it is common for fitness facilities to provide equipment orientation to new users. For more difficult activities, recreation facility managers could provide screening, testing, or certification for people to attain the appropriate license or experience before using a product. For example, it is common for people who are interested in scuba diving to complete a basic level of training before attempting a dive in uncontrolled conditions.

On the other hand, user knowledge of the specific recreation activity could be expected for less difficult activities, with managers only required to observe users or employees in a supervisory role. This difference in experience levels will influence employee assignments for product delivery.

User Behavior

Facility users come with a variety of interests, attitudes, and capacity to control their behavior. Although most users are responsible, sometimes things happen, altering their behavior and creating a negative situation. For example, participants competing against each other in an adult softball program may get into verbal or physical confrontations due to a hard slide to break up a double play. Although this type of behavior cannot be completely anticipated, management should be prepared to address these kinds of situations and any potential conflict that may result from user interactions.

Users' interests will vary, and users will each expect a different experience from a facility. For example, trails in a park system are viewed by some users as an escape to nature and a tranquil and peaceful experience. However, others use the trails for intense experiences such as mountain biking. If these users access the same areas at the same time, conflicts may arise. It is important to address these differences in behavior through rules and policies that are communicated through signage.

Recreation facility managers must be sensitive at all times to unexpected behavior and have a system in place to respond to it (see figure 12.1). This can be a significant concern if such actions involve a large group. Usually, these situations are uncommon; however, management should be aware of the potential for users to deviate from

Incident Report

Participants Involved

Name ______ Name ______
Address ______ Address ______
Phone ______ Phone ______
Date ______
Time of incident ______ a.m./p.m. (circle one) Time reported ______
Personnel present? ☐ Yes ☐ No
Name ______
Job title ______
Location of personnel at time of incident ______
General location ______
(List park site or facility.)
Specific room or area ______
Witnesses? ☐ Yes ☐ No
Name ______ Name ______
Address ______ Address ______
Phone ______ Phone ______
Description of incident ______

Record additional information on reverse side.
Action taken at time of incident ______

From R. Mull, B. Beggs, and M. Renneisen, 2009, *Recreation Facility Management* (Champaign, IL: Human Kinetics).

Record additional information on reverse side.

Activity

☐ Sports ☐ Youth
☐ Cultural activities ☐ Aquatics
☐ Social activities ☐ Rental
☐ Fitness ☐ Special events
☐ Other ______

Report filed by ______ Date ______
Approved by ______ Division Director Date ______
Review ______ Administrator Date ______
Follow-up recommended ☐ Yes ☐ No
Follow-up report

Completed by ______ Date ______
Review ______ Division Director
______ Administrator

From R. Mull, B. Beggs, and M. Renneisen, 2009, *Recreation Facility Management* (Champaign, IL: Human Kinetics).

Figure 12.1 Incident report.

normal behavior. These situations should be handled carefully, avoiding unnecessary escalation of the situation.

Environmental Conditions

Environmental conditions can affect the state of mind and possibly physical condition of users and employees. This is especially the case with outdoor recreation facilities where extreme temperatures or unexpected changes in weather can occur. In such situations, it becomes recreation facility managers' responsibility to make appropriate decisions to protect users and employees who face environmental conditions that could affect their well-being. An example of a common safety concern for outdoor recreation facility managers is inclement weather, particularly lightning strikes, that can cause the temporary closure of an outdoor recreation facility such as an aquatic, baseball, softball, football, or soccer facility. Rules and procedures need to be in place for closing the facilities quickly for the safety of users and employees. It is common for these recreation facilities to have access to weather information via television or other weather-alert devices. New technology even has presented options such as lightning-detection devices to assist facility managers in protecting the well-being of users and employees.

　　The comfort and satisfaction of users of indoor facilities revolves around the climatic conditions created by the HVAC system in an indoor facility. Very rarely do environmental conditions create an unhealthy situation in indoor facilities, but the potential exists. Recreation facility managers must be aware of the fact that their environment has the potential to create problems. Areas for concern in indoor environments include monitoring chlorine levels at indoor pools and monitoring ammonia or exhaust levels at indoor ice rinks. Detection devices serve as alarms when certain chemicals reach an unsafe level, including carbon monoxide detectors, which detect high levels of the toxic gas.

　　Recreation facility managers must also recognize unsafe situations and have the authority to take action to remedy the situation even if it means shutting down the facility or equipment. This could include removing equipment from an area where it does not function as designed. For example, if a weight machine is improperly functioning or loses a bolt, users should not have access to it. This situation must be addressed immediately by

© John T. Fowler

▶ Severe weather conditions will sometimes force an outdoor facility to close until the inclement weather passes through the area.

on-site facility personnel by using signs or taking the equipment to a maintenance or storage area. By consistently monitoring a facility and having maintenance schedules in place for equipment, such situations can be minimized.

Precaution

Facility **precaution** is a key safety function of recreation facility management. It involves analyzing the existing facility, evaluating the goals and objectives of the agency in terms of the product, and examining product utilization from user and employee perspectives in order to identify and minimize potentially hazardous situations. This precaution system attempts to eliminate injuries, accidents, and the potential for costly damages or lawsuits. Precautionary measures also raise awareness of potential risk among employees and users. They involve five basic components:

1. Leadership
2. Analysis
3. Education
4. Inspection
5. Reporting

Leadership

Recreation facility managers should establish a precautionary action program that includes a primary person, often called an officer, as well as an advisory group that could be referred to as a committee, to ensure successful delivery of the core product. These two sources serve as a team that accepts responsibility for administration of a facility risk management program. The risk management team develops a program of action by reviewing the facility, its core products, and its core product extensions and identifying any risks to users and employees. This team is responsible for implementing the precautionary system and also has the authority to take appropriate steps to avoid dangerous situations. Recreation facility managers often serve as the officer for precautionary responsibilities.

Analysis

One of the first steps of the risk management team, and specifically the officer, is to look closely at what exists in the facility. The following production considerations should be assessed:

- Scope of product
- Injury potential
- Conduct and behavior of users
- Level of product activity
- Activity instruction and supervision
- Hiring procedures
- Written guidelines and operation manuals
- Preventive techniques
- First aid availability
- Equipment requirement and use
- Training and meetings

The risk management team also should be aware of the history of the facility, which includes previous claims, accidents, or lawsuits on record. Inspections of the facility should be conducted, creating firsthand awareness of potential safety concerns. Information from this analysis should be documented, creating an overall analysis of the facility and any problems that exist.

Education

An important component of a precautionary program is educating employees and users about existing and potential problems in a recreation facility. This education could include formal training such as presentations on legal terminology, types of liability, standards of care, and evacuation procedures. Also, depending on the product, a standard of care could require training in first aid, CPR certification, and step-by-step emergency procedures. Management can reduce the chances of serious harm by teaching employees these techniques.

A secondary goal of a training program is to create a heightened awareness among employees regarding potential liability that could evolve from use of the facility. Potential liabilities could include claims of improper supervision, poor instruction, or failure to warn of a danger. The education process creates a consciousness about the potential

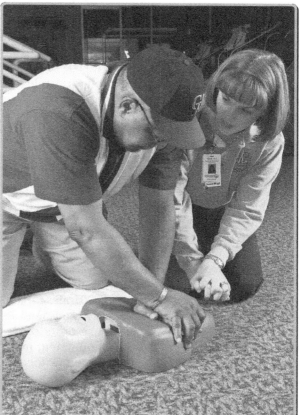

©Tom Roberts

▶As part of a facility's precautionary program, a recreation facility may require all employees to be trained in standard first aid, CPR, and step-by-step emergency procedures.

for injury and liability involved in the delivery of a product in a recreation facility.

Inspection

It is important to have a system of ongoing inspections where all facets of product delivery are assessed from a risk perspective. The inspection process can include instruments such as checklists that cover every aspect of a facility, including

- employees,
- equipment,
- maintenance schedule,
- policies and procedures,
- job descriptions, and
- operational items.

Inspections should be done regularly. The frequency of inspections can be daily, weekly, monthly, or annually depending on the facility and the product. The level and intensity of facility usage influences the need for more or less frequent inspections.

Recreation facility managers should routinely observe employees in the performance of their duties in an effort to minimize risk of injury. Employee education, certification, and relevant work experience all influence employee safety. Employee inspections should be conducted regularly to make sure they are doing their jobs correctly to minimize the risk of injury.

Equipment should also be inspected on a regular basis to ensure it will not wear out or break down. An equipment inspection checklist could be used to document equipment conditions. Checklists should be designed for each piece of equipment based on the characteristics of the equipment. For example, vehicles have a specified maintenance schedule. A vehicle may need its oil changed every 3 months or 3,000 miles (4,828 kilometers). Tires may need to be rotated every 10,000 miles (16,093 kilometers). A golf course mower may need its oil changed every 500 hours of use or its blades sharpened once every 2 weeks. Equipment maintenance and operational information is located in manuals that are provided by the equipment manufacturer. This information should be kept on file in the event of a malfunction. The amount and type of use should be considered when evaluating equipment and its replacement.

Inspection of facility areas and equipment should be done regularly. Recreation facility managers never know when an unsafe condition may develop. All indoor and outdoor surfaces should be checked for hazards before a facility opens for use. Other safety devices such as lighting, fire extinguishers, signage, storage, and exits should be inspected annually.

Finally, systems that contribute to an emergency process—exit doors, public-address systems, hallways, and stairways—should be inspected annually. Early warning systems and internal communication systems are essential elements of an effective precautionary system and should be inspected monthly. A meeting should be held immediately following all inspections and all monitors or committee members should report their findings as described in the next section. In addition, emergency procedures and drills should be practiced (see chapter 15).

Reporting

The final component of a precautionary system is making sure that any inspections, situations, conditions, and incidents are documented, reported, and stored for future use. These reports need to summarize what conditions exist or potential problems that could occur. Incidents should be documented, including the following information:

- People affected
- Witnesses
- Nature of incident
- Severity
- Medical attention required
- Comments by the injured and witnesses

One of the most important incident report forms that an agency should have on file is the accident report form (see figures 12.2 and 12.3). The accident report form can be used for medical, legal, and insurance purposes. This form should be completed in great detail and include the previously listed information. It should also provide the opportunity for a staff person to indicate specifically where on the body an individual was injured, the type of injury, the status of the injured person, how the injury occurred, and contact information for the injured person and all witnesses to the incident.

Other reports that are often part of a precautionary system could include facility and equipment maintenance logs and checklists (see figure 12.4) and reports for user concerns that reflect a pattern or a potential problem (see figures 12.5 and 12.6).

Accident Report

Complete this form for any reportable accident occurring at a park or recreation site during hours of supervision. Submit to safety and development director within 24 hours after accident.

Name _____ Sex ☐ Male ☐ Female

Address _____ Date of birth _____

City, state, zip _____ Phone number _____

Report by _____ Date of accident _____

Location _____

Time of accident _____ a.m./p.m. (circle one) Date of report _____

Describe how accident occurred (facts only) _____

_____

_____

Bodily Injury Status

Following is a numbered list indicating area of injury. In the box next to the numbers around the figure, show the type of injury that occurred, using the letter coding indicated under type of injury. If unsure or unknown, leave blank.

Area of Injury

Head	1	Thigh	11	Forearm	20
Face	2	Groin	12	Back	21
Eye	3	Ankle	13	Thumb	22
Tooth	4	Foot	14	Hand	23
Shoulder	5	Shin	15	Finger	24
Collarbone	6	Neck	16	Knee	25
Elbow	7	Chest	17	Lower leg	26
Ribs	8	Hip	18	Instep	27
Wrist	9	Upper Arm	19	Toe	28
Abdomen	10				

Type of Injury

Wounds
Laceration A
Incision B
Bruise C
Scrape D
Puncture E

Eyes
Foreign body F
Burn, chemical G
Burn, heat H
Burn, flash I
Wound J
Irritation K

Burns
Heat L
Chemical M
Friction N

Skin
Irritation O
Strain P
Fracture Q
Sprain R

Gases
Nausea S
Dizziness T
Irritation U
Pains V
Misc. W

From R. Mull, B. Beggs, and M. Rennelson, 2009, *Recreation Facility Management* (Champaign, IL: Human Kinetics).

Record additional information on reverse side.

Activity

☐ Sports ☐ Youth

☐ Cultural activities ☐ Aquatics

☐ Social activities ☐ Rental

☐ Fitness ☐ Special events

☐ Other _____

Report filed by _____ Date _____

Approved by _____ Date _____
  Division Director

Review _____ Date _____
  Administrator

Follow-up recommended ☐ Yes ☐ No

Follow-up report

_____

_____

Completed by _____ Date _____

Review _____
  Division Director

_____
Administrator

From R. Mull, B. Beggs, and M. Rennelson, 2009, *Recreation Facility Management* (Champaign, IL: Human Kinetics).

Figure 12.2 Accident report.

Employee's Accident Report

Date of report _____

Personal Information

Employee's name _____

Department and division _____

Social security # _____

Home phone _____

Address (city, state, zip) _____

Date of birth _____

Gender ☐ Male ☐ Female

Marital status ☐ Single ☐ Married ☐ Separated ☐ Divorced

Job Information

Hours worked per day: _____ Days worked per week: _____ Shift: _____

Date of hire: _____ Wage basis: ☐ Hourly ☐ Salaried wage: _____

Work status: ☐ Regular full time ☐ Regular part time ☐ Temporary full time ☐ Temporary part time
☐ Seasonal ☐ Other: _____

Accident Information

Date of accident: _____

Time of accident: _____ ☐ a.m. ☐ p.m.

Date accident reported to supervisor: _____ Was report delayed?: ☐ Yes ☐ No

If yes, why?: _____

Exact location (address) of accident: _____

City property?: ☐ Yes ☐ No

City vehicles involved?: ☐ Yes ☐ No   If yes, vehicle #: _____

Detailed description of accident (what was employee you were doing and what tools, equipment, structures, or fixtures were involved?)

From R. Mull, B. Beggs, and M. Rennelson, 2009, *Recreation Facility Management* (Champaign, IL: Human Kinetics).

_____

Nature of injury (e.g., bruise, cut, strain, etc.): _____

Part of body (e.g., wrist, forearm, toes, etc.): _____

Was medical treatment sought?: ☐ Yes ☐ No If yes, where?: ☐ Promptcare ☐ Hospital emergency room

Will you miss at least one day of work?: ☐ Yes ☐ No

If yes, what is your expected return-to-work date? _____

Was the accident due to unsafe conduct on part of the employee or on the part of another employee?:

☐ Yes ☐ No

If yes, explain.: _____

What should be done or has been done to prevent a recurrence of this type of accident? _____

Give name of witnesses to the accident: _____

Authorization and Release for Disclosure of Medical Records and Information

I, (employee name) _____ , by the following signature, authorize any and all medical providers, including but not limited to physicians, therapists, hospitals, and laboratories, to disclose all medical records and information concerning my physical and mental conditions relevant to worker's compensation benefits and coverage to the legal department and the risk management division. This authorization includes both past and present medical information and written and oral communications.

I hereby release any medical provider disclosing information pursuant to this authorization from any liability that may result from such disclosure.

Employee's printed name _____

Employee's signature _____ Date _____

Return this form to risk management within 24 hours of accident.

From R. Mull, B. Beggs, and M. Rennelson, 2009, *Recreation Facility Management* (Champaign, IL: Human Kinetics).

Figure 12.3 Employee's accident report.

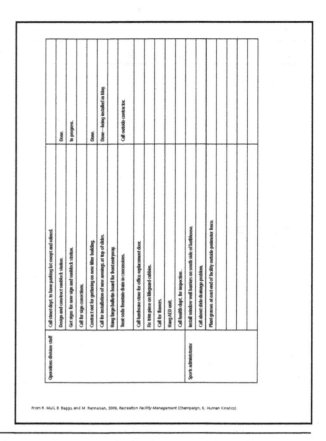

Figure 12.4 Pool facility opening checklist.

2008	Pool (Preseason)	Status
Facility maintenance staff	Remove plywood from bathhouse vents (upper and lower). Store in safe and secure area.	
	Hang clock in activity pool.	Probably already in pretty good shape.
	Clean out filter room, main pool, and activity pool.	
	Move ice machine to pool concessions.	
	Replace ceiling panel with new one by electrical box in front basket room.	
	Hook up floatables with locking devices; we will need these moved out of the bathhouse for pool cleanup.	
	Restock shower fixture that has broken away from wall on men's side.	New parts being installed by facility maintenance staff.
	Hang large bulletin board in front entryway.	Operations staff has the board.
	Install stainless-steel grab bars on both sides of frame bottom of bike waterslide.	Can be done after opening.
	Power wash block algae from south and south side of bathhouse.	
	Test all fixtures in bathhouse (i.e., lights, outlets, plumbing).	
	Hang sunblock station.	Get with operations staff for location.
Sports maintenance staff	Remove plastic tie wraps from skeletons and put canopies up.	
	Remove lounge chairs from inside of bathhouses.	
	Move stuff out from under roofed areas of concessions.	Discuss locations with operations staff.
Park maintenance staff	Repair hard areas of concrete deck.	
	Clean out drain in front entryway sidewalk and drain behind the office.	
	Fill in turf areas on south side of filter room.	
Landscaping staff	Make landscaping touch-ups to exterior and interior of facility.	
	Add mulch to landscaping areas in and out of fenced areas.	Done.
Operations division staff	Call street dept. to have parking lot swept and relined.	Done.
	Design and construct sunblock station.	In progress.
	Get signs for new sign and sunblock station.	
	Call for sign connection.	
	Contract out for guttering on new filter building.	Done.
	Call for installation of new awnings at top of slides.	Done—being installed in May.
	Hang large bulletin board for front entryway.	Call outside contractor.
	Reset soda fountain drain for front concessions.	
Sports administrator	Call handicrane stove for office replacement door.	
	Fix trim piece on lifeguard cubbies.	
	Call for flowers.	
	Hang AED unit.	
	Call health dept. for inspection.	
	Install window well barriers on south side of bathhouse.	
	Call about slide drainage problem.	
	Plant grasses at east end of facility outside perimeter fence.	

Citizen Report

Reporting Party

Name _____

Address _____

City _____ Zip code _____

Home phone _____ Business phone _____

Report taken by _____

Time _____ a.m./p.m. (circle one)   Date _____

Complaint

Suggestion

Info request

Commendation

Nature of Call

Building   Irrigation   Street furniture   Playground
Park   Path/trail   Programs   Other
Restroom   BBQ area   Floor

Details

Location of occurrence _____

Time _____ Date _____

Action Taken

By _____

Position _____

Time _____

Date _____

Action taken _____

_____

Reporting party notified by _____

Time _____ Date _____

Phone _____ a.m./p.m. (circle one)

Date _____ Letter _____

Was the citizen satisfied with your response?   1-Very   2-Satisfied   3-No response   4-Not satisfied

Review

Division director _____

Comments _____

Date _____

Administrator _____

Comments _____

Date _____

 Figure 12.5 Citizen report.

Figure 12.6   Vandalism and trouble report.

All analysis, education, and inspection information should be brought together in a formal plan for implementation. The plan should be conceived with the understanding that it should be flexible and sensitive to changing users, employees, facilities, and equipment. It should identify all risks and express potential effects and ways to minimize, control, or avoid them. The entire risk management plan should be available to all levels of management. It is the responsibility of the management to minimize these dangers and provide a safe and meaningful experience in all areas of the facility.

CONTROL

Control involves the practices that recreation facility managers implement because they are responsible for every person at their recreation facility. Whatever happens within a facility is ultimately the responsibility of management. Managers can demonstrate a caring attitude and take precautionary measures to avoid risks, but the bottom line is that they must exert reasonable control of the

activities at their facility at all times. Control of a facility takes into consideration internal influences and external influences.

Internal Influences

Internal influences involve ensuring proper use of the facility and its equipment. In order to accomplish this, certain guidelines, directives, and policies are created.

Policies and Procedures

Information must be developed that formally states limitations on what people are allowed to do while using the recreation facility. These administrative statements, known as **policies,** inform users and employees of what they may or may not do as they experience the product. Policies generally answer questions such as who, when, and what. They may limit certain types of use and establish fees and charges, type of use, supervisory statements, access requirements, capacity limitations, scheduling requirements, and so on.

At the same time, certain statements need to be shared that help people know how to use a facility and its equipment. These statements are called **procedures.** Procedures create user and employee awareness of how and where they may be able to use the facility as designed. Examples of procedures include directional information, time and place of activities, announcements, and user application requirements.

Rules and Regulations

Rules are controls that place limits on specific actions of users and employees. Policies and procedures can manage passive use of the facility, but active use requires additional limitations. A common example of this is a sport participation rule that limits the age of users who may participate in a certain program. For example, participants in a 12-and-under baseball league may not turn 13 years of age by December 31 and still be eligible to participate.

External Influences

In order to protect users and employees, local, state, and federal agencies, as well as professional associations, have established principles to protect people in recreation facilities. These forms of guidance are referred to as external influences. Recreation facility managers must be sensitive to how these external influences affect their responsibilities. External influences include liabilities, codes, and standards.

Liabilities

In the production process, potential liabilities may be created. A liability occurs when management had an obligation to protect the user or employee and failed to do so. This failure to exercise some degree of care by a reasonable person can be observed as negligence on the part of management. If negligence occurs, a user may make a claim, which could result in a lawsuit that provides damages equivalent to what the user may have experienced. These situations are often known as a tort or a civil wrong, a private wrong, or injury independent of a contract resulting in a breach of legal duty and responsibility to the user. These types of developments need to be avoided if at all possible. Potential lawsuits can place extensive demands on management, in addition to the possibility of significant financial loss for the agency.

Frequently, recreation facility managers accept the idea that all users are responsible for their usage of a facility. They take for granted that the users have the knowledge, experience, and willingness to accept responsibility for their actions. This can be a good legal defense in many situations. Regardless, management should take precaution and let this be the exception, not the rule. Additionally, assumption of risk is less of an option when providing a product to children and adolescents, as well as the elderly. **Assumption of risk** is intended to protect management; however it also implies significant responsibility for recreation facility managers.

Recreation agencies can make a viable defense claim when an incident results from an act of God, or certain facility and environmental developments outside the control of management. Again, this defense should be an exception and not the rule when determining appropriate risk management at a recreation facility. Forces of nature often create situations that facility managers could have avoided. Extenuating circumstances including floods, earthquakes, tornadoes, lightning strikes, and unforeseen sudden illnesses or death could be perceived by the court either as situations where management should have taken necessary

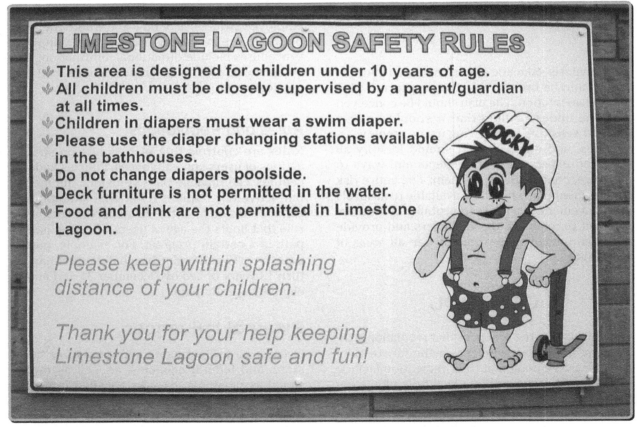

▶Signage can help inform users of rules and regulations of recreation facilities.

precautions or as acts of God that were beyond anyone's control.

An **attractive nuisance** is a condition that exists when a product that is not currently available is considered inviting or attractive to potential users. If the potential user could be a child or anyone else not realizing the hazard involved, management could be held responsible because the situation attracted the user. This is true even when the potential user should not have had access to the product. A common example of a recreation facility that is perceived as an attractive nuisance is a swimming pool. Recreation facility managers who are responsible for pools should always be sure that access is restricted by fences, lighting, and other reasonable control measures when the facility is closed.

A **standard of care** is usually established as a result of previous legal action or precedence. In this case, recreation facility managers who have the responsibility for supervising, instructing, or managing the facility must be familiar with information that is relevant to being responsible for use of the facility. Usually these standards are communicated by professional associations and organizations through meetings or publications. Often, standards of care are minimal. A recommendation to drag (groom) and line softball fields after every third game is an example of a standard of care often used by the Amateur Softball Association (ASA) for national tournaments.

Codes

Codes are legal guidelines or systems that set limitations or control mechanisms for recreation facility usage. They place restrictions and requirements not only on facility development, but also on daily operations. Codes change and it is important to stay abreast of these changes. One example of codes is construction codes, which are enforced during facility construction and can affect facility location, structural makeup, sizes of areas, entries and exits, and space requirements. Other common codes that apply to recreation facilities include fire codes and facility capacity codes designed to assist in the safe operation of a facility.

▶Enclosing an entire aquatic area of a facility with a fence is a good way to limit access.

Standards

Another external influence on recreation facility managers is national associations that create standards to provide guidance for the delivery and use of a particular product. Standards could also influence facility use, especially where a successful product is being delivered. Sometimes products can be so specialized that only the national association has the ability to oversee their proper application and use. Areas where standards can be observed include designing of spaces and areas, operation of a facility and equipment, ratio of employees to users, temperatures required for certain environment conditions, weather postponement, types of equipment for a job, level of attention and care to users and employees, and timing in getting specialized work completed.

SECURITY

Security can be one of the most important concerns when managing a recreation facility. Managers need to know that their facility and related equipment is safe from burglary, vandalism, and prohibited entry and use. Security is having a system in place to protect users as well as facilities and equipment from harm. Users and employees desire an environment free from the fear that they could be harmed or lose their belongings. When discussing security, the two most important aspects to consider are surveillance and access control.

Surveillance

A surveillance system allows management to keep close watch over space, equipment, and people. A variety of monitoring options are available. Although access control can play a large role in facility security, surveillance is a means of protecting a recreation facility—such as identification checks, gates, or security guards—without necessarily creating the discomfort that can occur with access control.

Lighting

Lighting can be a less intrusive option for securing a facility and can include providing adequate lighting in and around a facility. Regular lighting automatically contributes to facility security because it gives the appearance that people are present, making it unattractive to unwanted intruders during nonbusiness hours. Security lighting enables employees to view areas at a distance to see what is happening and have time to respond.

Surveillance Cameras

Another form of surveillance involves video cameras and monitoring systems. Cameras act both as a deterrent as well as a means for staff to view areas from monitors located at a control center. Two types of cameras are typically used in a security system. The first captures pictures in a still-framed format much like a typical photo camera captures pictures. The second type records action continuously. It can be fixed and only capture pictures from a limited area or mobile so that it can survey a wider area.

Surveillance cameras can be on continuously or triggered when motion, such as people walking through a door or crossing a trigger device, occurs. Strategic hiding positions of cameras are based on the nature of the facility and what is to

© Dale Garvey

▶Surveillance cameras may be necessary to provide a secure, safe environment for facility users and employees.

be recorded. Cameras can be hidden in overhead lights, in clocks, behind mirrors, or even within smoke detectors and ceiling speakers. Outside surveillance cameras can be placed on high poles and can have the capacity to zoom in on movement. As mentioned, cameras can also serve as a deterrent if they are positioned in areas where they can be seen. Multiple cameras can feed into one monitor and depict images from several locations. One disadvantage of this type of surveillance equipment is the cost. Some cameras are designed for night vision, which is even more expensive to purchase and maintain.

Surveillance Staff

Surveillance can also take place by staff designated to watch areas in and around a facility. This responsibility is part of the job for most employees but not their primary focus. In some instances, a recreation facility may include employees whose sole purpose is observing and guarding the facility. These security guards are valuable because the visibility that results from their uniform and sometimes a marked security vehicle can deter unwelcomed behaviors. Security guards usually have to meet predetermined qualifications, which can incorporate not only guarding but also emergency or disaster training. It is common practice for security guards to be fully evaluated before hiring, making sure they are properly trained for a particular recreation facility and product.

Watchdogs

An effective but inexpensive form of security guarding is watchdogs or guard dogs. This type of security is generally used at facilities during the evening hours. When using guard dogs, appropriate signs should provide warnings and the dogs should be behind barriers. Dogs can be much cheaper than electronic surveillance devices and they can as effective as police officers. Advantages of watchdogs are that they can intimidate intruders; they have a keener sense of sight, smell, and hearing than humans; and their bark can serve as both a deterrent and an alarm. A disadvantage of watchdogs is the considerable amount of time and expense involved in caring for them.

Access Control

Access control is a security concept where appropriate steps to influence who and what can enter an area or a facility are enacted. It keeps people out of a facility unless deemed appropriate for entry.

Generally, there are two areas of a facility, the perimeter and internal areas, where access control can be established. The perimeter is the outer area of the facility that may be enclosed by fences or other barriers, creating a boundary. Most facilities have a main entrance where perimeter control is maintained. Internal areas are enclosed by the walls, doors, counters, gates, or other barriers inside a facility. They include areas that are involved with the delivery of the core product and core product extensions. Different indoor areas may require different access control devices to limit access to the appropriate people.

Barriers or fences around the perimeter can be either natural or human made. Natural barriers include mounds, trees, bushes, and shrubs, whereas man-made barriers usually involve some type of fencing or gate. These barriers can prevent intruders from entering a parking area or from driving into areas that need to be protected.

▶Automated entry systems are common in recreation facilities and limit access to the facility without having to use the time of an employee to check in all facility users.

Barriers and fences can control entry to a facility, but access usually requires a system that identifies users and employees. Identification systems should be able to recognize people who have access to the facility or area. The most common system is to require a form of identification that has been authorized by management. Common forms of acceptable identification include

- driver's licenses,
- credit cards,
- school identification cards,
- work identification cards,
- birth certificates, and
- passports.

Often these types of identification are used to create a specific facility identification card or membership card. More advanced identification techniques include voice identification, fingerprint identification, and retinal identification.

At some point, security has to address door control, which involves a system of keying to create access to the facility. There are various means to accomplish this, including padlocks, mechanical or combination locks, or magnetically keyed locks. Each lock system provides a different degree of security in terms of the ability to remove the lock by someone who is trying to enter an area without authorization. Unfortunately, standard keys and locks no longer fulfill demands for maintaining access control. Keys can be a weak link in any security system because they can be lost, stolen, and duplicated. In addition, the process of changing locks and reissuing keys is costly and time consuming.

SUMMARY

Monitoring and guiding user and employee circulation, safety, control, and security is an important component of planning and operating a facility. By having good systems in place, a safe and comfortable environment can be created that not only protects users and the organization but also enhances the recreation experience.

Coordinating and Scheduling

Recreation facility management requires extensive insight into two key subjects: coordination and scheduling. Each facility has unique policies, procedures, and systems to meet administrative expectations. Recreation facility managers have the responsibility to coordinate and schedule space, people, and equipment efficiently. Because a variety of people as well as groups use a facility, coordination requires the careful integration of activities in the overall plan for use.

COORDINATING

The goal in coordinating a recreation facility is to create an effective system that provides for the efficient use of all areas, personnel, and equipment in a harmonious and timely fashion. Managing individual and group use of a facility takes time and effort. Inefficient coordination can reflect poorly on management and product delivery.

Competently coordinated facilities can enhance facility usage. In addition to providing a positive and satisfying experience for users, competent coordination also allows for maximum use of the facility. However, maximizing facility use can create conflict if not coordinated properly. Recreation facility managers should be sensitive to potential coordination problems and be prepared to respond to coordination challenges when they occur. Most facilities have different levels of usage interest from internal and external users and in some cases, employees. Multiple interests in facility use often create conflicts of interest, and recreation agencies must create policies to establish priorities for use. Even when policies are in place, ill will between competing user groups can occur and have a negative impact on facility operations.

Another issue related to maximizing facility use is allowing for the facility to be adequately prepared. The details for this preparation can be extensive. Typical arrangements to coordinate include the following:

- Dates and time commitment
- Setup and takedown
- Equipment needs
- Electrical needs
- Area load and layout
- Supervision
- Security requirements
- Access control

- Charges
- Food service
- Final written agreement

In the beginning, most recreation facilities have the available space to fulfill user needs. Over time, however, production areas can become crowded. Although this problem can be the result of demand for a product, it makes coordination challenging. Obstacles arise in meeting user needs when there are too many users or employees for the space available. Recreation facility managers should be alert to space limitations, anticipate solutions, and have appropriate responses that will help in the effort to coordinate facilities. An example of a space limitation is a golf course that has a waiting list for tee times. Managers can respond by limiting the number of tee-time reservations a person can reserve, altering the fee structure to encourage play at low-usage times, or adding facilities to meet the demand for additional golfers.

Obviously, coordinating maximal facility usage is important. There are five approaches to doing so:

1. Leadership
2. Stakeholders
3. Seasonality
4. Time
5. Place

Leadership

Leadership refers to how recreation agency leaders influence facility usage so that it fulfills the mission of the agency. Is the mission to serve people, to make a profit, or both? Recreation facility coordination evolves from administrative priorities and the style of the agency executive. People- or service-oriented leaders may be so sensitive to users, schedulers, and employees that technical responsibilities may be compromised. On the other hand, they could be so goal and profit driven that they lose sight of users' and employees' experiences. Understanding how leadership influences facility availability and coordination is fundamental for recreation facility managers.

Administrators have a philosophy about their product and how it should be produced and delivered. Often this philosophy is imparted in the form of a mission or vision statement. Employees should be familiar with this philosophy and it should influence decisions regarding facility

▶While space limitation might not be an issue when a facility is first built, demand for a core product can cause overcrowding in the facility's main area. Making changes in scheduling practices of a facility can help to solve this issue.

utilization. For example, a recreation agency may determine that a particular facility should be made available to tax-paying residents before other user groups. This philosophy would clearly affect the scheduling practices of the facility.

Stakeholders

Who are the users and employees, or stakeholders, who will use a recreation facility and what are their interests and needs? An appreciation for personalities, gender, race, social status, attitude, and motivation can make a big difference in facility coordination. Understanding the different people who may use a recreation facility and enhancing their usage can lead to harmonious use of a facility and can help anticipate and avoid coordination problems.

Seasonality

Seasonality is being aware of changes in recreation facility use as it relates to certain times of the year.

Busy times are the peak season and slow times are the off-season. For example, baseball or softball facilities are likely to be busy in the summer and not so busy at other times of year. Seasons could also be affected by changes in weather conditions, which greatly influence what users do, such as using an aquatic facility. Facility coordination efforts can change dramatically as seasons dictate product interest and support.

Time of Day

Facility usage also varies based on the certain times of the day. In coordinating a recreation facility, it all comes down to customer demand for a particular time. This is often referred to as prime time, and the opposite is nonprime time. Time could be divided into morning, afternoon, and evening time slots. Hours could be blocked into segments that are regularly scheduled for certain activities. For example, an ice arena may reserve weeknights from 7 p.m. to 9 p.m. for public skating. This time may be blocked regularly based on demand by users. Recognizing customer demand for facility time results in maximal use and revenue.

Place

It is critical that recreation facility managers be mindful of the type of facility and how it dictates certain use and coordination limitations. Depending on the facility, there can be policies, procedures, rules, and regulations that influence coordination. For instance, a community center caters to users of all ages. However, there may be some spaces that children are not allowed to access for safety reasons. Conflicting group usage could also arise in a facility that has multiple spaces that may be used at the same time, such as a convention center or park with pavilions.

SCHEDULING

Scheduling is the act of assigning a time, place, and date based on a request for a particular use. In many facilities, the agency schedules its own activities related to delivering the core product. In other instances, facilities may be reserved by users. Recreation facility managers are responsible for facility scheduling, which can be a tedious and difficult responsibility. Scheduling responsibilities will vary depending on the recreation agency, the facility, and the product, procedures, responsibilities, and policies.

Product

Each facility has scheduling needs based on the core product. A schedule may be required for employees to accomplish operational tasks, responsibilities, and functions related to the product. A different schedule may be necessary to coordinate use of the core product by participants. Scheduling practices for products are based on one or a combination of the following: users, staff, space, and events.

Users

Recreation facilities can have a number of users whose access to the core product may need to be scheduled. Depending on the use of the facility, varying degrees of supervision over users may be required. Understanding users, the product they want to use, and how the facility can best serve them is a function of recreation facility managers. Recreation facility managers' knowledge of users

▶Happy users are the main goal of any recreation facility.

can play a big part in how a facility is scheduled. User nature and status can be determined by several factors, including product popularity, socioeconomic status, gender, age, special needs and interests, skill level, and willingness to pay. Achieving customer satisfaction through needs assessment and appropriate allocation of space for their needs is an important goal of recreation facility managers.

Staff

Every recreation facility requires people to deliver and produce the core product and core product extensions. The type, number, and responsibilities of recreation facility employees can vary greatly by facility. A critical task for recreation facility managers is efficiently scheduling employees. Employee scheduling will vary depending on the nature of the facility and its operating hours and the nature of each position required to deliver the product. Product delivery personnel may have completely different functions than maintenance personnel. Recreation facility managers should be knowledgeable of these differences in personnel functions and scheduling practices in relation to employees' assignments, timing, and agency pri-

orities. Competent managers schedule employees so they can fulfill their obligation without conflict or interference.

Space

Another type of facility scheduling practice based on the core product is controlling facility use based on the area to be used. Recreation facilities may have any number of areas that need to be scheduled in a way that maximizes their use, whether they are hotel rooms, sport courts, theaters, classrooms, or outdoor areas. Some facility spaces require a completely different scheduling technique than others. Some spaces have laws that limit how many users can be accommodated at a given time. Each area of a recreation facility or even the facility itself can be viewed as unique space with its own requirements for accomplishing utilization expectations.

Special Events

Auditoriums, stadiums, convention centers, arenas, hotels, and other facilities have venues with the potential for holding events that can attract large groups of people, also known as *special events*. The coordination of special events is

▶Special events require a large amount of planning and preparing of the facility before the event and will usually last for the majority of the day.

one of the most complicated facility scheduling practices. Special events can originate in-house by recreation facility personnel, or they can be delivered by an outside agency requesting sole use of the facility. Event scheduling can be time consuming and require legal consultation regarding facility personnel responsibilities and limitations placed on personnel from an outside organization. Examples of special events that may take place in a recreation facility include weddings at a country club or church, concerts in an arena or stadium, tournaments at sport complexes, or lectures in an auditorium. Event scheduling requires a great deal of preparation and attention to detail.

Procedures

Recreation facility scheduling is challenging, so applying a system of sound procedures can be invaluable. These procedures may be applied informally or formally. In most cases where effective and efficient management scheduling is observed, the following scheduling procedures are applied: a request, log, review, response, and agreement.

Request

The initial **request** for use of a facility may require a letter or e-mail requesting the facility. Often, some type of form must be completed (see figure 13.1). The request demonstrates a sincere interest from a potential user that should result in a response from facility personnel. A reservation request form often includes the name of the group or person requesting use; a contact person, address, phone number, and e-mail; the date, time, and space desired; and a statement indicating the nature of the event. This document represents the beginning of an arrangement where both parties are attempting to come to an agreement on all the details for use of the facility. Agreements are commonly referred to as *permits, contracts,* or *facility use agreements* and can be detailed or simple depending on the facility and the use requested.

Log

When a request is received, it should be logged on a calendar, indicating the date and time of receipt. Recording the time of receipt can be important when there are multiple usage requests for the same time. If there are no predetermined policies establishing priority of use, a philosophy of first come, first served is often observed.

Golf Outing or Tournament Information Form

Name of group or event _____

Contact person _____ E-mail address _____

Address _____

City _____ State _____ Zip _____

Home phone _____ Work phone _____ Cell phone _____

Date preferred _____ Rain date _____

If your group includes 72 or more players, then players will have shotgun start with all teams teeing off at the same time. Please select the time of the shotgun start: ☐ 8 a.m. ☐ 1 p.m.

If your group includes between 24 and 71 players, what is your desired first tee time? _____

Check all services that are required:
☐ Scoring for the event
☐ Proximity markers for contests
☐ Names on carts (list of players required 48 hours before event)
☐ Scorecards
☐ Gift certificates for prizes (season passes, cart fees, and merchandise are available)
☐ Starting services
☐ Registration services
☐ Other _____

Figure 13.1 Golf outing or tournament information form.

Review

Each facility request should receive a complete review by appropriate facility personnel. More than one employee may review a request based on their area of expertise and level of authority. Depending on the nature of the facility and how often it is reserved for use by an outside party, some requests may not require an in-depth review and simply be scheduled into a date and time slot. Other requests may require that all variables and details be carefully considered before a determination of use is made. All final decisions regarding a request should be applied in a fair and equitable fashion.

Response

However a request is submitted, it should be responded to in a timely fashion. Each agency may have a policy stating the length of time that applicants can expect before receiving a response. Even if a request is denied, applicants deserve the courtesy of a prompt answer so that they can seek other arrangements. Acceptable response methods include a letter, e-mail, or telephone call to the person who made the request.

Agreement

A final, written agreement or contract may be necessary for some recreation facility uses. The agreement binds all details of the arrangement into a formal understanding between the potential user and the recreation agency. Some agreements or contracts may require the assistance of an attorney. The agreement should include details such as requirements for use of the space, equipment needs, food service, setup and takedown responsibilities, personnel requirements, safety and security concerns, length of use, and charges for use, misuse, or overuse. An agreement should clarify any specifics that are negotiated as the scheduling process evolves so there is no misunderstanding between the parties. Figure 13.2 shows a sample agreement.

Pool Rental Agreement

Name of group _____

Address _____

Phone _____

Representative of group _____

Reservation for *(circle one):*   Pool and waterslide   Pool   Wading pool only

Rental date____/____/____, from ____:____ a.m./p.m. to ____:____ a.m./p.m.

General description of group *(circle one):*   Youths 17 and under   Adults   Families   School group

Will your group need use of the wading pool for children aged 5 and under *(circle one)*?   Yes   No

Approximate # in group _____

Rental fee/hour $_____

Total fee $_____

I, as representative of the previously named group, hereby reserve the pool facility for the date and time indicated. As the responsible party for this group, I understand it is my duty to see that all pool policies and rules are followed by the group while using the facilities.
Please read carefully. We understand the following:

• Final decisions regarding closings and cancellations are at the discretion of the department staff only.
• Alcohol is not permitted.
• The premises are to be left in the same condition as when we arrived.
• All public rules and policies apply to private parties.
• Food and drinks may be brought into the facility but eaten *only* inside the concession area.
• Our party will be allowed to enter the facility no earlier than the confirmed rental time.
• The entire fee will be due at the time of reservation.
• Reservations will not be taken earlier than 3 business days in advance of the rental date.
• The entire fee will be forfeited if the aquatic director is not notified of a cancellation 3 business days in advance of the reserved date.

Signature _____   Date _____

Payment	
Cash	
Check/money order	
Credit card	
School group subsidy	

White copy—Office
Yellow copy—Pool
Pink copy—Patron

From R. Mull, B. Beggs, and M. Renneisen, 2009, *Recreation Facility Management* (Champaign, IL: Human Kinetics).

Figure 13.2 Pool rental agreement form.

Responsibilities

Scheduling responsibilities need to be understood before arrangements for use can take place. These responsibilities will vary depending on the facility and how it is utilized. Certain expectations for recreation facility managers and users need to be decided upon before finalizing the arrangements. Arrangements are often communicated in writing where both parties recognize their responsibilities. Users may need equipment, lighting, security, or other services provided by the agency. On the other hand, these needs may be the responsibility of the user and may include setup and takedown, security, supervision, equipment, and safety.

Setup and Takedown

Most arrangements to use a recreation facility or an area require recreation facility managers or users to perform some type of setup. It is important to define in advance who is responsible for what setup and takedown tasks. For instance, if a group is reserving a room in a convention center for a meeting, they will need tables and chairs. It should be established in advance whether the group or the convention center is responsible for setting up the tables and chairs. If the convention center is responsible for the setup, it is important that the users explain how they want the room set up. This is usually done when the agreement is signed.

Equally important is the need for a clear understanding regarding takedown responsibilities, especially if the users are responsible for this task. Users often do not have the same standards when it comes to returning a facility area to its original state. Recreation facility managers should clearly communicate, in writing, in what condition the facility should be returned to when the use is completed. Clearly communicating cleanup expectations can save a lot of trouble and inconvenience for recreation facility managers.

Security

Some facility uses require special security measures. A user's request should be reviewed and any security requirements established in advance. Some recreation facility uses can create concerns based on the size of anticipated crowds, the possibility of unusual or unexpected behavior, or other reasons. For example, a recreation agency may require security for a use that involves the consumption of alcohol at the facility. Security

▶ Recreation facility managers must ensure that it is clear in the final agreements who will be responsible for setting up a facility area for an event, as well as who is responsible for returning the area to its original condition, the facility staff or the users.

arrangements regarding protection of people, facilities, and equipment may be necessary based on a thorough review of the user's request. These needs and whose responsibility it will be to establish security should be discussed and agreed upon in writing before final scheduling takes place.

Supervision

Most recreation facility use will require some level of supervision, which can be provided by facility personnel or by the user. Details on facility supervision must be clearly communicated when the user is responsible for providing supervision. Supervisory arrangements will depend on the inherent risk associated with the type of use. Recreation facility managers need to make sure that users are fully aware of their supervisory responsibility, and in turn, users must demonstrate the capacity to meet this need. The most common arrangement is when the recreation facility provides supervision with facility staff. In this arrangement, the user typically is responsible for reimbursing the recreation agency for this service.

Equipment

With most facility requests, users will need equipment for whatever activity they have planned.

Recreation facility managers should communicate what equipment will be made available for use in addition to making sure the users know how to properly operate it. Users could also bring their own equipment to a facility, so a clear understanding of what equipment can be brought into a facility is important. In both cases, equipment damage could result. An understanding of each party's responsibility for equipment should be communicated in writing in the event that damage to the equipment or facility occurs. Equipment arrangements may warrant a separate written document expressing all obligations and financial responsibilities.

Safety

User safety is paramount in any recreation facility, especially when managers are scheduling a facility or delegating its use to an outside group. Aside from ensuring proper supervision, there should always be a safe environment, including safe equipment. If users are providing equipment, recreation facility managers need assurance that the equipment is in proper condition and is appropriate for the activity. Users must be aware of their responsibility for safety when providing their own equipment. In scheduling a facility for use, managers have to accept responsibility for safety of both the area and the equipment involved. They must make sure all the details regarding safety are reviewed and documented in writing, creating a clear understanding of the responsibilities of each party.

Policies

Facility scheduling practices require the establishment of policies to protect everyone's interest and involvement. Policies also provide the basis for consistent and fair review of facility requests. Scheduling policies can be related to charges or fees, prioritization, cancellation, damage, food service, and insurance.

Charges or Fees

An established and well-planned policy statement for fees and charges is a critical component of recreation facility management. Depending on the type of use and scheduling arrangements, the agency can incur costs that necessitate the assessment of fees for reserved use. Fees come in many forms. Each facility will have its own fee system for assessing charges to users based on the type and length of facility use. Other factors that can influence fees include special arrangements, equipment, supervision, time of day, and time of the year. These charges need to be established in advance in the a written policy, basing the amount on a fair assessment of all variables involved. Charges are usually intended to offset part of the construction costs, direct expenses related to the specific use, overhead, and a percentage for profit. Often, market conditions influence fees more than any other factor. Ultimately, fees and charges have a significant impact on the success of a recreation facility.

Prioritization

A typical user submitting a request for use of a recreation facility may not understand all the steps involved in the scheduling process. Further complicating this situation is when multiple requests are received for the same time and space. A policy stating how requests are received and prioritized should be in place to assist staff in determining which users' requests are to be granted and in which order. This policy should also be shared with users and outline how far in advance a request must be received. This allows time for making arrangements without excessive time pressure that can create misunderstandings and conflict.

Typical factors for determining priority of use include when the request is received, the nature of the group that is making the request, and the number of people being served by the use. The nature of the agency may also influence the priority policy. For example, a public recreation facility may prioritize local residents over nonlocal residents, whereas a private recreation facility may prioritize the group that will generate the most income for the facility.

Cancellation

There are times when cancellations occur, and a written cancellation policy is important for recreation facilities to be consistent in applying penalties or other consequences to the users. A cancellation policy should specify any acceptable reasons for a cancellation so that users are aware of their obligations in advance. The cancellation policy should include a clause that stipulates a time frame where financial penalties will be invoked.

Sometimes users make arrangements to use a facility but end up not showing up or using the facility as intended. Interested parties may also make a preliminary request to reserve a facility, taking a lot of time to discuss arrangements with facility staff, and then never follow through with a formal request. To deter facility users from wasting facility resources, sometimes advance deposits are required to reserve the facility. Agency policies should clearly define deposit requirements and stipulations. Typically a deposit is returned at the end of the use, providing the facility and equipment are not damaged. Reserving parties who fail to show for the intended use may forfeit their deposit or a portion of it based on a reasonable percentage of the full charges. This practice makes users think twice about not showing up. Advance deposits demonstrate good faith on the part of the potential user and protect administrative time and effort.

A refund policy should also be in place that indicates under what circumstances users may receive a partial or entire return of any fees paid. A policy statement should protect facilities from unwarranted requests while also returning to users all or part of a fee under certain conditions. A refund may be issued when user expectations are not met, an unforeseen change in the user's situation occurs, or the agency has a change in facility availability. Whatever the situation, the policy should include refund request details and be approved by the administrative authority of

Refund Request Form

Household name_____ Date_____

Address _____

City _____ State _____ Zip _____

Amount of refund _____ Participant name _____

Program _____ Class code #_____

Reason for refund _____

Requested by _____

Comments_____

_____

For Office Use Only

Approved by _____ Amount of refund_____

Account # _____ Project code # _____

Transaction fee amount _____ Return this form to refund clerk by_____

Check # _____ Date mailed_____ Receipt # _____

This form may be used *only* for refunds.

From R. Mull, B. Beggs, and M. Rennelson, 2009, *Recreation Facility Management* (Champaign, IL: Human Kinetics).

Figure 13.3 Refund request form.

the agency. The agency could also use a refund request form, as seen in figure 13.3.

Damage

Use of a recreation facility can result in damage to the facility and equipment. These developments are often unexpected and are seldom addressed during scheduling discussions. Unfortunately, damages do occur as a result of unruly participants, vandalism, weather, or accidents. The facility may have a difficult time recovering financial resources from the user group who caused the damage if there is no damage policy. A damage policy should be discussed in advance during reservation negotiations with users so that they have full insight into their responsibility in the protection of facilities and equipment. Usually, some type of facility inspection occurs with facility personnel and potential users before usage, citing all areas and equipment conditions so that neither party is caught off guard by preexisting damage. Facility personnel should also conduct an inspection after use and document any damages by the user. A deposit fee is often incorporated into the facility use agreement stating the conditions for the deposit to be returned to the user or retained by the facility after a final inspection occurs.

© Ezra Shaw/Getty Images Sport

▶A damage policy is often included in a scheduling agreement, and a deposit fee may not be returned if the users fail to return the facility to its original condition following an event.

Food-Service Policies

Some facility users may want food and beverage products available during their use. Requests may include the sale, purchase, or distribution of food and beverages, including alcohol. Any food-service arrangement should clearly stipulate the facility user's responsibilities. If a third party provides food service, facility management must be informed of the caterer's credentials and licenses and review the contract between the potential user and food provider. If food service is provided by the facility, all menu items and pricing should be reviewed in advance so that there are no surprises or misunderstandings between the facility and user.

Whether the food service is provided by the facility, the user, or a catering service, facility personnel should inform users of licenses, codes, and requirements dictated by state and local government. The sale or distribution of alcoholic beverages presents additional issues for both users and facility operators. Certain restrictions will be imposed by state and local agencies and a higher degree of supervision may be required. Additional liability to the user and facility operator due to the sale or distribution of alcoholic beverages may have financial or other implications. Food-service policies should clearly state limitations, restrictions, and expectations of the facility and the user.

Insurance Policies

Recreation facility managers may expect users to obtain insurance to cover their use of the facility. When this is necessary, the agency should have a policy statement that stipulates the type and amount of insurance coverage expected. The agency may also expect proof of insurance by requesting a certificate of insurance to ensure that the coverage is appropriate. The user's policy should cover all aspects of the use, including the areas and space used, interior and exterior equipment, people who are involved, and complete time span, from setup through cleanup. The certificate of insurance should state the limits of liability and type of coverage provided, and it should be presented by the user before final arrangements are made.

Scheduling Techniques

Scheduling can be accomplished using different concepts and practices. Computers play a significant role in the facility scheduling process. Certain techniques can be applied to efficiently manage facility requests, which can involve diverse interests and a large number of requests. Ultimately, whatever system is in place should be tied into a facility master schedule.

A **master schedule** is appropriate when there are many requests for facility use. It records all uses by date, time, space, and user contact information. The master schedule should be maintained and available for reference by facility personnel at any time. It helps keep scheduling organized and avoids overlapping conflicts. Master schedules can be maintained by using a reservation book or computer software that allows for review of any time and place that has or can be scheduled. It is important that a single system is used so that all of the reservations are available in one central location and that all entries are as accurate and up to date as possible.

▶Food and beverages may be supplied by the facility user at a special event, or for a fee, they may be supplied by the recreation facility or a third party caterer.

© Jeff Greenberg/age fotostock

SUMMARY

Recreation facilities often serve the needs of many activities and programs. It is critical for activities to be coordinated in a manner that maximizes facility use in an efficient and effective manner. Carefully coordinating activities can avoid conflict and result in positive experiences for both facilities and users. In addition to scheduling activities related to the core product and core product extensions, agencies often must work with their users in reserving and scheduling space for outside activities. By having procedures and policies in place for employees and users to follow, this process can run smoothly for all involved.

14

Maintenance

At the completion of this chapter, you should be able to do the following:

1. Explain the impact that maintenance has on facility usage and operations.

2. Recognize the categories of facility maintenance.

3. Understand the processes involved in maintenance requests.

Maintenance as a management function can be a critical contributor to facility utilization. If not performed properly and in a timely fashion, it can have a negative impact on the core product and core product extensions. **Maintenance** includes any function associated with keeping facilities and equipment in proper, safe, and functional condition. It is a support service and is often performed behind the scenes. Terms associated with maintenance activities include *clean, replace, repair, prevent, protect, preserve, fix, change over,* and *set up.* The goal of the maintenance function is to keep everything as close to its original condition as possible so that facility usage can take place as intended without safety concerns, distraction, delays, or disruptions.

In some agencies, maintenance functions are mistakenly regarded as a secondary responsibility that can be taken for granted and not given proper attention from management. This is unfortunate because poor maintenance practices can have a negative effect on user satisfaction and product delivery. In some cases, user safety is compromised due to lack of appropriate maintenance practices. Maintenance should always be a priority function. Recreation facility managers must be

committed to and involved in the maintenance process so that intended utilization can occur, bringing about positive user experiences with the product.

Maintenance can be observed as an indirect or direct function of product delivery. In most instances, maintenance is an indirect function because maintenance workers seldom come in contact with users. Recreation facility managers often intentionally schedule maintenance functions for times when the facility is not being used. Scheduling maintenance functions during these times is critical for the efficient and effective completion of maintenance tasks so as not to interfere with administrative and delivery operations. Scheduling maintenance functions can be challenging, particularly for recreation facilities that are in high demand. Maintenance tasks have to take place when the facility is not in use, which is often late at night or early in the morning. Recreation facilities that are extensive or have more complex products have unique maintenance scheduling challenges.

As mentioned, maintenance can have a direct impact on the delivery of the product. Because of this, it is important for maintenance leader-

▶Maintenance functions require unique scheduling practices to not interfere with user's utilization of a facility.

© Terry Wild Stock Inc.

ship to understand facility usage, including what activities it involves, volume of users expected, preparation efforts, and consequences, so that they can realize how their role and decisions will affect utilization. If maintenance is required when a facility is in use, then time and effort should be devoted to making sure that maintenance tasks do not negatively affect usage, keeping inconveniences to a minimum.

FACILITY IMAGE

The end result of the maintenance function will influence users' perceptions of the facility. Their impression of a facility may include a sense of comfort and belonging or a sense of uncertainty or discomfort. Recreation facilities that are not clean, are unsanitary, have broken equipment, or other poor maintenance practices can drive users away. For example, a person staying at a resort is much more likely to return to that location if the facility and rooms are clean and in good condition. The same holds true for users' experiences at a park or playground. If the area is clean and well maintained with no broken equipment, users are more likely to be satisfied with the experience than they would be if equipment didn't work or the area was dirty. Facility maintenance can make either a positive or a negative statement about the facility, the product, and management. Every effort should be put forth to maintain a positive image through good maintenance practices.

SAFETY

In addition to the image created by maintenance, safety is an important end result of good maintenance. Sometimes product usage results in the degeneration of the area or equipment, which can lead to hazardous conditions. For instance, playgrounds often have loose-fill surfaces such as wood chips or shredded rubber. If there are swings on the playground, usually children drag their feet under the swings, moving the loose-fill surface and creating an area directly under the swing with less surfacing for fall protection. By requiring the simple maintenance task of sweeping and leveling the loose-fill surface, safety in

▶Maintenance of the loose fill areas below the swings at a playground is crucial to maintain safety for the users and to diminish the risk of in jury.

the swing area is greatly improved and the risk of serious injury is diminished. Other examples of unsafe conditions can include a nail sticking out of a floor, security equipment that is not working, a hole in a playing field, a crack in a sidewalk, water on a floor, an emergency exit that is blocked, or ice or snow in parking areas. It is the maintenance staff that is usually in the best position to see hazardous situations and correct them. Maintenance staff should also conduct regular checks of smoke alarms, security alarms, emergency lighting, and other safety mechanisms in a facility. Their role in protecting users and employees is invaluable in keeping a facility free from unsafe conditions and serious emergencies.

Annual inspections of all life safety systems for emergency disruptions, including fire alarm checks, should be documented to ensure that the systems will function as planned. This would include a description of any maintenance practices that factor into the prevention process. In addition, any maintenance practice that is part of an evacuation plan should be included in the plan. For example, if an ice arena has an ammonia leak and the evacuation plan calls for a maintenance employee to shut down a series of equipment to limit further contamination, this should be documented in the evacuation plan.

MAINTENANCE CATEGORIES

Each facility and its areas and equipment can vary greatly with many challenging maintenance tasks. Maintenance can be broadly categorized into building maintenance, grounds maintenance, and equipment maintenance.

• **Building maintenance** involves indoor facilities or structures, including rooms, corridors, stairwells, lobbies, lounges, and offices that need to be kept clean, functional, and safe. Some specific building maintenance tasks include

- sweeping,
- mopping,
- picking up trash,
- window washing,
- watering plants,
- dusting,

▶ Infield grooming is a form of grounds maintenance.

- vacuuming,
- deep cleaning carpets,
- changing lights,
- repairing windows and doors,
- plumbing, and
- performing electrical or mechanical repairs.

- **Grounds maintenance** can have several meanings depending on the recreation facility. An outdoor facility such as a park or playground primarily requires grounds maintenance. In addition, exterior and landscaping care of a recreation building falls under grounds maintenance. Grounds maintenance is often the first thing users see and thus it affects their first impression of a facility and its curb appeal. This maintenance category incorporates all the necessary activities associated with keeping the outdoor areas attractive, functional, and safe. It includes tasks such as

- snow removal,
- leaf removal,
- tree pruning,
- watering,
- fertilizing,
- weed control,
- grass mowing,
- pest control,
- disease control,
- trash removal,
- shrub trimming, and
- grooming of infield surfaces.

- **Equipment maintenance** refers to items and mechanical systems that support a facility or help to make the product efficient and functional. It can include maintenance equipment and any equipment that fulfills product delivery. It can also include technical equipment for the efficiency support systems that provide comfort to users and employees as well as assistance with product delivery. Certain equipment can be susceptible to damage and wear, resulting in demanding maintenance work. Examples of maintenance in this category include

- repairing machines,
- replacing parts,
- cleaning,
- rotating and replacing tires,
- sharpening tools, and
- servicing HVAC equipment.

MAINTENANCE TYPES

In addition to the previous categories of maintenance, there are two general types of maintenance: routine and nonroutine. These two categories help to explain how tasks in each category may be described and organized.

Routine Maintenance

Routine maintenance is ongoing maintenance that represents efforts by management to keep facilities and equipment in proper condition from day to day or even hour to hour. There is a dependence on routine daily maintenance tasks to keep the production environment and equipment in its proper functioning state. Routine maintenance requires supervision, coordination, and attention to detail. These tasks are often performed around the delivery of the product and may include a daily or weekly checklist (see figure 14.1). Routine maintenance tasks should not be interrupted because delays can result in problems. The observation of routine maintenance usually indicates a well-organized and coordinated maintenance system and involves tasks such as cleaning, trash removal, and maintaining an aesthetically pleasing environment.

Nonroutine Maintenance

Not all maintenance is routine. There are many circumstances where nonroutine activities require maintenance attention, including projects and unforeseen, preventive, and cyclical maintenance. Nonroutine maintenance usually requires extra attention, especially as it relates to the coordination and scheduling of work that is needed. When these situations develop, a system is initiated that recognizes a need and then issues a response to take care of it.

Projects

From time to time, facilities and equipment require work resulting from damage, breakdown, or failure. This work, often called a project, may require planning and design. Nonroutine maintenance projects could include repair, renovation, or refurbishing of flooring, walls, turf, or equipment. These projects may or may not be preplanned and their accomplishment could require a short or long amount of time. As projects are scheduled, the work area must be blocked off from the public for their safety. It is a good idea to post a notice in advance about any projects that are being completed so

Facility Maintenance Inventory Form

Facility Items			Condition	Location of problem	Comments
General	Sport activity areas	Pool #1			
		Pool #2			
		Basketball court #1			
		Basketball court #2			
		Racquetball court #1			
		Racquetball court #2			
		Exercise or weight room			
	Office areas	Office #1			
		Office #2			
		Office #3			
		Break or meeting room			
		Reception or lobby area			
	Locker and storage areas	Women's locker room			
		Men's locker room			
		Storage area #1			
		Storage area #2			
	Safety	Fire alarm system			
		Security system			
		Sprinkler system			
		Back-up generators			
Structural	Interior	Ceiling			
		Floor			
		Walls			
		Windows			
		Doors			
	Exterior	Roof			
		Gutter and downspouts			
		Wall treatment			
		Windows			
		Doors			

Facility Items			Condition	Location of problem	Comments
Utilities	Water and sewer	Water lines			
		Sewer lines			
		Water heaters			
		Water treatment systems			
		Sink and shower fixtures			
		Toilets			
		Drinking fountains			
	Electric and gas	Electric lines			
		Gas lines			
		HVAC systems			
		Electrical fixtures			
Grounds	Vegetation	Trees and shrubs			
		Grass			
	Parking and walkways	Parking lot #1 (asphalt)			
		Parking lot #2 (gravel)			
		Sidewalk #1			
		Sidewalk #2			
		Mulch path			

Conditions: S = Satisfactory condition
  H = Hazardous condition
  R = Routine maintenance needed
  M = Large-scale maintenance needed (more than $500)
  m = Small-scale maintenance needed (less than $500)

Figure 14.1   Daily maintenance checklist.

users and employees are aware of the time frame during which an area or piece of equipment will be unavailable.

Unforeseen Maintenance

Often, nonroutine maintenance tasks fall under the category of unforeseen maintenance. Frequently they are the direct result of wear and tear due to facility and equipment usage. A maintenance system should be in place to repair areas or equipment when they simply reach a point where they do not function as intended. These developments can be an emergency, which means that the problem needed is taken care of as soon as possible, or they can be scheduled to be addressed when resources and time allow. Unforeseen emergencies could include

- trees falling over power lines,
- water leaks that affect delivery operations,
- toilet overflow, and
- electricity or light failure.

Other unforeseen maintenance tasks that may not require immediate action include

- locks not functioning,
- vehicles not starting,
- broken windows,
- water damage, and
- any area or equipment that can be scheduled for repair without disrupting facility usage.

Preventive Maintenance

Recreation facility managers try to avoid unforeseen maintenance through preventive maintenance. **Preventive maintenance** is applied in anticipation of what needs to be done to protect areas and equipment from wearing out, failing to operate, or breaking down. This nonroutine practice is usually planned, but it is most often results from a judgment based on the level of use and wear of areas or equipment. This preventive system recognizes potential problems and then attends to them, increasing the longevity of areas and equipment and ensuring their protection. When managed properly, preventive maintenance can decrease or even prevent area and equipment problems and possible hazards. Some examples of preventive maintenance include

▶Preventive maintenance can decrease or prevent facility problems. Pruning trees around the facility could prevent damage to the facility at a later date.

© Karlene V. Schwartz

- changing oil and rotating tires on vehicles or maintenance equipment,
- pruning trees around electrical wires and buildings,
- controlling insects and pests,
- refurbishing floors,
- painting surfaces, and
- repairing cracks in concrete and asphalt surfaces.

Cyclical Maintenance

Another type of nonroutine maintenance is **cyclical maintenance.** Although cyclical maintenance is performed on a schedule, it occurs infrequently and is not considered routine maintenance. Cyclical maintenance can be defined as a nonroutine application that is initiated as needed and performed with a complete set of tasks designed to restore an area or piece of equipment to its desired state. Cyclical maintenance incorporates several steps in order to complete a full process or cycle. An example of a cyclical practice is maintaining turf areas, which requires soil preparation, seed-

ing, fertilizer, watering, mowing, and aerating. These practices are repeated in a cycle, usually seasonally, and can be planned in advance.

MAINTENANCE SYSTEMS

The production and delivery process should not be subject to negative developments because of facility maintenance practices. A recreation facility is designed to create and deliver a product without disruptions. Recreation facility managers should ensure that a maintenance system is in place that attends to all nonroutine developments before they negatively influence operations. Maintenance systems should be created in the most effective way possible and should include planning, work orders, and work assignments.

Planning

Fundamental to a sound maintenance system is having a plan in place for addressing all potential facility and equipment maintenance concerns. A maintenance plan should incorporate both short-range and long-range planning. Planning is critical because so many details are involved with the maintenance responsibilities of a recreation facility. The key to planning is to anticipate deterioration, repairs, and replacements rather than having to react to them. This can be a demanding responsibility. However, not everything can be foreseen, and unexpected developments require a planning system that addresses whatever may occur. Planning must be evaluated regularly and modified as necessary. In order to keep facilities and equipment functioning properly, inventory, assessment, and task identification are often built into the maintenance planning process.

Inventory

A basic task of a maintenance system is creating and maintaining a complete inventory of everything that exists in the agency. This process creates precise records for reference whenever necessary so that accurate information exists, leading to proper planning. Detailed information about every aspect of a facility and its equipment is usually gathered to reflect quality, quantity, condition, number, type, size, cost, age, and location. This information can be used to help with planning various areas of maintenance, including budget, development projects, emergency assistance, preventive steps, production concerns, and the need for extra help.

Assessment

The facility assessment process allows maintenance employees to contribute to a systemized maintenance plan. This type of assessment does not address user needs, but focuses instead on the maintenance needs of a facility as identified by maintenance personnel. Maintenance employees can be scheduled to make a visual check of a particular area or piece of equipment. This inspection can be scheduled regularly as the maintenance employees perform routine tasks associated with their position. Maintenance employees are in the best position to recognize limitations that need to be identified for both short-range and long-range maintenance planning. These assessments can discover structural problems, unsafe situations, efficiency system failures, potential emergency situations, and other routine and nonroutine maintenance concerns. This information should be incorporated in a plan to address the facility or equipment problem. Assessment results can also be interfaced with formal feasibility studies or risk management plans and needs assessments that may be underway. Assessing facilities and equipment is a proactive effort that helps identify and solve problems before they can affect product success.

Task Identification

In order for nonroutine maintenance work to be initiated, information regarding the maintenance concern has to be submitted. This information can come from observation or assessment by three sources: maintenance employees, production staff, and product users. It can be presented through verbal complaints, user complaint forms, and staff requests for assistance. Each option should cite some type of problem that needs attention. Management should be prepared to receive this information, which may be relayed in a negative fashion, with sensitivity. This feedback is important because it offers information that could have a negative effect on delivery operations and customer satisfaction. Once maintenance situations are identified, they should be placed into a work-order system that addresses maintenance concerns in a timely fashion.

Work Orders

When a nonroutine maintenance issue is identified, it is necessary to have an action system that evaluates the problem, makes a judgment, priori-

tizes it with all other needs, and then assigns an employee to attend to it. This responsibility can be demanding, especially in a large agency. The response to a maintenance issue should be organized through a formal maintenance work-order system that includes a control center and job form and number.

In the work-order system, a formal documenting process should begin when a maintenance issue is identified. This request is a written or electronic form that identifies the category of work, its location, its nature, and whether it is an emergency (see figure 14.2). Some emergency situations may be handled by telephone, postponing the completion of this form until a later date. The request form usually requires a signature from the person completing it, along with additional information such as the department, telephone number, e-mail address, and detailed description of the nonroutine request for service. This request initiates a process that takes administrative time and effort and has a financial impact on the agency.

Maintenance Request Form

Facility and location _____ Date _____

Requested by _____ Date needed _____

Specific and complete nature of work requested _____
_____
_____
_____

Date request received _____

Assigned to_____

Date completed_____

Priority check _____

Comments_____
_____
_____
_____

Labor: _____ Hours: _____ Hourly rate: _____

Materials needed: _____
_____
_____
_____

From R. Mull, B. Beggs, and M. Renneisen, 2009, *Recreation Facility Management* (Champaign, IL: Human Kinetics)

Figure 14.2 Maintenance request form.

Control Center

After a request form is completed, it is often routed to a central place for review and assignment. This location for maintenance operations may be called the **control center.** This stage of the process is administrative in nature and represents the authority in receiving, reviewing, assigning, and supervising work. During this stage, an administrative judgment prioritizes all work, assesses costs involved, coordinates and assigns workers, and oversees work from beginning to end. This stage also includes keeping pertinent records and documenting all work performed.

Job Form and Number

A job form represents the official assignment of the work that needs to be done. As part of the form, a description of the work is included along with a job number, which serves as an identification code for the work. This number is usually logged in a sequence that can be applied to a written or computer-generated form. The job form and number assist in keeping accurate records, provide easy access for review, and track all work as

it is being completed. It authorizes and assigns the work to a specific maintenance employee or team that usually stays with the job through completion. Copies of the form are made available to the requesting person or unit, the maintenance employees completing the job, the control center, and the administration so that all parties can be updated on the status of the job.

Work Assignments

After the request form is processed by the control center, an administrative manager assigns the job. This can be influenced by the extent and degree of the work required, availability and ability of workers, financial resources available, and level of demand. A work assignment requires management to supervise the work in progress and make sure that it will get done correctly and in a timely fashion. There are various options for assigning work depending on the structure of the agency and the type of work to be completed. These options include assigning work to units, specialized crews, or outside contractors.

▸Trash removal can be just one of many tasks that a maintenance unit may be responsible for in a park.

Units

One approach to getting nonroutine work accomplished is to have it performed within a particular unit. A unit is a component of the maintenance division that responds to agency-generated work requests. It has the benefit of being familiar with agency facilities, grounds, and equipment and their respective maintenance needs. A unit could be a complete area or building with a crew that is responsible for all maintenance operations within that area. For example, a park maintenance unit may be responsible for mowing, trash removal, equipment repair, irrigation system repair, horticulture maintenance, and so on.

The advantages to a unit approach to work assignments include employees becoming familiar with maintenance of particular facility areas and ease of determining responsibilities. This type of system also breeds a high level of loyalty and pride within the unit. On the downside, employees need to learn a variety of jobs, supervisors must have diverse capacities to oversee work and equipment, and a unit approach may not make the most efficient use of expensive equipment.

Specialized Crews

Specialized crews consist of people who are trained to have specific skills. Examples of specialized crews include tree surgeons, mechanics, carpenters, locksmiths, plumbers and electricians. Because of their experience or certification, they are considered experts and their work is expected to be of the highest quality. These specialists could be the only ones who can competently complete a particular task. Large recreation agencies may have enough specialty work to keep these types of employees busy.

Specialized crews could be scheduled to move from one area or facility to another to perform their specialized work. The advantages of this system are that crews become extremely proficient at their work, expensive equipment is used efficiently, and the chance of accidents is less because of workers' experience and knowledge. Some disadvantages are that repetition of work tends to create boredom and mediocre work, and the assignment of a specialized crew to a variety of locations results in time lost for travel.

Outside Contractors

Depending on the management structure of certain agencies, some nonroutine work cannot be completed by internal maintenance staff. Recreation facility staff may not have the expertise to perform some facility maintenance needs. When this occurs, arrangements can be made with outside contractors to perform the work. These arrangements should always be completed through a formal arrangement. Special attention should be given to the contract to make sure the task is described so that there can be no mistakes or communication breakdowns. When work is contracted out, it is advisable to provide agency supervision of the task to make sure that the work is accomplished.

Contracting is frequently used by recreation agencies when a task cannot be accomplished internally, it requires specialized employees, or it is simply more efficient to contract out. The advantages of contracting out certain tasks include well-trained workers, no capital investment in equipment, no in-house personnel problems such as unqualified staff, appropriate insurance protection carried by the contractor, and decreased workload for in-house maintenance staff. On the other hand, there are some disadvantages for contracting out maintenance, including loss of control of when and how work is completed, higher costs, less vested interest in the facility and operations by external employees, and potential difficulty in coordinating contractor's time with facility usage.

OTHER MAINTENANCE CONSIDERATIONS

In addition to the maintenance responsibilities discussed thus far, there are many other considerations. Each maintenance consideration has a unique role that should be incorporated into a comprehensive maintenance system. In addition to the basic categories of maintenance, management must also account for supervising maintenance activities, keeping maintenance records, establishing maintenance manuals, housing maintenance shops and storage facilities, inspecting maintenance work, and maintaining efficiency systems.

Supervising Maintenance Activities

Supervision of all employees is paramount to effective recreation service delivery. Often nonroutine maintenance employees may work in a location where supervision is not present. In order to avoid a lack of effort, their work needs to be monitored regularly. The supervision of maintenance employees is not easy. Care and tactfulness is a high priority, especially with work that has demanding requirements. A system to monitor and control work performance needs to be established, especially with less trained or noncertified workers.

Keeping Maintenance Records

Records regarding assigned work should be kept to document the amount of time required to complete a maintenance task as well as track costs, including labor, material, and overhead. Keeping records helps with budgeting, maintenance accountability, and showing proof of work. Maintenance records can be extremely beneficial if legal action is taken against a recreation agency because they prove that routine maintenance tasks are completed. Records can also help with scheduling subsequent projects and employees because requests may parallel those for past work.

Establishing Maintenance Manuals

Maintenance manuals are instructional documents that provide written descriptions, photos, and diagrams that explain exactly what is required in the proper care of facilities and equipment. These manuals are particularly valuable for equipment or facilities that are highly technical. They provide details on everything required to keep the equipment or facility functioning effectively, often including a step-by-step checklist or system that guides employees through the work process. These manuals play an important role in effective maintenance operations. Manuals assist with keeping detailed information available to present and future maintenance employees and with keeping maintenance tasks organized.

Housing Maintenance Shops and Storage Facilities

Large, multifaceted recreation agencies that have both indoor and outdoor facilities could have an extensive maintenance operation that incorporates a specialized maintenance shop or department. Large recreation agencies sometimes have specialty areas that house particular maintenance functions in order to minimize the expenses involved with renting equipment, hiring outside expert assistance, and contracting out work functions. These shops can be created and maintained as independent departments with specific functions and equipment needs. Typical independent shops or departments can include

- paint shops,
- machine shops,
- carpenter shops,
- key shops,
- plumbing shops, and
- landscaping shops.

These areas could also be located in a maintenance control center or in a storage and warehouse facility, which is another space important to maintenance.

Storage facilities or warehouses contain equipment, bulk supplies, spare parts, and other maintenance items. Often they are incorporated with the control center for appropriate supervision, control, and distribution of the items. These areas often store items that require protection, including chemicals, flammable materials, paint, gasoline, fertilizer, paper goods, and production supplies. Some of these items are purchased in bulk in order to save money, and a storage area or warehouse houses them until they are needed. Some of the bulk supply items commonly purchased and stored include grass seed, light bulbs, toilet paper, soap, and hand towels.

Inspecting Maintenance Work

An important component of maintenance is keeping a facility and its equipment safe for users and employees. Any number of conditions can develop that could have a negative impact on delivery operations. In addition, codes, rules, and regulations that are enforced by local, state, and federal building inspectors must be followed.

External inspectors from local, state, and federal governing bodies regularly conduct formal reviews and write reports that reflect problems with facilities and their production process. Inspectors could require that corrections be made, issue a citation and a fine, and even shut down the facility for not meeting requirements. Maintenance employees are often looked upon to understand these requirements and be responsible for proper preventive maintenance. Regular checks are often conducted by in-house maintenance staff to avoid negative consequences during inspections. Areas that are frequently inspected for proper maintenance include fire codes, electrical standards, plumbing, area capacity, ventilation, and sanitary conditions.

Maintaining Efficiency Systems

The need to make a recreation facility functional and comfortable relies greatly on elaborate efficiency systems, which require maintenance employees to keep them working properly. Indoor recreation efficiency systems include HVAC systems, security systems, restrooms, plumbing, and lighting. Outdoor systems include irrigation, lighting, security systems, restrooms, and public-address systems.

How well these systems work, especially at times of high use, is a significant factor for recreation facilities. Whether this work is to be performed internally or contracted out, it is a crucial responsibility. Maintenance staff should also be familiar with utility monitoring and repair. Interruption of water or electrical service, waste removal, or communication systems could result in negative consequences for users and hence the recreation agency. Maintenance employees who have the ability to repair efficiency systems are valuable resources for a recreation facility.

SUMMARY

Although maintenance is not the focus of recreation facilities, it is an integral part of efficient operations. By establishing maintenance procedures and having policies in place governing maintenance, users can have a safe recreation experience. In addition, a well-maintained facility creates a positive image for the core product and the organization, and thus users are more likely to return.

Emergencies and Emergency Responses

In recreation facility management, the administration influences all operational functions to create a process that delivers a product as effectively and efficiently as possible. Whatever the product, recreation facility managers focus on influencing usage to lead to satisfaction and success. At some point, disruptions, either gradual or sudden, can throw the production process into disorder, interrupting the normal delivery of service. When a disruption occurs, the management response must provide appropriate attention to eliminate the disruption. Recreation facility managers play an important role in preparing a facility for disruptions and for executing emergency procedures.

DISRUPTION IN FACILITY ACTIVITIES

Delivery of a recreation product can occur daily, weekly, or monthly. Accordingly, operational efforts can become routine simply due to the repetition of normal responsibilities and tasks. Whatever the time frame, the product delivery has been planned, organized, and directed, and the users' perception is that all elements of the production process are under control.

One of the unfortunate aspects of facility management is that things do not always go as planned. In spite of the best precautionary measures and control practices, disruptions can still occur. It is management's role to anticipate these potential disruptions, accept the responsibility for every situation, and be prepared to respond in an organized fashion.

Degrees of Disruption

Disruptions come in varying degrees and in a wide range of conditions. Minor disruptions could include concerns such as toilets overflowing, lights not working, negative user behavior, equipment malfunctioning, comfort systems (such as HVAC) breaking down, weather problems, crowd control, and so on. Even these minor unexpected situations can often be time consuming and challenging to resolve. If they are not dealt with properly, they could escalate into more serious situations. It is usually the responsibility of management to address unexpected disruptions and implement appropriate action. Responses to unexpected disruptions could include a call to maintenance to fix an equipment-related problem,

a call to security to deal with user behavior, or a verbal warning given face-to-face or over a public-address system to caution against unacceptable user behavior. Whatever response is required, recreation facility managers have to be in a position to address the disruption so that the production process can continue.

One reality of recreation facility management is that unexpected disruptions can also be severe. These unexpected situations extend beyond normal circumstances and could affect users' and employees' physical or emotional well-being. They may be perceived as minor at first, but they can quickly escalate to a dangerous level. Extreme disruptions can place both users and employees in a situation that requires emergency attention and assistance. Examples of major disruptions include severe weather, equipment breakdowns that stop product delivery, extremely negative user behavior, crowd panic, or severe health problems such as heart attacks, strokes, or accidents leading to bodily injury. Recreation facility managers should have an appropriate precautionary plan and response in place to address any development of an extreme nature. Disruptions that are not managed appropriately can evolve into serious injury, emotional trauma, defamed reputations, damaging lawsuits, or sanctions of irresponsibility. Ultimately, a disruption of this nature could lead to the demise of a recreation facility. Plans for emergency response are discussed later in this chapter.

Unfortunately, not every extreme situation can be completely anticipated or controlled, and some can result in life-threatening situations. This is a worst-case scenario for recreation facility managers that can end in the death of a person or group due to an extreme condition such as a fire, tornado, hurricane, earthquake, flood, violence, or crowd panic. In some cases, investigations reveal the lack of a planned emergency response system. Although the production process can be time consuming for recreation facility managers, it is vital to be prepared for extreme conditions that can cause life-threatening situations.

Catalysts for Disruption

Normal delivery of a product is what every user expects. Employees also expect the routine of providing the same product day in and day out. However, situations develop that cause disruptions, and these disruptions have unique characteristics in different parts of the world. Certain

▶Recreation facility managers need to be prepared to address out of control behavior from users. One way to do this is by using security staff to control the crowd.

© John Rowley/Stone/Getty Images

regions may be more susceptible to earthquakes, floods, mudslides, rockslides, avalanches, tornadoes, or other natural disasters. These factors must be considered when management creates a plan to respond to disruptions. The nature of the product may also affect the planned response to a potential disruption. For example, the sheer physical size or geography of a ski resort may require a specific planned response to a participant injury or natural disaster, such as an avalanche. In contrast, the limited physical size of an indoor facility may require a much different response to a participant injury. Each facility, its location, and its type of product must be evaluated to plan for potential disruptions.

The evaluation process includes being aware of the catalysts that create disruptions, especially those that affect participant and employee safety and well-being. The disruption catalyst could be the product itself, maintenance, weather, fire, threats, crowd behavior, or a combination of two or more catalysts. Initially these catalysts could be perceived as relatively harmless, yet they could evolve into something more severe and challenging to management.

Product or Service

The very nature of the product may create disruptions. These situations may not necessarily be part of the normal production process, but they can create delays that need to be addressed. Some examples include mechanical breakdowns such as lighting failures, spectator misbehavior, and equipment malfunction. Any of these occurrences can create delays and frustration. The most common disruptions are when users become ill or injured. These events may require medical or emergency treatment, which can disrupt product usage. Recreation facility managers should keep their focus on the production and delivery process and be aware of how the intended use may result in disruptions for those who are using the facility.

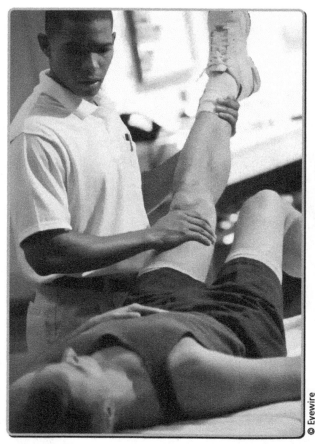

▶ Recreation facility managers must be prepared for any type of injury that may occur while a user is participating in a core product's delivery; this may even include contacting medical staff outside of the facility for help.

Maintenance

Maintenance functions not performed in a timely and efficient manner can disrupt facility operations. Examples of disruptions include unfinished facility repairs, nonfunctioning equipment that needs to be fixed or replaced, setup that has not been completed in a timely fashion, and sidewalks not cleared of snow. Maintenance disruptions are unfortunate because they are usually preventable if they are identified in a timely manner and appropriate action is taken. Maintenance disruptions can be minimized through proper planning, good communication, and the presence of a sound maintenance system. Management needs to communicate with maintenance and production personnel to coordinate and anticipate maintenance-related disruptions. Applying preventive measures, conducting inspections, and initiating a well-thought-

out and documented preventive maintenance plan should minimize these concerns, as described in chapter 14.

Sometimes the use of chemicals may be necessary in the production and maintenance process of recreation facilities. Recreation facility managers must be aware of the potential danger to users and employees that could result from the use or storage of chemicals. Incidents involving chemicals occur when there is inappropriate use or an unexpected release of chemical agents. This type of disruption negatively affects the production process, creating potential harm for users as well as employees, and should be avoided at all cost. Chemical spills may require an evacuation or the activation of an emergency plan. The following are general guidelines for responding to chemical spills:

- Notify facility manager on duty.
- Evacuate area of spill or facility depending on the size of the spill and the chemical.
- Contact the fire department or dial the emergency number (911).
- Attend to people who may have come in contact with the chemical. Removing clothing and flush skin with water.
- Follow chemical guidelines for cleanup.

A more detailed plan for dealing with chemical situations should be in place for all recreation facilities. The Centers for Disease Control and Prevention (CDC) provides guidelines for chemical storage which should be incorporated into this plan. Facility management should be aware of the responsibilities associated with the use and storage of chemicals.

Weather

One of the most common outdoor recreation facility disruptions is inclement weather. Even when inclement weather is anticipated, it can have far-reaching negative implications for the facility. Recreation facility managers could even be held responsible for not providing appropriate warnings as dangerous weather situations develop.

Each facility has its own potential weather situations that require a plan of action to protect participants and employees. Some of these extreme conditions may include tornadoes, hurricanes, earthquakes, landslides, floods, and avalanches, depending on the region. In some parts of the world, extreme heat and humidity or cold can affect participants' and employees' physical and emotional well-being.

Seemingly normal weather conditions can quickly become extreme. Light snow can turn into a blizzard with excessive snow that can limit access to and from a facility. Excessive rain can create flooding that can have severe ramifications. Heat or humidity can reach such high temperatures that people's health becomes compromised through heat exhaustion or heat stroke. When weather conditions deteriorate while an indoor or outdoor recreation facility is in use, managers must remember that they are responsible for the people at the facility.

Fire

Another common yet unexpected disruption in facilities is fire. Lightning, electrical problems, human carelessness, spontaneous combustion, and intentional arson can cause fires. Fires in recreation facilities are extremely dangerous, not only from the fire but also from the resulting smoke and crowd panic. Every precaution should be taken to prevent fires and to extinguish them if they occur. Fires have resulted in innumerable deaths throughout history. Evidence has shown that many of these deaths could have been avoided with proper management or preventive measures. Typically, city, state, or federal laws require indoor facilities to have fire response mechanisms, including fire alarms, fire extinguishers, sprinkler systems, and other devices to protect facility participants and employees. Management must be aware of potential fire hazards and take every precaution to prevent them and respond accordingly. Standard procedures in the event of a fire include the following:

- Activate the fire alarm system.
- Call the fire department or 911.
- Notify facility manager on duty.
- Evacuate the building.

Facilities are usually required to post these procedures. Once the building has been evacuated, the manager should meet the fire department as they arrive at the facility to provide information about the fire and the facility. If the fire is small, facility staff may use a fire extinguisher to put out the fire. However, if they have any doubt about whether they can put the fire out, they should not attempt to extinguish the fire and should evacuate the facility.

© Gary Irving/Stone/Getty Images

▶A fire is an extreme emergency that may have life threatening consequences. Recreation facility managers should minimize fire risks and have a response system in place in the event of a fire.

Threats

In recent years, a new form of disruption has emerged. Since September 11, 2001, the term *terrorist threat* has increasingly become common. This type of disruption can occur with or without warning. In some cases, a disturbed person or group informs a facility of a bomb or other dangerous device in a facility. This action could create a disruption that could lead to the evacuation of the facility. In other cases, the threat comes without warning. In this situation, management is forced to respond to the threat after the action has occurred. After September 11, 2001, the Department of Homeland Security recommended that federally protected parks and monuments increase security and devote more resources towards doing this. These threats have become more common in recent years as evidenced by shootings at community centers in places such as Los Angeles, San Francisco, and Washington, D.C.

Unfortunately, little can be done to deter such actions. The greatest challenge to recreation facility managers in this case is making the judgment to accept the terrorist threat as reality and not just a hoax. In situations of this nature, it is best to be proactive and evacuate the facility and call emergency personnel to assess and contain the potential threat. Virtually all communities have an emergency management response system in place as a result of the terrorist attacks on September 11, 2001. The United States Department of Homeland Security regularly updates the status of threat and guidelines for dealing with threats on their Web site (www.dhs.gov/index.shtm). Information can also be obtained by contacting the local emergency response agency.

Crowd Behavior

Anytime the core product draws a large number of people in one place, the potential for a crowd-related incident becomes a concern for recreation facility managers. In normal circumstances, crowds can be a positive part of a facility, generating energy and enthusiasm for a product. However, recreation facility managers should be prepared to make efficient and effective decisions to ensure safety when crowds begin to get out of control or participate in disruptive activities. Crowds can be dangerous because disruptions can trigger panic or irrational actions. Crowd behavior can range from supportive and participatory to rebellious and hostile.

Deaths have occurred in the past as a result of crowds that are out of control. In some instances, people have been trampled and killed at concerts with large crowds. There have also been instances at crowded nightclubs where people have been unable to evacuate in a fire, resulting in death. These situations can be one of the most demanding facility responsibilities to plan for and control. Management should take every precaution to assess crowd behavior to avoid the development of inappropriate behavior and when necessary, take appropriate action to prevent crowd behavior from getting out of control.

User or Nonuser Behaviors

Certain people come to a facility with disruptive attitudes and behavior. For whatever reason, these people regress to a behavior pattern that lacks maturity, reason, or logic. There is a tendency for these facility users to abandon their normal restraints and to lose their sense of social responsibility. Alcohol, drugs, and event enthusiasm can influence their behavior, or they can have psychological disorders that affect their behavior. Any number of circumstances can provoke this unexpected negative behavior.

In some cases, people are looking to create disruptions through excessive drinking, fighting, and verbal harassment of other facility users or employees. Behavior of this nature can include throwing food, pushing and shoving, and insulting or antagonizing other participants, employees, or spectators. Even more severe disruptions include impulsive self-gratification through theft, vandalism, or social explosiveness where one person's negative behavior can cause group violence and rioting.

Recreation facility managers may also experience damage, vandalism, or stolen equipment by facility users and nonusers. These incidents may not cause as serious a disruption as other catalysts, but they do require attention from management. Sometimes damage or theft could impede the production process. In such cases appropriate and rapid action should be taken. Security lights or alarm systems in addition to routine patrols of the interior or exterior of facilities help discourage theft and vandalism.

EMERGENCY RESPONSES

Recreation facility managers should have a system in place to appropriately respond to whatever disruptions occur. Emergency responses vary greatly and are dictated by the type of facility, the catalyst, and the product that is being delivered. It is vital that management be fully aware of not only the potential disruption but also the coordination of an appropriate emergency response.

Each recreation facility should have a system in place that can respond to disruptions when necessary. This action must be effective and efficient to minimize the damage to facilities and equipment and most importantly to attend to situations that could affect participants and employees. In order for this to take place, recreation facility managers must provide leadership and take action in handling disruptions, requesting support from law enforcement and medical personnel as judged appropriate, and facilitating steps to evacuation if needed.

Leadership

Management must demonstrate leadership in making appropriate judgments for action when a disruption occurs. As discussed earlier in this chapter, all facilities and equipment can experience varying degrees of disruption. Recreation facility managers must make the appropriate decision, anticipate potential disruptions, and have proper procedures in place for dealing with these situations.

Some recreation facilities will respond with a few special arrangements, whereas others will need to provide the highest level of security and medical care. The cost to provide appropriate responses could be prohibitive for some recreation facilities. However, proper precautions can result in cost avoidance. Failing to take any precautionary steps can result in more serious and costly problems. Management should be aware of potential disruptions. Supervision and warnings are two key actions that help fortify recreation facility managers' leadership role in responding to disruptions.

Supervision

Recreation facility managers cannot be in all places at all times. Often, responsibilities for reacting to emergencies are delegated to qualified employees. The delegation process authorizes the appropriate person to represent and take appropriate action on behalf of management as necessary. Possible employees who might be delegated this responsibility include supervisors, ushers, guards, attendants, and officers. Generally, these employees or volunteers should be in a position to manage disruptions or emergencies at the facility. Depending on the product and potential situations, various levels of training and certification could be required of employees in these supervisory roles. Facility supervisors are typically certified in CPR, standard first aid (SFA), and the use of portable defibrillators. Other certifications may be necessary for certain facility personnel, including lifeguard training, water safety instructors training, or certified pool operators training. Supervisory employees usually function as observers, requesting assistance, taking appropriate action, reporting

▶Pool lifeguards, supervisors, and managers are delegated by the recreation facility manager to represent their facility and respond to disruptions. These employees are trained for their responsibilities and are certified in standard first aid and CPR.

disruptions and emergencies, and responding to any incident that arises.

Warnings

Every facility, equipment included, should be designed to minimize accidents or injuries. Occasionally, the design, construction, or renovation of a facility can result in unintended disruptions to the delivery of a product. Often, these unintended consequences are not discovered until the facility is in use. It is incumbent on recreation facility managers to notify users or employees when they discover a part of the production process that can lead to injury. In these cases, managers should provide advanced warning. These warnings should be displayed and accurately worded so that all users and employees are fully aware of the potential for injury.

Taking Action

Some disruptions can escalate to the point that immediate action is required. The degree to which this action is required depends on the disruption and its severity. The response of recreation facility managers should be responsible and neither excessive nor incomplete. The three basic steps for taking action are

1. assess,
2. attend, and
3. refer.

Assess

Supervisory staff, along with other employees involved with the production process, should have the ability to observe and evaluate what is going on in the delivery of a product. If a disruption happens to occur, staff should remain calm and assess the situation. Hopefully, previous employee training will provide proper knowledge and techniques to accurately assess and address the disruption. The ability to accurately assess and respond appropriately is important. An inappropriate assessment can sometimes lead to a response that is worse than no response at all.

Attend

An emergency response plan should exist that attends properly to any disruption. Appropriate action could be as formal as SFA, CPR, preventive disease transmission (PDT), or announcing warnings. Other responses to less threatening situations include resolving conflict, repairing

equipment, or diverting attention from disruptions. When proper attention is not taken, the consequences could be extensive for all involved. The importance of this aspect of facility management cannot be overstated.

Refer

In most cases, supervisory staff can handle disruptions by providing appropriate attention. However, sometimes these developments need to be referred to outside parties after the initial action is taken. A referral may entail bringing investigators to the site, an ambulance for medical assistance, or police to assist with people who may need to be removed. Occasionally, a referral is necessary when a disruption exceeds the ability of management to respond.

Law Enforcement Some disruptions can be anticipated because of large crowds, social tension, high intensity, or skill level of participants. Even with qualified staff, recreation facility managers can anticipate disruptions that exceed their

© Paul McMahon

▶Sometimes facility use requires the assistance of law enforcement personnel to control the area and help avoid any emergencies.

capacity. In these instances, proactive managers may have security guards or police at the facility to assist with potential disruptions and to serve as a deterrent. The use of law enforcement should not be excessive, however; too much police presence can have the opposite outcome of what is desired.

Medical Assistance The delivery of some recreation products can create situations that require responses beyond SFA, CPR, and PDT. Although these activities may have inherent dangers, their popularity and participant involvement is not diminished by the potential danger. When necessary, management may have medical personnel on site to assist with any injuries. Some examples of medical personnel used in the recreation environment include trainers, paramedics, nurses, EMTs, and doctors. These medical personnel have varying degrees of training that would allow them to attend to a more severe situation. Depending on the type of activity, some or all of these personnel may be warranted at a recreation facility. It is management's responsibility to anticipate these developments and make sure the appropriate assistance is available.

Evacuation

Catalysts such as chemical spills, bomb threats, threats of violence or death, fire, hurricanes, floods, and earthquakes can be so serious that management must have a system established for evacuating the facility. Catastrophic developments require immediate action to remove people from a facility or place them in a position that protects them from harm. Disruptions of catastrophic proportion are infrequent, and most recreation facility managers have never had to initiate an evacuation plan. Even though such occurrences may be rare, they can still occur. Recreation facility managers should have an established and practiced evacuation plan in the event an evacuation is necessary. This evacuation plan should describe employee responsibilities, include basic facility information such as location of emergency exits and safe locations, and list other actions that should be taken in the event of an emergency.

When developing an evacuation plan, it is important to keep it as simple and concise as possible. Disruptions can vary so greatly that the plan could require unique and immediate interpretation by staff in tenuous circumstances, which means keeping the plan simple and concise is a must.

There are three general components of creating an evacuation plan.

1. Assessment or inquiry
2. General information
3. Action steps

Assessment or Inquiry

One of the first things that recreation facility managers should do when creating an evacuation plan is to check with fire, law enforcement, and emergency personnel for any local requirements regarding an evacuation plan. Fire, police, or other municipal agencies often have requirements for building evacuation. Local codes or ordinances can also stipulate what kind of plan should be in place.

Recreation facility managers should also ascertain if an emergency planning group is available. As a result of the terrorist attacks on September 11, 2001, many communities have a designated emergency planning group that has developed an emergency response and evacuation plan. This group is a resource whose guidance should be followed with any facility evacuation plan.

Recreation facility managers can also obtain evacuation plans from similar facilities as an additional resource. Although these plans will not always duplicate the facility plan, they could help with format, resources, and general information.

General Information

Any evacuation plan should be in writing and placed in a highly visible and accessible location where facility personnel can locate it in an emergency situation. The evacuation plan should state general information identifying the users, core product, core product extensions, mission, and goals and objectives. These statements help emphasize the activity level, involvement of staff, and interaction that takes place in the facility during an emergency situation.

An emergency and evacuation plan should include a specific policy statement that ensures the safety of users during an emergency. In addition, it should show the relationship and coordination with all local emergency service agencies (fire, police, medical, emergency). The information should reflect a full description of the facility, making references to architectural drawings, space capacities, physical layout, entrances and exits, primary and secondary communication systems, and the location of any emergency command center. The architect or a fire marshal can help

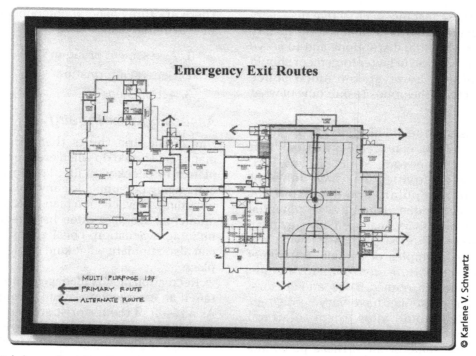

▶ It is important to post an emergency plan where it is easily accessible by all facility staff and users.

with understanding this information and assisting in preparing the emergency and evacuation plan. It is also prudent to provide local fire and police agencies with copies of the facility blueprints for use in emergency situations.

Action Steps

When an evacuation is required, certain action steps need to be initiated. Responsibilities should be identified, delegated, and explained to facility personnel before emergencies occur. In addition, specific situations should be addressed:

- What happens if main entrances are blocked?
- How do disabled users and employees safely exit?
- Should certain instructions be disregarded if conditions change rapidly?
- What happens if electrical power is lost?
- If a child care facility is on site, how will children be evacuated, especially if they are too young to move independently?

The procedures for executing the evacuation need to be clearly documented for full understanding. All employees need to be knowledgeable of what the procedures are and how their role relates

to other steps in the process. Ongoing training and rehearsals should be conducted to reinforce employee knowledge and practical application of the evacuation plan.

An evacuation plan should include any forms or reports necessary to assist with revisions or improvements to the plan. Documentation should include details of simulation exercises, all staff training, and inspections in case a critique is necessary either before or after an evacuation.

Finally, potential serious disruptions should be defined based on the location of the facility, its structure, and the product usage. It is important to recognize that each disruption may have different factors for recreation facility managers to consider when determining the appropriate action steps to implement.

SUMMARY

Disruptions or emergencies in providing the core product and core product extensions are not common; however, they do occur. It is the role of recreation facility managers to provide leadership for employees and users in responding to these situations. A prepared response and an evacuation plan for catastrophic disruptions can lead to a safer response for all involved.

PART V

Auxiliaries of Recreation Facilities

Recreation facilities have auxiliary spaces that support or enhance the core product. Auxiliary spaces are classified as ancillary spaces (such as parking, locker, and reception areas) or core product extensions (such as food service and child care areas). Some spaces, which may be classified as auxiliary, may also be a stand-alone facility. These types of facilities include parks, playgrounds, and aquatic parks. Each of these types of facilities can be a source of revenue generation. They also have several unique characteristics that must be managed for effective operation.

Parks and Playground Facilities

LEARNING OBJECTIVES

At the completion of this chapter, you should be able to do the following:

1. Recognize the various types of parks and their characteristics.

2. Understand the design factors that make each park unique.

3. Recognize maintenance and safety practices used in parks.

4. Understand the various types of playgrounds and their purposes.

5. Explain the concept of use zones and fall protection in playgrounds.

6. Recognize the characteristics of various types of playground surfaces.

Parks and playgrounds are outdoor amenities that are part of every community. These facilities can be core products or core product extensions of another facility. Parks are outdoor spaces that provide an opportunity to connect with nature, whereas playgrounds are facilities with equipment and structures that provide physical challenges and are primarily geared toward children. It is common to see playgrounds built within a park, but it is important to distinguish between them because they have unique characteristics.

PARKS

Parks are prominent in the fabric of communities all over the world. A **park** can be defined as an outdoor space made available to the public, often provided by a public agency, for the benefit of the citizens of a community, state, or country. Public parks are owned and operated by tax-supported government agencies, including local municipality, state, or national systems. Private parks are typically owned and operated by either corporations or private organizations that provide opportuni-

ties for employees or members. Parks have many benefits:

- Parks offer a respite from urban areas, congestion, pavement, and other man-made features.
- Parks provide natural habitats for wildlife and plants.
- Users may appreciate the ability to connect with nature in park settings.
- Users may also be able to use park areas to improve physical fitness through running, walking, hiking, biking, and other outdoor activities.
- Parks can have economic benefits; they may be designed to generate revenue if they have fees associated with them.
- The value of property in the vicinity of parks is higher than property not located near parks.

Parks can exist in a variety of settings, including woodlands, mountains, deserts, rain forests, beach areas, and underwater reefs. Or, they simply

▶Neighborhood parks are located in a specific neighborhood, which is often densely populated.

can be a neighborhood area that has a playground or ball field available for residents.

Types of Parks

Parks range in the size, shape, function, and amenities. Most parks are owned and operated by some form of government system that is supported by tax dollars, fees and charges, donations, or all of these. The most common public parks can be classified as neighborhood, urban, community or regional, linear, state, and national parks. Specialty parks can be public or private, depending on who owns them. They include theme parks, aquatic parks, and sport parks and are operated with the primary objective of generating revenue.

Neighborhood Parks

Neighborhood parks serve relatively small areas of a community, and by definition they are located in a neighborhood, often in a densely populated area. Generally, users or neighbors can access neighborhood parks by walking. These types of parks are generally 15 acres (6 hectares) or smaller in size and offer amenities such as a playground, park benches, a picnic shelter, and an open area for multipurpose use.

Urban Parks

Urban parks serve the most densely developed areas of a community. Urban parks tend to be fairly small and are usually bordered by a combination of residences and businesses. These types of parks often include hard surfaces such as concrete or pavement due to the high traffic expected. Park benches, tables, and occasionally performance stages are common in urban parks. Depending on the location of the park, a playground may also be included.

Community or Regional Parks

A **community** or **regional park** is larger than either neighborhood or urban parks. Typical acreage can range from 15 acres (6 hectares) to several hundred acres. This type of park consists of a broader range of amenities that attract users from a greater geographic area. Users are more likely to have to drive to a community or regional park. For this reason, large parking facilities are common. Typical features may include all of the amenities commonly found in neighborhood parks, in addition to sport fields; hiking, biking, and skating paths; aquatic facilities; formal gardens; water features; zoos; museums; and other recreation attractions.

▶Urban parks create a place in an urban area where people can take a break in the middle of an otherwise busy area.

▶A community or regional park may offer all the amenities of a neighborhood park with the addition of other amenities, including sports fields, formal gardens, zoos, and other recreation attractions.

▶Linear parks are often long or linear and located next to a trail system.

Linear Parks

The linear park is generally found along a stream, river, or wetland area or an abandoned railroad bed. By definition, **linear parks** are long or linear in nature and may connect to other similar parks. When two or more linear parks are connected, they are called **greenways.** Often, a trail system is incorporated in a linear park. Recently there has been a significant movement in the United States by the Recreational Trails Program to convert abandoned railroad corridors into trails for use as alternative transportation routes as well as for recreation. Funding from the federal government passed down to state and local governments assists in the development of these trail systems throughout the United States.

State Parks

A state park is usually larger than a community or regional park but may have similar amenities. **State parks** are owned and operated by a large government unit and serve those within the boundaries of the state and others who come to visit from outside the state. In the United States, state parks are operated by the Department of Natural Resources (DNR), a state department. In Canada, the system of parks similar to state parks are provincial parks. These types of parks are usually created

© 2007 Drake Fleege

▶ This beach on the shores of Lake Michigan is just one of thousands of state parks located across the United States that preserve the unique features of its area.

to preserve natural areas such as water features, deserts, trees, and other unique attributes of the geographic area where the park is located.

National Parks

National parks share many similar characteristics with state parks. **National parks** are usually owned and operated by the national government and serve all those within that nation, as well as other visitors from around the world. In Canada, these parks are administered by Parks Canada. In the United States, national parks are operated by the National Park Service (NPS), a division of the Department of the Interior. These types of parks are usually created to preserve natural areas that include unique features of the geographic area where the park is located. Users typically have to drive or fly a considerable distance to access a national park. Some well-known U.S. national parks include Glacier National Park in Montana,

© Jim West

▶The Grand Canyon is one of the United States' National Parks, which is operated by the National Park Service, and people drive from hundreds or even thousands of miles away to visit each year.

Carlsbad Caverns National Park in New Mexico, Yellowstone National Park in Wyoming, Hawaii Volcanoes National Park, Grand Canyon National Park in Arizona, Everglades National Park in Florida, and Rocky Mountain National Park in Colorado.

Specialty Parks

Some facilities include the word *park* in their name or description. Although not generally considered to be parks in the same way as the parks described earlier, they do have some similar characteristics.

Unlike the parks previously discussed, specialty parks may be operated in the public or private sector, and many are constructed with the intent to generate revenue. In addition, specialty parks are designed with a specific purpose in mind, including theme parks, aquatic parks, and sport parks, just to name a few.

Theme parks offer an entertainment experience that is designed to attract visitors. Though this same description could apply to other parks, a theme park is a constructed facility that doesn't

© David R. Frazier / Photo Researchers, Inc.

▶Specialty parks, such as Disney World, may be operated by the public or private sector, and they are mainly constructed to generate revenue.

usually rely on natural features. Common examples of theme parks include Walt Disney World, Disneyland, Six Flags America, Holiday World, and Kings Island. These types of parks are operated by a management system and are designed to produce a profit.

Aquatic parks may also be designed to produce a profit. They may be operated by a municipal government or a private company. At aquatic parks, water features or aquatic facilities are the main attraction. Aquatic parks may offer water slides, activity pools, wave pools, serpentine waterways for rafting, jet sprays, splash pads, lap pools, and other amenities that allow users to interact with water. Chapter 17, Aquatic Facilities, is devoted solely to aquatics and aquatic parks.

Another type of specialty park is the **sport park,** which features a sport or a combination of sports as the core product. Sport parks may be operated by a municipal government or a private company. They may provide multiple sport areas for one

▶The main area at an aquatic park consists of a pool or other large water features.

particular sport or for various sports. These parks are often constructed to host community, state, or national sporting events that may attract numerous participants and have a significant economic impact on the community where the park is located. Sport parks also include professional sport venues that are owned and operated by professional sport organizations. These facilities also have a significant economic impact on the community.

Park Design

The design of most park areas relies on the natural features of the area. Landscape designers and design architects, the expert consultants often hired to design parks, attempt to complement the natural features of the area in their design. Every park has a unique design based on its intended location and size, flow, amenities, and programs.

Location and Size

The location and size of a park will influence its design. The topography of the area must be taken into consideration as well. Slope, valleys, soil types, and existing vegetation can be used as part of the design or may have to be altered to create the park. Natural features including mountains, lakes, streams, rivers, oceans, beaches, trees, and rock will affect where park features can be located. Often these features are the attraction that creates customer interest. Competent landscape architects incorporate these features into the design of a park and attempt to minimize alteration of the natural conditions.

Parks can vary in size from less than an acre (.4 hectare) to thousands of acres. Generally, urban areas have smaller acreage for parks due to the density of the population and the value of land in densely populated areas. However, this is not always true. In some major cities, civic leaders and landscape architects had the vision to preserve significant acreage in their communities for the future use and enjoyment of their residents, such as Central Park in New York and Forest Park in St. Louis.

Urban or neighborhood parks may have limited land mass that affects the amenities that may be included in the design of the park. Since these types of parks often serve smaller geographic areas, there may be limited or no parking areas. In contrast, larger parks, including community, state, or national parks, may incorporate significant parking areas in their design to accommodate a large number of patrons who have to drive to the park.

A common practice in park design is to locate certain areas together. For example, playgrounds or other activity areas, such as sport fields or courts, typically have restroom and parking areas nearby. Parks where wooded areas, rock formations, trails, water features, or other natural elements of interest exist should be designed for appropriate access while limiting the possible negative impact of that access on the features that make the park unique. Railings, pathways, gates, and other barriers may be necessary to limit access to these features and to protect visitors from danger.

Parks that attract a high volume of users, particularly specialty parks, will need numerous parking areas and extensive restrooms to accommodate visitors. Pathways, either hard or soft surfaced, should be placed in high-traffic areas to lead visitors to various features of the park. Exterior lighting may be necessary in parking areas, around restroom facilities, and along pathways to increase user safety in the later hours of the day. Regardless of size, parks must take into consideration how patrons will use the site. Landscape architects and other consultants often assist with the design of park facilities.

Flow

The design of the park entrance or reception area should consider the maximum flow of user traffic, including what the load will be at any single moment, and ensure that there is adequate space to handle user needs in entering and exiting a facility. A reception or entrance area naturally has the potential to cause lines to form. In certain park facilities, users may have to wait a significant amount of time to access the product. Adequate space to accommodate customer waiting should be incorporated into the design of any park facility. Special consideration should be given to park facilities that attract large numbers of users and long lines with considerable waiting time, as discussed in chapter 12.

Amenities

Most park users have expectations for basic furnishings, including benches, tables, trash receptacles, signage, dog waste stations, water fountains, cooking grills, and other so on. These products are commonly called *amenities*. Because they enhance the core product, they are therefore core product extensions. The vast size of certain parks often requires many amenities spread out over the entire park. Due to the extensive use of amenities, a replacement plan that factors in the life span of each amenity is an important management consideration.

Programs

Park areas are generally designed for unstructured leisure experiences. That is, they are designed for people to use at their own pace and for individual reasons. However, park areas may be used for programmed activities. Programs that take place in a park can include nature programs, sport programs, camp activities, special events, youth programs, and senior activities. A park can be an excellent resource for activities that take place in the outdoors, and they are typically used for programs during times of the year when the weather is warm.

Park Areas

Parks contain a variety of areas that enhance the core product and are important to users. These areas can include a welcome center, shelter buildings, food service, restrooms, equipment rental or checkout, retail outlets, trails, and playgrounds.

Welcome Center

Some park areas combine a reception area, sometimes known as a welcome center, with administrative offices. Welcome centers serve several functions, including fee collection, information exchange, and emergency personnel access. These areas may be combined to maximize available space or simply because it is more efficient for the operation of the facility. Combining these areas into one location provides access for administrative personnel to assist customer service staff and respond quickly to customer questions or emergencies. In many respects, a reception area is an extension of administrative offices.

Shelter Buildings

It is fairly common for most parks to have some type of physical structure that provides shelter from the elements. Shelter buildings may be fully enclosed for the comfort of users or may be open to the elements, only providing cover from rain, snow, and sun. Occupancy of shelter facilities can be controlled with a reservation system or allowed on a first come, first served basis. Park agencies often charge a fee to reserve a shelter and base the

▶Conveniently locating a welcome center at the front area of a park will make it easy for users to pay fees, receive information, or locate emergency personnel.

amount of the fee on the shelter size and amenities provided.

Food Service

Parks may choose to incorporate vending or **food-service areas** depending on the location and type of park and the likelihood that patrons would benefit from vending or food service. Park areas such as state, national, or specialty parks that draw a substantial number of visitors may choose to offer full-service restaurants to serve customer needs. Smaller parks such as community, neighborhood, or specialty parks may offer a limited service concession or vending option. The agency that is responsible for the operation of a food-service area must consider the added responsibilities it requires, including waste prevention and removal from natural park areas, and balance those responsibilities with their goal of service or profit. Food services are discussed in more detail in chapter 19.

The high visibility of a welcome center, park entrance, or major attraction makes for a good food-service location. This service should be located near the main thoroughfare of the park in order to capitalize on the traffic in this area. High visibility can be important to the success of food service.

Restrooms

Restroom facilities are often a fundamental need at parks. Restroom options can range from portable toilets or outhouse pits to the customary fully plumbed system. When selecting restroom facilities, park administrators should consider the typical length of stay of visitors in addition to the environment of the park. Natural areas may have attractions in locations that have limited plumbing access. In these areas, the more primitive restroom facility may be the only option. Parks in urban areas or theme parks that attract a large number of visitors with children are more likely to offer fully plumbed restroom facilities.

Equipment Rental

Park operating agencies should analyze the potential equipment needs of visitors. Equipment rental or checkout should be considered where possible to provide a service and generate revenue. Managers of theme parks may provide stroller rentals to visitors with children. Aquatic parks often offer

▶Food service areas can used as a way to increase revenue at an outdoor facility, but including a food service area also requires waste prevention and removal from the park areas.

cabana or lawn furniture for rental, as well as snorkeling or diving equipment, boats, Jet Skis, canoes, paddleboats, kayaks, and necessary safety equipment such as life preservers. Parks with cross-country or downhill ski areas may offer ski equipment rentals. Each park area should analyze the rental opportunities available based on the core product.

Retail Outlets

Some park areas offer retail outlets, pro shops, or gift shops that serve as core product extensions. Depending on the type and size of the park, the retail outlet may be as simple as counter space within the welcome center, or it may be a separate area located close to the welcome center or the core product area. Visitors to state, national, or theme parks may wish to remember their visit with a souvenir. A variety of products including T-shirts, sweatshirts, hats, coffee mugs, key chains, stuffed animals, calendars, DVDs, and other items may be sold at a retail outlet.

Incorporating these retail functions into a high-traffic area increases user awareness of the retail outlet. It is also a good business practice that enhances the functionality of the facility.

Trails

A common element in a park is a trail. Trails are paths or tracks in a natural outdoor area that are designed to be used by park users for a variety of activities, such as walking, jogging, hiking, horseback riding, cross-country skiing, or biking. Some trails are also designed for use by motorized vehicles. An important consideration in trail design is to make sure the trail is properly sloped for water drainage. If water settles into places on a trail, the trail can erode and become unsafe for users. Trail designers need to make sure that there is a gradient of 3 percent to 4 percent in a trail to allow water to run off the trail.

Playgrounds

A play area or playground can greatly enhance the park experience and serve as a major attraction, particularly in neighborhood and urban parks. Play areas can provide many physical challenges and opportunities for social interaction for children. Equipment in a play area can range from swings and slides to climbing walls and jungle gyms. The type of equipment in a play area will dictate the type and age of users. There are a number of

▶Retail outlets at recreation facilities allow users to purchase items of convenience, such as food, or they may allow users to purchase a souvenir to help them remember their visit.

considerations regarding play areas that will be presented later in this chapter.

Park Operations

Operating a park requires that a management system be in place to coordinate basic park functions. Park operations functions include access control, fee collection, maintenance, safety, and security. The implementation of these considerations varies depending on the type, location, and size of the park.

Access Control

The process of managing customer or visitor entry into a park area is called **access control.** Access control can vary based on the type of facility. For example, a state or national park may require users to enter the facility through a gated area staffed by park employees who limit access by charging a fee or restrict access to limit park usage or for safety purposes. Certain restrictions or policies may limit access to a particular park area. For example, local community or neighborhood parks may have no

physical access controls in place but may have policies that identify park hours. Specialty parks are likely to incorporate park hours, an access control system, and admission fees.

Various access control systems may be used, including gates, turnstiles, counter areas, and ticket booths. Some of these areas may use card-reading equipment and metal detection or X-ray screening devices. Personnel involved in facility access control include attendants, receptionists, customer service representatives, security personnel, ushers, and ticket takers.

Fee Collection

As mentioned earlier, some park facilities collect a fee before permitting access and use of the area or product. Access control or reception areas can incorporate this function by using a staff person and equipment, including a cash register, credit card machine, or computer, to assist with fee collection. Park facilities may collect fees each time a user accesses a facility, or admission fees, or they may collect fees in one lump sum, such as memberships or season passes.

Maintenance

Most people visualize open spaces with trees, grass, flowers, water features, and other amenities when they think of parks. However, as described earlier, a wide variety of park areas exist. Each area may incorporate man-made structures that provide a core product or a core product extension to support the purpose of a user's visit. These park areas can be vast and have a number of areas and facilities that require a great deal of maintenance. The following facilities may be located in a park setting, and each may require specific maintenance, as discussed in chapter 14:

- Restrooms
- Concession or food-service areas
- Shelter buildings
- Parking facilities
- Roads
- Paths
- Trails

Parks usually have vegetation to maintain. This vegetation can include trees, flowers, shrubs, aquatic plants, and grasses, in addition to other flora. Vegetation maintenance can vary greatly depending on the region. Park employees need specific knowledge of vegetation management based on the location of the facility. For example, vegetation in arid areas may require different irrigation practices than vegetation located in climates where rainfall is more consistent. Qualified arborists and vegetation specialists should be employed when vegetation requires specialized maintenance.

Nearly all parks have the basic responsibility of maintaining some type of surface area. There are a wide variety of surfaces that may need to be maintained, as discussed in chapter 6. In areas where grass is prevalent, simply mowing grass areas on a regular basis may be a basic maintenance practice. In park areas where snow is prevalent or even necessary to deliver a product such as downhill or cross-country skiing, the maintenance of this surface will require specific equipment and maintenance practices. The grooming of snow for skiing requires specialized practices and equipment to provide the desirable surface for park users. In most cases, snow removal is required to allow use of parking areas, roadways, or trails.

Trails also require considerable maintenance attention. As mentioned previously, one of the most important parts of trail maintenance is to make sure the trail is properly sloped for water drainage. Trail slope should be considered in the design phase of the trail construction, and trail maintenance crews should examine the trail on a regular basis, after periods of high usage or periods of inclement weather. By maintaining moving soil to divert drainage areas or to build up areas, maintenance crews can ensure that the trail will provide a safe experience for users.

Safety

Park users have a basic expectation that their visit to a park will be a safe one. It is incumbent on management to limit the risks associated with delivery of a service in a park area. Common safety practices include signage that warns users of potential risks, brochures or other literature designed to educate users of risks, and barriers that limit access to areas that may pose risks.

Management can also institute regular inspections and maintenance of park areas to ensure that surfaces and amenities are safe to use. This variety creates a significant responsibility for recreation facility managers, who must assess risks and then implement maintenance and management practices to protect park users. A typical example of this practice is the routine inspection of park playground equipment for safety concerns. This practice is so common that park maintenance employees are often required to take courses offered by professional associations to become certified playground safety inspectors. Playground maintenance will be discussed in more detail later in the chapter.

Security

Park security is a significant concern for management. The sheer size of some park areas makes security a challenging aspect of recreation facility management. It is common for parks to have staff on site to provide assistance to users or to enforce park rules and regulations. These employees may be patrol personnel, park police, or other security personnel. Other personnel, including gate attendants and maintenance employees, may also have some basic security responsibilities.

Some larger parks face tremendous challenges in limiting access to their areas. At best, parks may have perimeter fencing or other barriers that limit access and keep park assets secure from those who would poach resources within the park. Signage indicating park boundaries may also warn those who would enter that they are trespassing on park property.

PLAYGROUNDS

Playgrounds are an integral part of a community and can be found as an auxiliary to many types of facilities. Playgrounds are typically located in parks, schools, child care facilities, housing complexes, and community centers. It is becoming more common for playgrounds to be included in the design of restaurants, resorts, and other commercial establishments that attract families.

On the surface, playgrounds appear to be a fun attraction for children to play on. However, there is much more to a well-designed playground than just an area to play. All playgrounds should be designed to foster the physical and social development of children. Physical development takes place as children climb up, down, and through play equipment. Social development takes place as children learn to play together and get along with each other. A well-designed playground provides spaces and amenities that allow for these opportunities and more.

Playground Equipment

Playground equipment varies in the type of physical challenge provided. The equipment selected for a playground should reflect the age of the users. Typically, playground equipment is designed to meet the needs of two age groups: preschool and school-age children. Guidelines established by the CPSC are typically adopted by state departments and dictate safety recommendations for playground equipment for these age groups.

In many playgrounds, children of both age groups may be using the equipment. When this is the case, the age-specific equipment should be kept in different areas of the playground. Since most playgrounds are not supervised, it is the responsibility of adults to make sure that children are using age-appropriate equipment. If a preschool child climbs up a larger slide or uses an overhead climber, there is a greater chance of injury. It can also be problematic if older children use preschool equipment because they can

▶Playgrounds allow children to develop social skills as they learn to play with other children and take turns using the equipment found on the playground.

© Janet Horton

▸Preschool playground equipment should not be more than 5 feet high, should have very small stairway areas, and should offer children the opportunity to play together.

damage the equipment that is not designed for larger users.

Preschool Equipment

A playground designed for preschool children (aged 5 and younger) should include equipment that is less than 5 feet (1.5 meters) high, which is typically no higher than the average preschool child can reach. Any elevations in the equipment should be accessible by ramps or small stairway areas. In addition to being low to the ground, equipment should be selected that provides opportunities for children to play together.

School-Age Equipment

For children aged 6 and older, playground equipment should provide a greater physical challenge than preschool equipment, such as more opportunities for climbing. In addition, equipment should also include chances for children to develop arm strength by providing overhead ladders and arm swings. School-age equipment should be no higher than 8 feet (2.5 meters) above the ground.

Playground Safety

Safety should be the top priority of recreation facility managers when designing a playground and selecting playground equipment. The CPSC tests and evaluates playground equipment, and agencies should strongly consider choosing equipment that has been certified by the CPSC. The CPSC tests equipment to ensure that it doesn't have entrapment areas where children could get their limbs or heads stuck. According to the CPSC, there have been hundreds of incidents over the last decade where children have been maimed or killed by entrapment areas on play equipment. The CPSC also tests the material that equipment is made from to make sure it is durable and can support the stress that children impose during play.

Playground Use Zones

The CPSC also provides guidelines for equipment use zones. A **use zone** is the space below and around a piece of equipment that should have

© Janet Horton

▶School-age playground equipment should not be more than 8 feet high and should provide children ages 6 and above the opportunity for greater physical challenges.

some type of fall-absorbent surface and be free of other equipment. The use zone, which is also called the *safety zone,* provides adequate space to prevent injury should a child fall from the equipment.

Use-Zone Size

The size of the use zone is typically dictated by the height of the equipment, the ground, the type of play or movement taking place on the equipment, and whether the equipment is stationary. For equipment that is stationary, the standard use zone is 6 feet (2 meters) beyond the perimeter of the structure. Equipment that is not stationary will require a larger use zone, and in most instances, the use zone is specific to the equipment.

One type of standard nonstationary playground equipment that has specific use-zone guidelines is a swing. The use-zone guidelines for swings require the use zone to extend twice the height of the swing structure in front and back of the swing. So, a swing structure that is 8 feet (2.5 meters) high should have 16 feet (5 meters) of use zone on the back side of the swing and 16 feet of use

zone on the front side of the swing. On the sides of the swing where no movement is taking place, the standard 6 feet (5 meters) of use zone applies.

Use-Zone Surfaces and Accessibility

As mentioned, use zones also include surfacing. Although cost plays a role in selecting a surface, the most important factor for selecting a safe surface is fall protection. Fall protection refers to how absorbent a surface is, or how much give there is in a surface. Each surface provides a different degree of fall protection. There are two basic categories of surfaces that may be used on a playground: loose-fill surfaces and unitary surfaces.

- Loose-fill surfaces are the most common and include materials such as sand, pea gravel, wood chips, shredded rubber, and synthetic wood fibers. These surfaces require containment and maintenance on a regular basis to prevent displacement. As a loose-fill surface is moved around, it becomes displaced and its fall-protection qualities are altered. Each loose-fill surface varies in fall-protection

▶Playground use zones help to prevent serious injuries to children if they should fall while playing on the equipment.

qualities and the depth of material that should be maintained. Typically, shredded rubber and synthetic wood fibers are more absorbent than other loose-fill surfaces and do not need to be maintained at a depth as great as sand, pea gravel, and wood chips.

- Unitary surfaces typically take the form of tiles with a rubbery quality that are interconnected and provide a surface that cannot be displaced. Unitary surfaces are much more expensive to purchase and install, but they keep their fall-protection qualities and are much easier to maintain.

The type of surface selected also affects the accessibility of the play area. Unitary surfaces and loose-fill surfaces of shredded rubber and synthetic wood fiber are considered accessible. The surfaces of sand, pea gravel, and wood chips are not considered accessible and do not meet ADA guidelines. In regards to playgrounds, ADA guidelines can be applied to the accessibility of playground equipment. An entire playground area is not required to be accessible, but people in wheelchairs must be able to access play equipment.

Playground Supervision

Playgrounds are primarily supervised by adults visiting the area with children. Most playgrounds are not equipped with staff to supervise use; however, recreation facility managers must design the play area in such a way that adults can easily supervise it. Several factors in the planning phase can make supervision easier:

1. In selecting a playground site, management should consider locations that minimize potential hazards, such as busy roads or areas near water that could be attractive nuisances to children.

2. Sight lines are an important element in being able to supervise a playground. Spaces should also be avoided where sight lines are restricted by vegetation or man-made structures. When equipment is placed in a playground, it should be located in such

a way that the equipment doesn't limit the sight lines.

3. Signage is another way that management can assist in supervision of a playground. By providing signs that communicate age-appropriateness of equipment and rules for a play area, adults may better understand how to supervise play on the playground.

4. Management can also facilitate playground supervision by providing support amenities in the playground area for adults. Permanent benches in predetermined areas informally direct adults to those areas where they will be better able to supervise. In addition, adults will be more likely to sit in the playground area instead on sitting on benches in areas outside the playground.

5. Providing other amenities such as trash receptacles, water fountains, or restrooms makes adults and children more likely to stay in the playground area and leads to fewer instances of inadequate supervision.

Playground Maintenance

Playgrounds must be maintained in order to ensure a safe user experience. As mentioned in the earlier section of playground surfaces, it is important that the depth of loose fill surfaces be maintained in order to keep fall-protection qualities. An example of this is the area directly below a playground swing. It is common for users to drag their feet and displace a loose-fill surface below the swing. By raking the area and adding loose fill surface material, depth can be re-established. Maintenance crews should examine surfaces in fall-protection areas on a regular basis. Maintenance crews should also be aware that rain can erode loose-fill surfaces. After inclement weather, crews should examine these surfaces.

Maintenance for playgrounds also applies to playground equipment. Most pieces of playground equipment have bolts or screws that should be tightened on a regular basis. When purchasing playground equipment, manufacturers usually provide maintenance guidelines. However, it is good policy for maintenance crews to establish a

▶ To ease supervision by parents at public playgrounds several actions can be taken during the planning stage, such as not building the playground near a busy traffic area, not limiting the sight lines in the playground, posting signs that include rules for play, providing benches for parents in the play areas, and providing amenities nearby.

schedule for checking equipment and surfaces to ensure the safe experience of playground users.

SUMMARY

Parks and playgrounds provide opportunities to participate in a variety of recreation activities in an outdoor setting. Parks can take a number of forms and can be an effective source of revenue generation. Playgrounds are prevalent in many settings and play an important role in the physical and social development of children. Attention should be given to the planning of parks and playgrounds to ensure that users have a safe and satisfying leisure experience.

Aquatic Facilities

LEARNING OBJECTIVES

• •

At the completion of this chapter, you should be able to do the following:

1. Recognize the various types of aquatics facilities and the experience that each is designed to provide.

2. Identify the type of staff required for operating an aquatics facility.

3. Understand the practices used at an aquatics facility to ensure a safe experience for users.

4. Explain terminology associated with aquatic maintenance.

5. Recognize the various types of delivery areas in an aquatics facility and the types of programs that might be offered.

quatic facilities provide opportunities for users to engage in activities in spaces where water is a part of the experience. Similar to parks and playgrounds, aquatic facilities can be core products or core product extensions of another facility. **Aquatic facilities** are becoming immensely popular and are a common amenity in many recreation facilities. They can vary from a small 8-lane lap pool to a large multiattraction aquatic center with slides, wave pools, child swim areas, and other unique attractions. Aquatic facilities generate revenue, offer diverse aquatic opportunities, and provide participants with a unique leisure experience.

TYPES OF AQUATIC FACILITIES

Aquatic facilities can be found in indoor and outdoor settings and may be natural or man-made. Typically, aquatic facilities fall into one of three categories: waterfronts, pools, and water parks.

Waterfronts

A **waterfront** is an outdoor aquatic facility located at a lake, beach, river, or quarry. The aquatic space includes all open water; that is, the facility is not contained in a closed environment. Weather plays an important part at all waterfront facilities. It determines what activities are offered, when the activities are offered, whether the facility opens, and where participants can swim. Waterfront facilities are commonly used for swimming, boating, and fishing. Beach facilities and marinas must be aware of changing tides and varying aquatic animals and have staff members who are trained to deal with swift currents and safety concerns.

Pools

Pools are the most common and basic aquatic facility. Pools may include a diving board or slide, but for the most part, they offer few amenities. The traditional pool may include lap swimming areas

▶Water parks have become more and more popular recreation areas each year. They can be indoor or outdoor facilities.

© iStockphoto/Kenneth C. Zirkel

and a diving well, an area of deep water suitable for diving. Detached diving wells are becoming more common, and because they are a separate pool, they tend to be much deeper. A current trend in aquatics is **leisure pools.** This type of pool moves from the traditional square or rectangle shape to a variety of formats and does not include areas for competitive swimming. Pools can be located indoors or outdoors and are frequently found in recreation centers, health clubs, country clubs, and hotels.

Water Parks

Water parks are becoming more widespread across the United States every year. These facilities incorporate different water features designed for maximum entertainment. Features at these types of facilities include water slides, wave attractions, spray features, slow-moving water attractions (for example, a lazy river), toddler play areas, and shallow entries. Similar to traditional pools, water parks can be indoor or outdoor facilities.

AQUATIC FACILITY CONSTRUCTION AND ACCESSIBILITY

Water parks and pools are man-made aquatic facilities. Basic construction is usually a concrete basin with a few options for liners. Sometimes tile is installed on the pool basin and deck. Both concrete and tile can become a slippery surface hazard. To combat this, tiles should be one square inch (2.5 square centimeters) and all decks should be slightly sloped toward a drain to prevent standing water.

Facility accessibility is also important. Accessibility enables all participants to use facilities regardless of disabilities. The ADA outlines accessibility requirements that should be followed for

▸Construction of most aquatic facilities starts with a concrete basin.

▶The Americans With Disabilities Act (ADA) sets forth requirements to make aquatic areas accessible for people of all abilities.

aquatic areas. There are a few ways to make a pool or water park accessible.

1. Moveable ramps and stairs allow access to the facility through an easier entry point for those with limited mobility.
2. A chair lift runs on electricity or hydraulics to move participants from the deck to the water with ease.
3. Moveable floors are becoming popular in new facilities. This feature allows the floor of the pool to be moved to any depth to allow various groups of participants the opportunity to be in the water.

AQUATIC FACILITY OPERATIONS

Aquatic facilities require a number of key management functions to efficiently operate. The facility must be adequately staffed, safe, and well main-

tained. In addition, it must have proper mechanical systems and quality aquatic equipment.

Staffing

Staffing is the one of the most important concerns that facility managers will encounter when managing an aquatic center. The most important consideration when hiring staff is finding properly trained and certified employees. Certification must be obtained before employment occurs. Aquatic staff may include lifeguards, instructors, and additional staff.

Lifeguards

Lifeguards are the lifeblood of an aquatic facility. Most facilities have lifeguards and head lifeguards. Lifeguards are first and foremost responsible for the safety of participants in the aquatic area. This can include enforcing facility policies, administering emergency care, surveying the water, and performing other duties as assigned. Head lifeguards perform basic personnel management responsibilities and are also responsible for standard lifeguard duties. It is important to make sure that lifeguards they are properly certified. This should include lifeguard training, CPR, SFA, PDT, automatic external defibrillation (AED) training, and lifeguard supervisor certification. These certifications ensure that lifeguards are properly trained in handling emergency aquatic situations.

Instructors

Aquatic facilities rely on many types of instructors for their programming needs, such as swim instructors, water exercise instructors, and aquatic therapists. There may also be aquatic classes that warrant instructors for scuba (self-contained underwater breathing apparatus), sailing, canoeing, and kayaking. When dealing with a large number of instructors, recreation facility managers may find it beneficial to hire an instructor supervisor or coordinator. This position is closely related to that of head lifeguard and is in charge of supervising the instructor staff and scheduling aquatic space for each class.

Swim Instructors The most common type of aquatic instructor is a swim instructor. These instructors are responsible for teaching participants the skills needed to be a swimmer. All swim instructors should be certified as water safety instructors as well as in certified in SFA, CPR, and AED use.

Water Exercise Instructors Fitness instruction is another key aspect of aquatic operations. Water exercise is a low-impact fitness option that offers an alternative to traditional land-based aerobic and weight training. To properly teach these classes, water exercise instructors are needed. They should be certified as water exercise or exercise instructors and hold the same safety certifications as the swim instructions, including SFA, CPR, and AED.

Aquatic Therapists Closely related to water exercise is aquatic therapy. These instructors are specialists in rehabilitation or therapy with older populations or people with disabilities. Aquatic therapists' certifications should be based upon

▶Swim instructors are the most common type of instructors at an aquatic facility.

industry standards for therapists and should include certification for safety standards such as CPR, AED, and SFA.

Other Instructors   Although the swim and fitness aquatic programs are the most popular, many new courses are becoming successful that require many types of instructors. Some facilities offer scuba classes, which require not only SFA, CPR, and AED certifications but instructors knowledgeable in local diving locations. Club sports—which include swim teams and dive teams—may have instructors or coaches depending on the facility and the availability of funds for the club. Sailing, canoeing, and kayaking instructors should be knowledgeable about their type of water craft. All of these instructors should also be trained in CPR, AED, and SFA.

Additional Staff

Aquatic facilities may have additional staffing needs. Maintenance personnel are essential to any facility, but especially to aquatic facilities. These professionals are tasked with making sure the mechanical, chemical, and sanitation systems of the facility are functioning properly, efficiently, and in accordance with health and safety codes. In addition, janitorial staff are vital to the upkeep of the aquatic venue. Custodians take care of all cleaning, supplying, and beautification projects. If an aquatic facility operates concessions or pro shops, it may become necessary to hire staff to manage and operate these amenities as well.

Fee Collection

Aquatic facilities are revenue-generating facilities. Revenue is typically generated through fee collection where users pay a fee before permitting access the aquatic area. Access control by staff persons and equipment, including a cash register, credit card machine, or computer are utilized to assist with fee collection. Aquatic facilities may collect fees each time a user enters a facility, or they may collect fees in one lump sum in the form of memberships or season passes.

Aquatic Facility Safety

Safety is a primary concern in aquatic facility management. When working around a water environment, each decision regarding safety is one of life and death. Safety has many components, including standards, codes, and safety training for all staff. Not only are these workplace practices designed to protect the aquatic users but also to keep staff members healthy and safe as they perform their duties.

An important aspect of aquatic safety is **access control,** the process of managing entry into an aquatic area. Because aquatic facilities offer an inherent risk of drowning, it is important to limit access to the aquatic area. In most settings, this is done by fencing the aquatic area and establishing an entrance area staffed by facility staff. This entrance area is also where admission fees are collected or passes are checked.

Standards and Codes

Standards and codes affect not only aquatic facilities, but many other businesses, agencies, and organizations that people come into contact with every day on the job. Standards are the broad guidelines that facilities strive to follow in their everyday operations. Codes are rules and regulations that are mandated by the federal, state, and local governments. These regulations state minimum standards that must be met for a facility to remain open. They are usually enforced by random inspections that help to determine state or local licensure.

State and local bathing codes vary, so it is important for facility managers to check with local and state government offices to ensure that they have the most up-to-date copies of all codes and regulations pertaining to aquatic facilities. State codes cannot be less stringent than federal codes, and local codes cannot be less stringent than state codes. The codes can become more regulatory as they move down the governmental chain. Typically, bathing codes contain information regarding safety, sanitation, equipment, and bather loads.

The Occupational Safety and Health Administration (OSHA) protects employees in a variety of work settings. It plays a major role in regulating jobs that have primary responsibilities involving chemicals, drugs, bodily fluids, and other potential health hazards. Employees at an aquatic facility have the potential to come into contact with bodily fluids and chemicals on a regular basis.

Safety Training

Paramount to safety is certifying staff to respond to and effectively manage accidents. There are many agencies that provide basic certifications in SFA, CPR, PDT, AED, lifeguard training, and so on. One agency that provides many of these certification necessities is the American Red Cross (www.redcross.org). Two other agencies that provide many aquatic certifications are the Young Men's Christian Association (YMCA; www.ymca.net), and Jeff Ellis and Associates (www.jellis.com). All CPR guidelines are passed down by the American Heart Association (AHA; www.americanheart.org), and they also offer their own certification in this skill. Obtaining these certifications is crucial for all staff, not just aquatic personnel, because it enables anyone who works for the aquatic facility to help participants in need of assistance.

The key to effective emergency management is a solid emergency action plan. This plan allows staff to assist participants in emergencies in the best possible way. In aquatic facilities, these plans can encompass near-drowning experiences, spinal injuries, and non-life-threatening emergencies. Proper supervision should be part of any plan. Lifeguards practice supervision every time they sit down in their chair. By taking steps to ensure that participants are following the rules, lifeguards practice **preventive supervision.** Children need to be given special consideration in the aquatic environment. They often do not understand the serious threats imposed by an aquatic facility. Because of their curiosity and willingness to try anything, they need to be given the utmost attention during supervision of a facility.

Maintenance and Hygiene

Maintenance and hygiene are essential to maintaining safety at an aquatic facility. These two factors can take on many facets. Minor repairs come up almost on a daily basis, including anything from replacing a broken handle on a bathroom stall to restringing a lane line. A critical aspect when dealing with minor repairs is addressing them as quickly as possible, because the costs can be greater if they turn into major problems later. Locker room sanitation must be done every day. This can include scrubbing toilets, cleaning sinks, scrubbing floors, and hosing showers and other surfaces. Similar to locker room sanitation is deck sanitation. Every day, both before the facility opens and after it closes, the deck should be sanitized with a water and bleach mixture. This will keep bacteria and other parasites from

▶An aquatic area must be sanitized every day with a water and bleach mixture to kill bacteria and other parasites and keep them from contaminating the pool water.

contaminating the pool water and ensure that the pool deck is user friendly.

To keep a facility looking professional for many years, preventive facility upkeep is essential. A fresh coat of paint each year on the walls and pool (manufacturers' guidelines for pools should be accounted for first) will lengthen the life of the facility. Appliances such as air conditioners, toilets, sinks, and hand dryers should have routine maintenance performed on them per the manufacturers' guidelines to ensure a long life span. At times, it may be necessary to make updates to an aquatic facility. These modernizations will keep users satisfied with the facility and wanting to come back. Before undergoing any major renovations, check with local government agencies for the proper building codes and permits. It is also imperative to make sure updates meet the ADA.

Mechanical Systems

The heart of any aquatic facility is the mechanical system that filters and sanitizes the water. The first consideration in an aquatic mechanical system is the pump. This piece of machinery circulates the water throughout the aquatic venue. Pumps can be placed before or after the filter, which is the next key component of a mechanical system. There are various types of filters, but the two main types that recreation facility managers may encounter are sand filters and diatomaceous earth (DE) filters. Both of these systems trap loose materials in the water and put the filtered water back into circulation. The last main part of a mechanical system is the sanitation system. The two most recognized chemicals used in aquatic sanitation are chlorine and bromine. Chlorine is the most widely used sanitation chemical and can come in three forms: gas, liquid, and tablet. Tablets are the most common form used in systems today. Gas chlorine is not commonly used because of the dangerous properties it possesses when under pressure in a cylinder. It is important that all three aspects of the aquatic mechanical system—the pump, the filter, and the sanitation system—work together to provide a safe and clean environment for participants.

To ensure that the aquatic mechanical systems are running efficiently, routine maintenance should be performed on the system. **Backwashing** the pump and filtration system is a process that should be done every week. This process involves putting the pump on in reverse to stir up the sand in the filter and remove the buildup of materials

▶Filters are just one type of three aquatic mechanical systems used to keep pool water safe for aquatic facility users.

from the system. Sanitation systems also require basic maintenance. They must be cleaned and refilled regularly, according to the manufacturer's maintenance guidelines. Failure to clean a system can lead to buildup of the sanitizer and hinder the performance of a system. Seasonal pools have the added burden of winterizing or closing the facility for the off-season. This can include draining the pool, cleaning and dismantling the sanitation system, cleaning the pump, putting away all moveable pool equipment, and locking down the facility.

Certain safety concerns arise when dealing with pumps and chemicals. For instance, it is important for all personnel to know the location of the emergency pump shutoff and how to operate it. This switch will shut off all mechanical systems in the event of an emergency. Additionally, some pool chemicals can cause burns and other health problems. Extreme care should be taken when handling these chemicals. Recreation facility managers should provide proper safety equipment and information to all employees who may come into contact with these chemicals. When storing chemicals, it is necessary to read the labels and fact sheets to make sure that the chemicals can be stored together and where they should be stored. All chemicals should be stored in a cool, dark area. Improper storage can lead to anything from corrosion of the storeroom to health hazards.

Aquatic Facility Equipment

Without the equipment that goes inside of it, an aquatic facility is just another body of water. There are many types of equipment that allow recreation facility managers to provide almost unlimited types of programming, including rescue and safety equipment, instructional and fitness equipment, swimming and diving equipment, and general aquatic equipment.

Rescue and Safety Equipment

The most important equipment in an aquatic facility is rescue and safety equipment. This equipment can include items such as rescue tubes, ring buoys, reaching poles, backboards, rescue boards, and various other pieces that a lifeguard may need when performing a rescue. Part of the rescue equipment, called personal protective equipment, is extremely important because it keeps employees safe from disease transmission. Such equipment can include rescue masks, gloves, aprons, and other items that put a barrier between the rescuer and the victim. Rescue and safety equipment also includes first aid supplies, including band aids, blood spill kits, gauze pads and bandages, slings, antibacterial cream, ice packs, glucose, and general safety supplies.

Instructional and Fitness Equipment

Instructional and fitness equipment form the core of aquatic programming equipment. Instructional items can range from water noodles to water toys. Instructors use various products while teaching, so it is best to find out what the instructors need and order equipment accordingly. Fitness equipment at an aquatic facility can include anything from kickboards and pull buoys to aqua jog belts and wrist weights. Many people mistake aquatic fitness for swimming laps. This misconception leaves out the many aspects of water that make it a perfect medium for fitness. Fitness in aquatics can include programs such as aqua aerobics, classes

▶ Being well-stocked with rescue equipment and first aid supplies is especially important for having a safe aquatic facility.

for participants with fibromyalgia, and aqua step aerobics. These aerobic classes can provide a low- or high-impact workout and tend to be less stressful on bones and joints. Facility managers should take this into consideration and provide equipment accordingly.

Swimming and Diving Equipment

Swimming and diving clubs and teams also have a great deal of equipment at an aquatic facility. Swim groups have the usual kickboards and pull buoys, but they also have specialized equipment such as fins, resistance trainers, weight sets, and hand paddles, to name a few. Dive groups may have dry-land boards, crash mats, trampolines, and other equipment to help them practice a dive before trying it on the real board where serious injury can occur if the dive is not done correctly. Recreation facility managers may not be responsible for the team or club equipment, but they should be aware

▶Having the essential equipment for swim instruction and fitness instruction will help you provide a successful aquatic instruction and fitness program.

of the equipment used because it may be stored or brought into the facility.

General Aquatic Equipment

Aside from the specialized aquatic equipment, every facility has general equipment that should be taken into consideration. Tables, chairs, and lounge chairs are the most widely used nonprogramming equipment at aquatic facilities. They are useful for people participating in aquatic activities and for those who would like to bring participants or watch them. Such pieces of equipment should be checked daily to make sure they are in working order because they are the most likely to wear out. Other equipment that recreation facility managers may find at an aquatic venue are benches, umbrellas, cleaning equipment, lane-line spools, computer timing systems, bleachers, trash cans, office supplies, and so on.

AQUATIC FACILITY PRODUCT DELIVERY AREAS

As mentioned in the section on aquatic staffing, there are a number of production delivery areas within an aquatics facility. Restrooms are ancillary production delivery areas at aquatic facilities that support the core product and are often included in locker rooms. Another type of production delivery area is the retail outlet. Retail outlets are core product extensions where users may purchase merchandise or equipment as a part of their aquatic leisure experience. Production delivery areas that focus on the core product include areas for informal swim, instructional swim, fitness programming, special events, intramurals, clubs, and athletic teams.

Informal Swim Area

Informal swim is the easiest area to schedule and the most crucial to any aquatic facility. Most people think of informal swim as lap swimming. Although lap swimming does occur during informal time, the concept encompasses all types of activities that participants might chose to do. Whether the activities involve swimming laps, jumping off the diving board, aqua jogging, or just chatting with friends, informal swim should be the primary focus of recreation facility managers because it is where a facility will see the most participation.

Instructional Swim Area

Instructional swim is the second most popular activity at aquatic facilities and the one that will garner the largest profits if promoted, offered, and run properly. Swim lessons make up the bulk of instructional swim time, and scheduling them is of great importance to the success of instructional swim. These programs are typically offered during peak times, which include the late afternoon, early evening, and weekends, so as not to conflict with school schedules. During the summer, it is more common to see instructional swim offered throughout the day. Swim lessons for preschool children can be offered on weekday mornings and early afternoons, but they should also be offered during peak times to account for working parents.

Swim lessons can be offered to children as young as 6 months to adults who are 100 or more years old. It is imperative to keep the instructor-to-student ratio low but cost effective. In addition to group swim lessons, private and semiprivate lessons are another great service to provide. They give participants either one-on-one instruction or lower instructor-to-student rations. They also bring in extra revenue because their fees can be relatively high.

Swimming and diving lessons represent the traditional instructional programming offered at aquatic facilities. However, new forms of instructional programming are being offered. Scuba instruction is growing rapidly. Sailing, canoeing, and kayaking are popular at facilities with outdoor capabilities, and innovative classes such as surfing or water skiing can add to the diversity of programming. When deciding what programs to offer, it is important for recreation facility managers to think about what they can actually do within their facility. Although participants may desire a surfing class, if there are no facilities where the class can be conducted, it is illogical to offer it.

Fitness Programming Area

Fitness is becoming a popular dimension in aquatic facilities and is often referred to as water exercise. Water exercise can incorporate many facets of aquatic activities. Lap swimming can be considered water exercise, but most consider it to be a traditional class with an instructor. Water exercise includes swim conditioning, aqua jogging, water aerobics, and aquatic yoga. An interesting spin-off concept from traditional fitness programming

▶Water exercise is quickly gaining popularity among users at aquatic facilities.

is personal aquatic training. Similar to personal training, personal aquatic training is one-on-one exercise with a certified trainer in the aquatic environment. This is a more recent trend in the field of aquatics, but recreation facility managers should be aware of it because it is gaining popularity.

Closely related to fitness programming is aquatic therapy. As mentioned earlier in this chapter, water has many properties that make it the ideal environment for people who may need less impact on their joints. Seniors are finding benefits from classes aimed at strengthening the body to help alleviate the symptoms of arthritis. Athletes are using the water to help recover from injuries and surgeries. And people with disabilities are able to use the water to gain range of motion that makes everyday life easier.

Special Events Area

Special events are a prime time to showcase a facility and what it has to offer. These programs can range from a daylong event to a once-a-month community offering. During special events, partici-

pants who would not normally be using the facility have the opportunity to do so. Family swim time is the easiest special event to program, but it will need the most attention from a risk management standpoint because small children will be using the facility. It can be scheduled daily, weekly, monthly, or at other designated times. Family swim is just what it sounds like: It's a time for families to have fun exploring aquatic activities together. Facility rentals are another type of special event that can bring in large revenue. There are many groups who may want to use the facility, and it is the job of recreational facility managers to prioritize these groups and schedule space accordingly. See chapter 13 for more details on special events and facility rentals.

Intramural, Club, and Athletic Programming Area

The next tier of aquatic activities delves more into competitive swimming and diving. Intramurals is the most informal form of swimming competition. All levels of swimmers partake in competition

▶Many details go into planning a swim or diving meet, including coordinating schedules, timelines, and preparation. The recreation facility manager should request help from people who have knowledge of this type of event to make sure all details for the event are covered.

based on cooperation and fun. Events can range from traditional competitions to more inclusive events such as a doggy-paddle or cannon-ball competition. This type of event is usually a day-long tournament with men's, women's, and coed teams.

Club programs are a more formalized system of aquatic competition. Clubs can be formed for not only swimming and diving but also for water polo and synchronized swimming. They typically have weekly, if not daily, practices and a set meet schedule. A club schedule can also include invitational meets, championship tournaments, and other national competitions.

Athletic teams are the traditional varsity swimming, diving, water polo, and synchronized swimming teams. These teams practice daily and sometimes up to two or three times a day. Meet schedules can vary based on the season of the sport, so recreation facility managers should be aware of the season of each sport that they supervise. At times, a facility may be called upon to host a championship meet or competition. These meets

can range from a local all-city meet to an international championship. Each event has different needs and concerns, so facility managers should surround themselves with people knowledgeable of the event. The meets require much attention from facility managers in coordinating schedules, timelines, and preparation, which can take weeks or even months to develop and implement. These types of events can raise revenue not only for the facility but also for the surrounding community as an economic stimulus.

EXTERNAL SUPPORT

Certain services are vital to an aquatic facility, but facility employees may not be able to provide them. This is where external personnel such as emergency medical personnel; police, security, and fire personnel; food services personnel; computer and information technology personnel; and maintenance services personnel help to fill in where needed.

Emergency Medical Personnel

Critical in the emergency action plan, emergency medical personnel are the next link in the chain of survival for an accident victim if on-site staff are unable to handle an emergency on their own. EMTs and paramedics can provide a standard of care above that of the lay rescuer. They can also transport victims to a medical facility where they can receive advanced care faster. Aquatic facility managers should have contact with local emergency personnel to review the facility emergency action plans and figure out the logistics of possible emergency scenarios.

Police, Security, and Fire Personnel

Police and fire rescue services are integral to emergency services systems. Facility managers should have contact with these services because they are important to all emergency action plans. Fire rescue services can help address where participants should go in the event of a fire or other emergencies. Police have their obvious job of upholding the law, but they can also be brought into a facility to provide security. Security services can also be performed by a third-party organization that specializes in them.

Food-Service Personnel

Aquatic facilities may have an area where food service becomes important. Recreation facility managers must decide whether the service will be done in-house or contracted by a third party. In either case, it is important to consider the health and safety codes that are part of food service. This section will not delve deeply into the components of food service, but facility managers should be aware that such services do exist at aquatic facilities. For more detailed information on food services, see chapter 19.

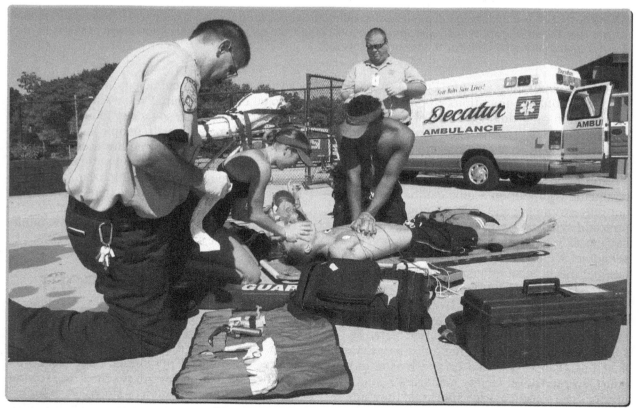

▶Aquatic facility managers should establish contact with emergency local personnel and review the facility's emergency action plans.

Computer and Information Technology Personnel

As technology grows, more and more aquatic facilities are using computers and the Internet in their everyday business. Although some aquatic and recreation facilities may have their own information technology (IT) services, this may be a service that is provided by a third party. Computers and IT services are a useful tool for facility managers in programming, personnel management, marketing, and many other areas. Aquatic facilities are beginning to take computer usage to a new level with drowning-detection cameras that run on computer programs. Recreation facility managers must become aware of such technologies through continued professional development and training and must also surround themselves with experts in the field.

Maintenance Services Personnel

As mentioned earlier, the mechanical systems of aquatic facilities can be extremely intricate and sometimes frustrating for recreation facility managers. If a properly trained aquatic specialist is not on staff, managers can hire a third-party contractor who specializes in aquatic maintenance. Contracting these services can be more expensive, but it ensures that a trained professional is working on the systems. General maintenance can also be obtained from third-party vendors. Facility managers should make themselves aware of the costs associated with these services. If the laborers are in a union, facility managers should also keep up on union policies.

SUMMARY

Aquatic facilities have many unique properties that will overwhelm recreation facility managers who do not understand the intricacies of successfully running a facility of this type. With the increased revenues being generated by pools and water parks today, it is of great importance that recreation facility managers understand how to adequately staff these facilities and create a safe aquatic environment.

18

Ancillary Spaces

All facilities have a primary purpose or core product designed to meet management mission and goals. This purpose constitutes the basis for construction of the recreation facility. However, rarely does a facility exist by providing only a core product. Facilities are supported by **ancillary spaces,** areas that support the core product. In most facilities, the core product could not be made available to users were it not for the supporting ancillary areas. Ancillary areas do not exist as sources of revenue; the spaces that support the core product and generate revenue are called *core product extensions* and will be discussed in chapter 19. It is important for recreation facility managers to understand ancillary areas, such as parking and locker rooms, and how they affect recreation facility management.

PARKING

Fundamental to almost all recreation facilities is the availability of parking for users and employees. As an ancillary area, parking provides users and employees with a place to leave their vehicle and can prove to be a valuable convenience. Inadequate parking facilities can have a negative impact on the use and revenue generation of a recreation facility.

Two kinds of parking areas can be used for recreation facilities. The most common form is **surface parking,** an area consisting of a single, level surface. The second type of parking area is a parking structure or garage. These structures contain multiple levels of parking and create more parking area using less land. Parking structures are useful in cities and other areas where there are space restrictions. However, they are much more expensive to construct than surface parking.

Parking Options

Three types of parking options are typically offered at recreation facilities: self-parking, gated parking, and valet parking. Each type has unique considerations. The nature of the core product typically determines which parking option will be used and to what extent.

Self-Parking

Self-parking is the most common parking option, and it is when owners park their vehicles. This option is typically used when a recreation facil-

ity has access to public streets or a parking lot in close proximity. It may be free of charge for facility users or charge a fee based on length or time of use, which typically is regulated by parking meters. In some instances, such as a campus recreation facility or health club, users may be required to purchase parking permits.

Gated Parking

Gated parking can be designed to combine self-parking and a system that controls vehicle access and security. Gated parking is often controlled by one-way access and exit with an attendant to check vehicles in and out as well as to collect fees. This option often incorporates a gate that is controlled by access cards. In this instance, the user swipes a card through a magnetic card-reading device or a device is attached to the vehicle that trips an electrical signal. These systems activate the opening and closing of the gate. They often have a variable fee structure and membership options. Higher fees offer benefits that may include specified parking spaces, with spaces that are closer to the facility having a higher fee than more remote spaces.

Valet Parking

Valet parking provides maximum customer convenience. A valet service provides staff members who greet customers at the entrance of the facility and take the vehicle to a different location or parking area. This is a convenient form of parking, requiring little effort on the part of the vehicle owner. A numbered ticket is given to the owner, who gives the ticket to the valet upon leaving. The valet matches the number and returns the vehicle. Generally, there is a higher fee for valet parking. Management must have access to nearby parking areas and provide vehicle security. Management must also have insurance coverage for this type of service. Valet parking is most common in urban areas, country clubs, hotels, and resorts.

Parking Operations

It is generally understood that recreation facilities should provide some form of parking as part of the facility or at least nearby. Usually, community-planning agencies require facilities to provide on-site parking to prevent congestion and overflow on local streets. The efficiency of a parking area projects a message about the management of the facility. This can be reflected in parking access, signage, maintenance, and security.

a

b

▶The two basic kinds of parking areas are (a) surface parking and (b) parking structures.

Access

It is important to consider how accessing and exiting a parking facility occurs. If a large parking area connects to a main street in the community, it may cause considerable delays for customers exiting the parking area. There should be a system of control and communication in the event that there is heavy use created by a special event or when the parking area is full. This may require the use of parking attendants to direct vehicles to appropriate parking areas or security personnel to facilitate safe entry and exit of a parking facility that connects to a busy street.

Signage

Signage provides critical information for drivers using a parking facility. Recreation facility manag-

▶Parking area signage should be easy to read and, if applicable, may provide information on time limits, parking rates, and where to pay rates.

ers should provide readily identifiable directional indicators so that drivers know how to find and enter the designated parking areas. Signs that need to be considered include directional, handicapped, visitor, compact car, and space or lane restriction signage. Signs also can be used for advertising, indicating rates, and communicating rules, regulations, policies, and how to pay. Some community ordinances place restrictions on the size, location, and amount of signage that may be allowed. Signage in a parking area should be consistent in size, color, and location throughout the parking area to provide easily identifiable information.

Maintenance

There are three major considerations when it comes to the maintenance of a parking area.

1. **Attend to structural needs of the parking facility as required.** This requires management to respond to harsh conditions, extreme weather, vehicle weight, and general wear and tear on the parking area.

2. **Keep up with the daily maintenance functions required to keep a parking facility in working order.** These tasks include ensuring that the surface is in good shape, parking lines and signage are visible, and meters and gates are operational.

3. **Attend to the appearance of the parking area by keeping the area clean and attractive.** This can include attending to landscaped areas and providing adequate water to support vegetation in addition to providing trash receptacles and removing waste.

Security

Parking operators need to be concerned for the safety of users and prevention of vehicle theft and damage. Special attention is required to provide complete protection of vehicles and personal property. Courts could hold an agency liable for damage and criminal acts if adequate security is not provided. A key factor in parking security is the provision of proper lighting. Overhead lighting with adequate brightness can limit security concerns. Where feasible, security guards can supervise parking areas. In the event of an incident, some form of emergency communication device should be available, such as an alarm, intercom, telephone, or security camera.

▸Recreation facility managers need to make user and employee safety a priority in parking areas, and one way to do this is install an emergency alarm, intercom, or phone in the parking lot.

© Salvador Alvaro Nebot/age fotostock

Parking Design

Recreational facility managers often dedicate little time to parking once a facility has been designed and is operating. However, it is vital that time and effort be devoted to the design of the parking area during the planning phase of parking operations. A variety of details must be considered in parking design, including shape, angles, codes and ordinances, space size and number of spaces, sidewalks, landscaping, and drainage.

Shape

The shape of a parking area can be greatly influenced by topography and architectural requirements. A rectangular parking area is the most efficient and most common. Irregularly shaped lots are often the product of site constraints and usually result in an inefficient design.

Angles

Parking spaces are usually at 90-, 75-, 60-, or 45-degree angles. In some cases local ordinances require spaces to be at designated angles. However, the angle of a parking space is most frequently dictated by the amount of space available for parking and the desired number of parking spaces. Ninety-degree spaces allow for the most parking spaces in two-way traffic flow; however, in one-way traffic flow, angled spaces require less row width and may use space more efficiently.

Codes and Ordinances

Codes and ordinances can affect parking areas. They usually apply to areas with more than six parking spaces. Codes and ordinances depend on the interpretation of community planning agencies, each community having its own requirements. Codes may require a ratio of parking spaces per facility user tied to the capacity of the facility. For example, a code could require one parking spot for every six potential users and employees. Other factors that could be affected by codes include the appearance, overall design, entrance and exit locations, and location of the parking area in relation to the facility. Management should inquire about codes and ordinances in order to be in complete compliance. Accessibility for users who are disabled is governed by the ADA accessibility guidelines.

Space Size and Number of Spaces

A parking space needs a minimum of 20 inches (51 centimeters) of door clearance, preferably 24 inches (61 centimeters). The general width for most parking spaces is 8 feet (2.5 meters). The ADA establishes guidelines for handicapped-accessible parking spaces (see figure 18.1). In addition to being located at the shortest walking point to building access points, accessible parking spaces should be at least 8 feet (2.5 meters) wide. Parking access aisles should be 5 feet (1.5 meters) wide for standard cars and 8 feet (2.5 meters) wide for vans and should be part of an accessible route to the facility entrance. Two accessible parking spaces may share a common access aisle. Parking spaces and access aisles must be level, and at least one space must be van accessible.

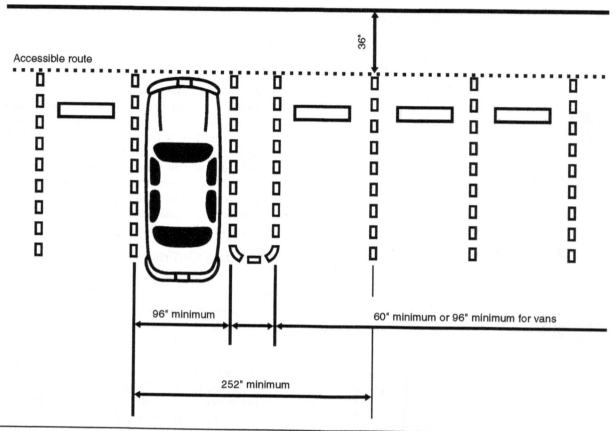

Figure 18.1 Sizes and access aisles for accessible parking spaces.

Reprinted, by permission, from Ladies Professional Golf Association, 2005, *Accessible golf: Making it a game fore all* (Champaign, IL: Human Kinetics), 191.

The number of parking spaces required for a facility is also often dictated by local ordinances; however, there are some general guidelines to follow:

- Universities: 1 parking space for each employee and 1 parking space for every 4 to 6 students
- Community or recreation centers: 1 parking space for every 200 to 250 square feet (18.5-23 square meters) in the facility
- Stadiums: 1 parking space for every 3 to 4 seats
- Parks: 1 parking space for every 4,000 to 5,000 square feet (371.5-464.5 square meters)

The ADA also includes guidelines for the number of handicapped-accessible spaces, which is based on the total number of spaces at the facility (see table 18.1).

Generally, parking areas should be located in close proximity to the facility. Typically, users do not want to walk far to access a facility. However, in instances where there is inadequate space or an event where a large number of vehicles need to park, management should provide perimeter parking options, which require a longer walk or even a shuttle service to and from the facility.

Sidewalks

Sidewalks are essential for safety, especially with large parking lots. Sidewalks should be distinguished from the roadway and parking areas and should be raised 3 to 6 inches (8-15 centimeters). In situations where sidewalks are not raised, they should be properly painted, placing adequate emphasis on them for easy visibility, especially in crosswalks.

Landscaping: Shading, Screening, and Buffer Zones

Landscaping greatly contributes to the appearance of a parking area and can even increase

Table 18.1 Minimum Accessible Parking Requirements

Total number of parking spaces	Required minimum number of accessible parking spaces
1-25	1
26-50	2
51-75	3
76-100	4
101-150	5
151-200	6
201-300	7
301-400	8
401-500	9
501-1000	2% of total spaces in lot
1,001 and above	20, plus 1 for each 100 over 1,000

Reprinted from the United States Access Board (www.access-board.gov).

property value. Landscape design can also help control traffic and increase safety in a parking area. In addition, the planting of berms, trees, and other types of vegetation can assist in shading a parking area. This is not only helpful in keeping vehicles cool, but it also helps maintain asphalt by limiting direct sunlight. Vegetation is also useful in screening neighboring areas and creating buffer zones from the parking area, which in many cases is required by local ordinances. Screening or buffer zones can also be created with walls, fencing, or other types of dividers.

Drainage

It is important that parking areas have proper drainage to prevent pooling and flooding from rainwater. The parking area should have a flat surface with a slight slope (1-4 percent) to allow for water runoff. The slope should be minimal and not create a hazard for users. In most cases, the slope is not noticeable to the naked eye.

RECEPTION AREA

A reception area is an ancillary area that can be vital to recreation facility usage and product success. The reception area represents an extension of the administration and delivery operations, cre-ating initial contact with customers and providing a first impression of the facility. A reception area should establish a comfortable, noncongested, and nonconfusing atmosphere that helps users gain access to the product.

A reception area serves as a transitional area from the outside boundaries of the facility to inner operations. How well the reception area functions can make a lasting impression on users. This section includes some critical points for placing emphasis on a reception area.

Initial Appearance

An aesthetically pleasing reception area creates a favorable first impression by being well maintained and organized. A disorganized and unattractive reception area can cause users to draw negative conclusions about the facility and its management. A positive image projected by the reception area can recruit new users and help maintain repeat use from current users.

Efficiency

The efficiency of a reception area may be more important than its appearance. Efficiency refers to how well the staff communicates with users. A knowledgeable staff that is properly trained and

▶A reception area has many functions for a recreation facility, and an aesthetically pleasing and comfortable reception area can create a favorable first impression of the facility for users.

▶Attitude of reception desk staff is equally as important as the appearance of the reception area.

understands organization procedures is vital in order to maintain consistency at the front desk and share correct information with users.

Attitude

Information and aesthetics go a long way in creating a positive impression in the reception area, but attitude is equally as important. Guests should feel as though staff members are friendly and helpful. Reception staff members are often asked the same questions over and over. It is important for them to make users feel as though they are pleased to answer their questions and enjoy the interaction. A smile and a warm greeting go a long way in making users feel welcome.

Functions of Reception

The reception area may serve a variety of functions depending on the facility. In a health club,

the reception area may just provide a point to sign in or get information. In a hotel or resort, the reception area will also include a check-in area. Regardless of the facility, there are certain reception commonalities, including access control, fee collection, communication, schedules, and other functions.

Access Control

The reception area controls user access. Nearly all indoor and many outdoor recreation facilities require some way of limiting user access. Not all areas of a facility are appropriate for users to enter. Outdoor recreation facilities may have sensitive environmental areas where user access should be limited to protect the area. Indoor facilities may have mechanical or other equipment areas that users should not enter for their safety and to prohibit tampering with important equipment.

If the facility has a requirement for controlled access, much thought should be put into the design of the reception area and any lobby or atrium that complements the reception area. The reception area can play a major role in the security of the facility because many reception areas are responsible for opening and closing functions. Most importantly, a reception area is often designed to limit user access by the use of gates, barriers, or controlled doors.

A variety of access-control systems may be used. Spectator sport facilities such as college and professional arenas or stadiums may require tickets, passes, or names on a pass list to gain entry. Community centers, YMCAs, and public and private fitness centers may also limit access by requiring some type of identification card or pass.

The facility access area can fulfill this obligation through several techniques. Typical access-control devices include gates, turnstiles, counter areas, card-reading equipment, and metal detection or X-ray devices. Typical personnel involved in the facility access process include attendants,

receptionists, customer service representatives, security personnel, ushers, and ticket takers.

Most facilities exercise some degree of access control. These measures are implemented to protect the safety of users and employees in addition to protecting the benefits associated with membership. Security concerns resulting from the impact of the September 11, 2001, terrorist attacks have dramatically affected access procedures for many facilities. It is common to see extensive use of security personnel at recreation facilities that attract large crowds. Even recreational sport facilities may limit access or provide additional scrutiny of potential users by using some of the measures listed earlier. Regardless of the facility, access control is often the responsibility of the reception area where facility employees identify and welcome users.

Fee Collection

Some recreation facilities collect a fee before permitting access. Reception areas can fulfill this

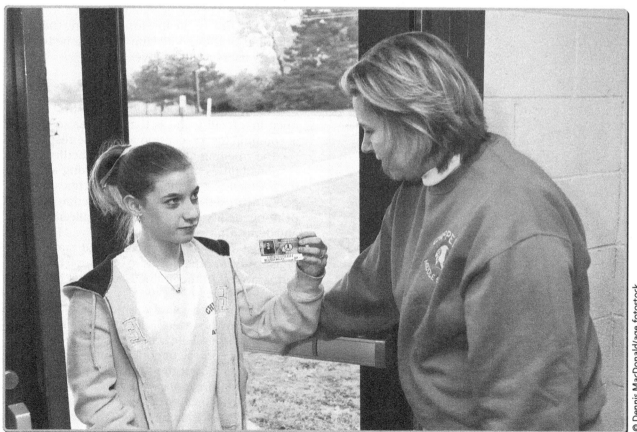

© Dennis MacDonald/age fotostock

▶Many recreation facilities have an attendant or receptionist check photo identification cards to control access into the facility.

obligation with an attendant using a cash register, credit card machine, or computer to assist with fee collection. Other types of fees can also be collected, including membership fees, late fees, registration fees, rental fees, or fees from the sale of merchandise. Recreation facilities may collect fees each time a user accesses a facility (admission, participation fees) or in one lump sum (memberships, season passes) to allow access and use of the core product or core product extensions.

Information and Communication

Facility reception and access areas are commonly where facility information is shared with users. Facility hours, policies, procedures, rules, regulations, fees, registration deadlines, and any facility control policies are often communicated from this location. Information on the core product, the core product extensions, and all relevant details are also communicated when a user inquires. Information

Copyright Shullphoto

▶ A bulletin board is a common item used to communicate information.

exchange can occur face to face, through verbal contact on the telephone, or through a Web site. Additional communication techniques include signs posted in the reception area. It is common for employees in a reception area to receive positive or negative feedback about anything that goes on in a facility. Customer service employees should have forms available to record customer comments. These comments should be provided to management, who may consider altering policies or procedures to improve customer satisfaction. For more information on comment cards, refer to chapter 4 and the online student resource.

Schedules

Recreation facilities require use coordination and scheduling practices that can be quite involved. These arrangements or reservations for use result in a schedule that can be maintained and communicated at the reception area. Types of schedules can include employee schedules, area and space schedules, and access and use schedules. A reception area can also facilitate schedules for simple or major maintenance tasks that need to be done on a particular day at a certain time. Reception area staff could be responsible for producing the actual schedule, or they could simply post schedules for view by users and employees.

Other Functions

Typically the reception area is the first area to open in a facility and is the last area to close. It is common for a reception area to be responsible for the opening and closing of a facility. These responsibilities may include unlocking and locking the facility, turning on and off lights and other equipment, setting alarm systems, compiling and printing facility usage or other required reports, and depositing receipts from daily use. Many facilities have a variety of activities that may require registration or other forms to be completed. These forms are often maintained and filled out at the reception area.

Response to a facility emergency could also originate in this area. Reception staff could be responsible for taking action in the form of first aid, CPR, crowd control, or contacting other facility or external staff about the situation.

Reception areas may present an opportunity to assist with facility control by using a public-address system to communicate announcements and use considerations. Reception areas may also be the location where lost-and-found items are turned in, stored, and claimed by users.

Contributing Areas

Reception areas vary in function, size, and location from facility to facility. Several areas contribute to the reception area. These areas may include the lobby, administration offices, and other contributing areas.

Lobby

The most common space in a reception area is the lobby. All recreation facilities have some type of entrance that makes the initial presentation of the product to its users. There may be an atrium that includes a small or large lobby area with furnishings coordinated with the reception area. Lobbies can be thought of as welcoming areas that may include special decorations, displays of awards and achievements, play areas for children, and reading materials for those who are waiting for other users or employees. A lobby should be designed to help the user feel comfortable and to create a positive impression of the facility.

Administration Offices

Another ancillary space located near the reception area is administration space. Some facilities have a combined reception and office area. These areas may be combined to maximize available space or simply because it is more efficient for facility operation. Combining these areas allows administration personnel to assist customer service staff and respond quickly to customer questions. In many respects, a reception area is an extension of administration offices.

It is also common for core product extensions to be located in the reception area, including revenue-generating amenities such as vending machines, equipment rental, and retail sales spaces. Core product extensions will be discussed in greater detail in chapter 19.

Other Contributing Areas

Facility directories and bulletin boards are often in the reception area and are maintained by the reception staff. There may also be some type of showcase displaying facility information including its history, successes, promotions, or awards. A child care area could be incorporated in a reception area as a service for users. Child care areas are discussed in more detail in chapter 19.

Reception Area Design

Recreation facility managers should be aware of the importance of a reception area and how its design enhances the functionality of the facility. Most important in the design of the reception area is its location, especially if the area is intended to perform numerous functions. It should be in the center of activity so that users can easily identify it.

The reception area should also be located in such a way that it guides users through the facility. A reception area by nature has the potential to cause lines to form. In certain recreation facilities such as amusement parks, users may have to wait a significant amount of time to access the product. Adequate space to accommodate customer waiting should be incorporated into the design of any recreation facility. Special consideration should be given to recreation facilities that attract large numbers of users and long lines with considerable waiting time.

The ability of a recreation facility to effectively receive its users can have a tremendous impact on user satisfaction. Recreation facility managers and those involved in the design or renovation of a facility should pay attention to the number and type of doors, ADA requirements, and how users can make their way through the reception area without difficulty or unnecessary delays. The desk or counter needs to be designed in such a way that the space, size, height, and working area are conducive to users' reception and employees' ability to do their job. For example, ADA requirements necessitate a counter height of 30 inches (76 centimeters) to accommodate users with disabilities. Receiving all users properly and creating a sense of comfort in the receiving process is an important consideration in the design of the area.

LOCKER AND SHOWER AREA

In some recreation facilities, such as health clubs, aquatic parks, or campus recreation centers, facility managers could be responsible for operating a locker and shower area. Whatever the setting, this area can present unusual management challenges. As an ancillary space, it could be a support service that is a key to the success of the core product. Locker and shower areas are usually a service provided to users and employees. They require specialized knowledge and attention to detail that should not be taken for granted.

Functions of Locker and Shower Areas

Certain locker and shower functions are compared with other areas of a recreation facility. This space should be secure, private, and where necessary, supervised to protect the users. Many of the following locker and shower functions will vary from facility to facility. These functions are fundamental to the provision of locker and shower areas and include hygiene, grooming, lockers, showers, restroom areas, therapy, and information and communication.

Hygiene

A basic function of any locker and shower area is to provide an area for users to perform personal hygiene functions after using the facility. A locker and shower area becomes a necessary service where physical exertion creates a need to shower, clean up, or perform other personal hygiene functions. All areas and surfaces must be kept clean and sanitized at all times. If not attended properly, this function can create an unsafe environment and have a negative impact on the success of the core product.

Grooming

Grooming, or performing tasks associated with maintaining personal appearance, requires space in a locker and shower area. This activity usually requires a sink, mirror, electrical outlets, shelving, hair dryer, and other personal items such as shaving cream, hair spray, hand cream, brushes, and combs. Most facilities require users to bring personal grooming items to the facility. However, some upscale country clubs or private fitness facilities may offer these products as a benefit for members.

Lockers

Lockers are important when the core product requires users or employees to store their belongings in a secure space. Typically, users are responsible for providing their own lock, or they can rent or check out a lock at the facility. Lockers vary in size and are typically smaller at outdoor facilities where users may only be storing valuables, such as at a water park or amusement park. Lockers should be larger at facilities where users may be

changing clothes and showering. A facility should include enough lockers to serve all users during peak hours of operation. This number should be planned before the locker room is designed because adding lockers at a later time can be expensive.

Ample space should be provided in and around lockers to allow for users' comfort as they dress before or after using a facility. The space around the lockers should be adequate and include seating such as benches or chairs. Enhancing user comfort also includes paying attention to the color of the locker area, lighting, music or television, and type of floor covering. The flooring chosen for a locker area should provide comfort for users and be a safe, nonslip surface. Users will often be coming from the shower area and may still have wet feet, which can lead to injuries related to slipping on a surface that does not absorb or displace water.

Showers

An adequate number of showers should be available for the number of potential users at any given time. Shower systems can be provided in several ways. To maximize space, sometimes showers are placed in a group in an open area. There are also circumstances where privacy is of greater importance and individual showers are separated with partitions to provide privacy. Appropriate hardware for dispensing the water should be available with adjustable showerheads. Water temperature and velocity should be adequately regulated so users do not have to feel the discomfort of irregular water pressure or temperature. Soap dispensers or bars can be provided. The showering area should be separate from but proximate to the locker area.

Restroom Areas

All locker and shower areas should provide appropriate restroom facilities, including toilets, urinals, and sinks, as appropriate. In general, these facilities should include partitions to provide privacy. Other considerations include whether to use automated or manual mechanisms for toilets and sinks; what type of and how many paper towel dispensers to provide; and the provision of scent-enhancing devices to keep areas fresh. Restroom areas must be kept clean and sanitary at all times with disposable covers for toilet seats where necessary or required. The ADA requires that restroom areas comply with specific dimensions to accommodate users with disabilities. Recreation facility managers and administrators must consult ADA regulations before designing or renovating any restroom area. A link to this information is available in the online resource guide.

Therapy

In more elaborate locker and shower facilities, therapeutic functions may be provided for users. Therapeutic services could include access to massages, a hot tub, a steam room, or a sauna. A training area may also be provided where users can receive prescriptions for health concerns; weight and blood pressure checks; and treatment for injuries. Some private health spas and centers design their services around these needs. It is becoming more common to see indoor recreation facilities feature therapeutic services, including heart rehabilitation services and customized exercise and nutrition programs. Provision of therapeutic functions greatly depends on the nature of the facility and should be managed appropriately.

Information and Communication

The final consideration for the locker and shower area is using the space to communicate information to facility users. A locker and shower area is an excellent place to convey a message because it is a location where people congregate. Bulletin boards and signs can be placed in highly visible locations in a locker and shower area to disseminate information about upcoming activities, services, deadlines, and so on. Public-address announcements could also be incorporated along with other creative methods for conveying information.

Locker and Shower Area Design

Each subarea of a locker and shower area has unique needs in terms of its function. These factors should be addressed in the design phase of a facility project. Proper circulation of the areas and user safety should be a primary consideration in the overall design. Spacing of a locker and shower area should be considered in terms of user circulation or flow; users' ability to move from one area to another should be facilitated and easily monitored. Additionally, there should be adequate space in each functional space—lockers, showers, grooming areas, and restroom facilities—so that there

is no interference with personal comfort zones. User movement should be safe and free of objects, barriers, and slippery surfaces. Entrance and exit traffic should be anticipated to control unwanted intrusion and congestion.

Locker and shower areas are generally contained units with minimal or no windows. The activities of a locker and shower area, by their nature, create odors, humidity, and other by-products, so ventilation is also critical. Ventilation systems must accommodate adequate air circulation, especially during times when a lot of showers are in use. Humidity can build up and temperatures can increase without proper ventilation, which can have a negative impact on the structure and fixtures in the area, not to mention the comfort of users. Appropriate ventilation should be maintained at all times with regulated temperature and humidity checks to prevent odor and moisture containment.

The surfaces in a locker and shower area are also important for maintenance and safety. Showers can create wet surfaces that are hazardous for walking. Where wet conditions exist, slip-resistant surfaces should be incorporated. Management must be particularly sensitive to floor surfaces in this area because they can be a liability if not designed and maintained properly.

Lastly, security needs should be a top priority in locker and shower areas since users will be storing personal belongings, showering, and changing. Valuable belongings are often stored in lockers, so security measures should be implemented to minimize theft. Locker areas should be designed to have open sight lines and provide easy angles for observation from facility staff to help minimize inappropriate activities. Surveillance cameras may be used to assist with security; however, they are limited to the entrance of locker areas, and they can be expensive to install and monitor. However, theft in locker areas is usually due to users not using locks or leaving personal items out in the open. Ultimately, it is the responsibility of users to ensure that they keep their belongings in a secured locker.

SUMMARY

Many functions in facilities support the core product. These functions are essential for efficient facility operations and providing users with services that are typically expected in a recreation facility.

Core Product Extensions and Areas

LEARNING OBJECTIVES

At the completion of this chapter, you should be able to do the following:

1. Define the term *core product extension*.

2. Recognize factors of commodity outlet operations.

3. Explain the various types of food service operations used in facilities.

4. Understand factors associated with child care operations.

5. Understand operating procedures for equipment rental and checkout.

A recreation facility manager's primary focus is on providing the core product to users. However, users often seek additional services when using a facility. These additional services may enhance the use of a facility or enable a user to use a facility at all. Services such as child care can make it possible for some users to use a facility, while products such as recreation equipment, merchandise, or food and beverage simply enhance a facility. These additional services are also sources of revenue. Revenue-generating products and services that complement the core product are called core product extensions. These extensions play an important role in meeting user needs. Core product extensions are similar to ancillary spaces in that they support the core product of the facility, as discussed in chapter 18. The difference is that core product extensions are designed to generate revenue. They can take the form of commodity outlets, food services, child care, and equipment rental or checkout.

COMMODITY OUTLETS

A core product extension that can enhance revenue generation for a recreation facility is a **commodity outlet,** which sells gifts, supplies, apparel, equipment, and specialty items. These outlets can provide purchasing opportunities to regular users as well as facility visitors. Common terms used to describe these operations include *retail outlet, store, pro shop, specialty shop,* and *gift shop.* They can be found in a variety of recreation settings with a variety of systems and layouts.

Before opening a commodity outlet, it is important to create a written business plan. This plan should document a mission statement, goals, objectives, and timetable or action plan. The business plan should include details such as items to be sold, item quantities to be purchased, prices of items, expected expenses by category, and anticipated revenue. Recreation facility managers should try to anticipate and analyze every

© Rhoda Peacher

▶Including a commodity outlet in a recreation facility provides the facility with another means of revenue generation.

aspect of the commodity outlet before opening for business. Situations that should be reflected in a plan include when to offer discounted sales, staff hiring and training, item layout adjustments, merchandise return policy, purchase and delivery timing, inventory system, security measures, and advertising and promotions. Detailed planning can help avoid problems before they occur as well as provide the necessary background to make good decisions.

Commodity Outlet Operations

The delivery responsibilities for a commodity outlet are to prepare and enhance the sale of items to users. Recreation facility managers should be aware of the following principles: merchandising, vendors, pricing, staffing, sales, displays, and enhancement of success.

Merchandising

The core product plays a key role in determining the commodities that can be merchandised to facility users. There should be a complete understanding of the items being sold and customers' needs and interests, as well as some expectation of how the product will be received. For example, selling ice skates, sticks, athletic tape, and other hockey supplies makes sense at an ice arena, whereas selling athletic shoes and apparel may not be well received in the same facility.

Merchandising requires a sincere commitment and enthusiasm from facility managers and employees in bringing the product to customers. Those responsible for purchasing merchandise for resale should remove emotion and personal preferences from their decisions to buy products. Some items do not sell, and an emotional buyer could make a bad decision. Purchasers must also remember that they may not be able to accommodate all customer interests. Accepting that accommodating a small niche is better than trying to offer too many items will lead to fewer unsold items and greater profit for the agency.

Purchasers should take special interest in understanding product lines and how they might appeal to a particular customer base. They should also recognize that men and women have differing purchasing habits regarding styles, types, quality, and price points. As an example, a fitness center may be tempted to purchase and resell a wide variety of nutritional supplements to try to meet

the needs of all members. However, this approach could lead to some products selling and others rarely selling. It's better to tell customers that the facility doesn't carry their preferred item than to have too much inventory of items that don't sell enough to make a profit.

Vendors

Vendors provide a wholesale service to commodity outlets. Maintaining a good working relationship with vendors is a key component to the success of commodity outlets. When considering which vendors to use, recreation facility managers should carefully assess vendor pricing, delivery, financing terms, consignment terms, product availability, and overall service. Ask questions such as the following: Do they provide a display for the product line? Do they advertise locally, regionally, or nationally? The size of a commodity outlet will determine how many vendors are necessary to supply the appropriate merchandise. It may be wise to keep the number of vendors to a minimum to simplify operations.

Pricing

Pricing is critical to the success of a commodity outlet. It simply comes down to whether the user will purchase what is being sold for the designated price and whether the outlet can afford to sell the items for that price and make a profit. There are some things management can do to allow some flexibility in pricing merchandise. As appropriate, the manager of the commodity outlet may offer quantity purchases (large numbers) and special sales (buy one, get one free). These tactics are often used to move items that have not sold well or are outdated.

Commodity outlet operators can also look at the standard in the industry for the sale of comparable items and maintain similar pricing. Different regions, settings, and facilities are able to set prices based on their unique environments. For example, a golf course at a resort in Hawaii is going to be able to charge more for the same piece of logo apparel than a municipal golf facility could charge. Operators should continually evaluate competitors' prices.

Assessing customers' willingness to pay and product popularity will have a significant impact on setting a price for a product. Prices should meet the cost of the operation, which includes the cost of goods to be sold, labor, and any overhead such as utilities, insurance, and equipment, as well as build in a margin of profit. A common pricing strategy employed is to keystone or double the cost of the goods to be sold. Applying the keystone strategy for a golf shirt that costs $20 from the vendor would result in a retail price of $40.

Staffing

All staff should show sincere interest in customers by greeting them in a friendly fashion. They should also be capable of attending to customers in a competent manner and answering questions about the products. Sometimes when a commodity outlet has been operating for awhile, staff enthusiasm wanes, personnel become complacent, and even management loses sight of responsibilities. Facility managers may want to consider scheduling regular training sessions that include techniques for motivating staff to maintain a positive and professional approach to their responsibilities. Staffing is critical to the success of any commodity outlet. Emphasizing training and supervising and evaluating employees is vital because staff members play such an important role in the purchase transaction, satisfaction of the customer, and ultimate success of the commodity outlet.

Sales

The goal of all commodity outlets is to sell or move a product. A variety of methods can be used to accomplish this goal. Even unpopular items, known as *dogs,* need to be moved. Unpopular items often can be moved by creating sales opportunities for customers. Items could be sold at a discount, or a lower price for quantity purchases could be offered. For example, a sleeve of golf balls, with three balls per sleeve, may sell for $10. However, a quantity discount scenario would offer four sleeves of golf balls for $35. This encourages customers to purchase a larger quantity and helps reduce the inventory of a commodity outlet.

Another option for moving difficult products is to offer special payment plans. An example of this option would be to offer a monthly payment plan of $50 per month toward the purchase of a set of golf clubs priced at $600. The $600 price may be too much for potential buyers to pay at once, but $50 per month may allow the buyers to purchase the desired product. All customers like to believe they're getting a good deal when they purchase an item. Being creative with sales and promotions can greatly enhance the success of a commodity outlet while at the same time creating customer satisfaction.

Displays

Most commodity outlets arrange, present, and display their products for two purposes:

1. Displays present opportunities to store items.
2. Displays attract potential customers.

Displays can be set up to create a flow of traffic that contributes to sales. They can also be set up with items that complement the main product of the outlet so that the buyer recognizes the extra item and may choose to make a purchase. This technique can also be applied by displaying impulse items at a cash register or entrance. Examples of impulse items might be athletic socks, sweatbands, and water bottles at a fitness center or golf balls, gloves, and tees at a golf facility. Impulse buys might also include key chains, magnets, or pens at a resort or gift shop. These displays should always be attractive and complement the decor of the facility. Displays should be modified, adjusted, and moved to various places in the outlet to keep the environment from becoming stagnant. Moving displays also generates interest in products that were previously out of the main flow of traffic.

Enhancing Success

Not all items sell as readily as others. Additional options can help customers become aware of what is available and encourage them to make a purchase. All staff associated with a commodity outlet should be knowledgeable about products and able to share information about their benefits. This may include providing demonstrations of the product or offering assistance in any way possible. Some options to entice the customer into making a purchase include gift wrapping, free or discounted shipping, extended warranties, quantity discounts, open houses to feature certain items, liberal return policies, special deliveries, trial uses, and reminders (newsletters or e-mails) of sales or activities associated with the commodity outlet.

It is important to analyze what techniques have previously produced successful results. Repeat what has been effective in the past, anticipate trends that could affect the product, and make adjustments as necessary. For example, tight-fitting athletic shorts for men have been replaced with loose-fitting, long shorts. Moisture-wicking fabrics are currently more popular than standard cotton blends. Knowing what trends are popular is critical to making appropriate purchase decisions and thus enhancing the success of a commodity outlet.

Commodity Outlet Design

A number of design elements are associated with a successful commodity outlet. An architect or consultant who may be part of the design process of a commodity outlet can provide this information. Often, commodity outlets are added to a facility during a renovation project. On these occasions, recreation facility managers may be responsible for making recommendations for the design of the commodity outlet. It is imperative that facility managers be cognizant of design elements in order to enhance the success of this core product extension.

Location

A commodity outlet needs to be located where users of the facility see it and can take advantage of it. This location should be in an area with significant user traffic flow. Successful locations are typically close to reception areas where fees, tickets, or other admission-based fees are collected, such as at entrances to facilities or near spectator areas in stadiums. Making a commodity outlet visible and easily accessible to customers improves the likelihood of success.

Appearance

Another factor that parallels location in terms of importance is the appearance, image, and decor of the commodity outlet. All elements of aesthetics dealing with decorations, wall and floor coverings, paint colors, windows, and lighting should receive attention to enhance comfort of the customer and contribute to product sales. Often customer moods can be affected by appearance. The image of the product and the appearance of the commodity area should be designed carefully with this in mind.

Signage

Commodity outlets can use a variety of internal and external signs to influence sales. Internal signs can communicate a message or help feature a sale. External signs help potential customers become aware of the location of a commodity outlet as well as communicate sale opportunities. External signage should be considered during the design phase. Local codes can affect what size and type of signs are allowed. Both internal and external signage should be attractive, well laid out, and

presented in a fashion that creates a positive impression and draws customers' attention.

Security

Unfortunately, most commodity outlets have to deal with theft of products. Theft can occur both internally by staff and externally by customers. In the design stage of a facility, security should be planned for the commodity outlet in order to observe customers and staff and to help prevent theft while the facility is open or closed. Some security options include mirrors, security doors, motion lights or sensors, monitoring cameras, and alarm systems. Additional options include affixing special sensors to items that must be removed by a salesperson or they will set off an alarm located at the exit. Internal theft can be minimized simply by limiting employee access to keys to certain parts of a facility. In addition, strict and frequent inventorying of products can limit employee theft. Although it is not easy to think about this responsibility, it is a reality and one that should be addressed during and after the design phase of a commodity outlet.

Changing Area

Most commodity outlets include the option of purchasing some type of apparel. An area that is set up for customers to try on apparel should have adequate space, hangers, benches, and mirrors, even if it is incorporated into a restroom. If changing areas are offered, security measures should be implemented. Changing areas present the opportunity for customers' personal items to be stolen and also present the opportunity for customers to steal merchandise. Additional staff may be required to monitor changing areas, particularly in larger retail operations.

Other Design Considerations

Other considerations for commodity outlets include area lighting to enhance certain products. Enhancing customer comfort by controlling the temperature of the commodity outlet encourages customers to stay longer. Providing appropriate seating encourages longer visits by providing nonshopping family members with an option for waiting. Commodity outlets require a higher number and different type of electrical outlets to accommodate displays, special lighting, counters, and other equipment. A commodity outlet is a specialized facility that can become very expensive if not designed and managed properly. It can also be very profitable if the right items are sold at the right price in an environment that encourages customers make the purchase.

FOOD SERVICES

A common core product extension in a facility is food services. Food services can be a demanding responsibility for recreation facility managers. At the same time, they can be a vital part of the overall product delivery and increase user satisfaction by meeting a need.

Food and beverage operations could range from simply selling candy, ice cream, and sodas to a complete restaurant with hostesses, waiters, cooks, a full menu, and a comfortable environment. No matter what type of food service is offered, the operation should be customer-service oriented and be sensitive to health issues and requirements related to this type of service. All food and beverage environments are regulated by local and state laws.

Types of Food Services

Food and beverage outlets can vary in size, length of season, menu, and even mobility, moving from place to place or facility to facility. The most common food and beverage outlets are snack bars, vending machines, cafeterias, full-menu restaurants, and catering.

Snack Bar

A common type of food-service outlet is a **snack bar,** which usually features a limited menu, provides fast service, requires a small staff, and is relatively easy to operate. These operations can be observed at golf courses, stadiums, theaters, resorts, hotels, arenas, public pools, and community recreation centers. They are often called *concession stands* and may include a grill or a small cooking area for short-order items such as hamburgers, hot dogs, or sandwiches. Usually, items are served that require less food handling, such as candy, sodas, popcorn, and ice cream. In some applications, snack bars also sell alcohol, placing greater responsibility on management. Although alcohol sales can produce significant profit margins, they require additional staffing and supervisory measures in addition to creating greater risk for the agency. Agency policies and goals should be carefully considered before offering alcohol at a food-service outlet, and a liquor license will be required.

▶Snack bars or concession areas are common in many recreation facility settings.

Vending Machines

Many facilities may not have enough customer demand, sales volume, or space for a snack bar that would require staff. In this case, vending machines may best serve the needs of the facility. Vending machines allow for certain food, beverage, and specialty items to be offered with no staffing or extended management responsibility. Vending machines can contain a variety of food and drinks. They require little maintenance, create few health concerns, and require minimal security or management attention. Some vending machines can offer nontraditional items such as sandwiches, milk, fruit, and juices that may require additional attention. These types of machines are usually maintained and stocked by the vendor who owns the machine. Vendors typically have a schedule for stocking machines based on purchasing habits at the facility. However, should there be an unforeseen increase in vending machine use, a recreation facility manager can notify the vendor to restock machines prior to the normal schedule. Usually, the gross earnings from the vending machine go to the vendor with a negotiated percentage of the sales being paid back to the recreation agency. Purchasing habits of facility users can be catered to by selecting the products that will appeal to the user base. For example, a fitness center may choose to stock vending machines with nutrition or energy bars, sport drinks, and bottled water.

Cafeteria

A cafeteria is a food-service option that is slightly less involved than a restaurant. This option allows customers to select food and beverages by serving themselves or being served by staff as they go through a line. Such operations generally require the same food preparation as a restaurant. Benefits of cafeterias include no wait staff, a less diverse menu, and patrons serve themselves and clean off their own tables. Facilities where this type of food service can be observed include golf facilities, cruise ships, fitness centers, and community centers.

Full-Menu Restaurant

Some facilities offer a full-menu restaurant as part of their conveniences. Restaurant operations are typically found at hotels, resorts, stadiums, arenas, and country clubs. They require a much greater level of responsibility compared with snack bars and vending machines. Restaurants also require a greater commitment from management in terms of food preparation, quality, and service. Restaurants can be thought of as a separate management unit, particularly at extensive facilities. Careful analysis of the customer base along with specialized knowledge and training should precede any attempt to provide a restaurant operation.

Catering

Many agencies, because of the product, lack of food preparation area, or users they attract, have to make arrangements for food to be brought to the facility and served. This situation may necessitate the use of a **caterer.** Arrangements of this nature require advance planning. Hiring a catering service delegates all food responsibility to an independent operation that is committed by contract to providing food service for the facility. A typical example where a caterer might be used is for a golf tournament or outing at a golf facility. This type of event usually creates demand beyond the ability

of a typical food-service outlet at a golf course due to the number of participants and the need to provide food service within a limited window of time. All details should be discussed in advance, leading to a written agreement or contract. Many decisions should be considered during planning stages, including the users' food and beverage interests, the time of the event, the location of the food-service area, and the number of people to be served. The menu and food quality for such occasions can be diverse. Catering costs can be extremely high, and guarantees for food quality, quantity, timing, and service should be stipulated in the written agreement. Sometimes additional accessories and equipment may be necessary to ensure that all expectations of the catering service are met.

A fundamental consideration when offering food and beverage service at a facility is whether the service can or should be provided in-house or outsourced. Each option has benefits and drawbacks. Generally, the benefits of in-house operation include control of the food and beverage products offered and a higher income potential. Drawbacks include additional staffing and training requirements and more risk associated with preparing and serving food. The benefits of outsourcing include reduced risks, a more experienced and knowledgeable staff, and a guaranteed revenue stream. Drawbacks include lack of control of operational concerns including hours of operation, menu, price, and staff selection and training, and in general, less income from the operation.

External Influences

Food-service outlets are regulated by predetermined codes, standards, and laws, or external influences. Any facility that offers food and beverage service accepts a responsibility that can affect people's health. This is a serious responsibility with far-reaching implications involving people's well-being. Negligence can result in lawsuits that can be extensive and damaging to a management system and its reputation. These standards and codes are provided by OSHA, public health agencies, state liquor agencies, and local ordinances.

Occupational Safety and Health Association

OSHA checks various elements in the food-service industry. It enforces laws that ensure safety of employees, conducting inspections to assure compliance with these laws. It regulates how workers function in preparation and service, as well as the condition of the food-preparation environment. It also observes functions such as storage, cooking procedures, food handling, and employee protection. OSHA can require adjustments to be made, or if a facility is not in compliance, fines can be levied or the facility can be closed.

Public Health Agencies

A public health agency is an extension of the state, federal, or local government that stipulates requirements, provides assistance, and performs inspections for food-service operations. These agencies influence many aspects of food service, including food preparation, food supplies, storage, food temperature, personnel, equipment, sanitation, water, waste removal, restrooms, personal hygiene practices, and insect and pest control. Each state has a publication that outlines this information and any local requirements. Public health agencies also conduct inspections to check the quality of food as it relates to health problems that can result from food consumption.

State Liquor Agencies

State liquor agencies are involved in the licensing required for serving alcohol at a facility. They place limits on the distribution of alcohol at a food-service outlet. State liquor agencies control the minimum age of customers, consumption levels, and server rules and regulations. Significant legal implications can result when a food-service outlet does not follow state liquor agency requirements. Management should carefully consider the pros and cons of offering alcohol products before including this option in a food and beverage operation.

Local Ordinances

Most communities have governing bodies that observe food-service outlets. Local ordinances supersede all other laws and agencies when immediate action is required in the event that food and

▶OSHA conducts periodic inspections of food services establishments to assure that the establishments are in compliance with the laws.

beverage requirements are neglected. Situations and conditions can vary considerably from community to community. It is recommended that recreation facility managers be knowledgeable of local ordinances before opening a food-service operation.

CHILD CARE

Child care is a core product extension created to provide the service of caring for children while adults use or work at a recreation facility. It is planned as an extension of the facility, providing a supplemental service and when possible, additional revenue. It is crucial that parents feel confident that their children will receive proper care. Child care operations often do more than just watch children; they also provide activities that are designed to enhance the children's development and experience.

Child Care Age Levels

The child care industry is extensive. For some, it is a professional career that can be managed within an existing facility or independently delivered as a separate operation. The child's safety and well-being is a primary responsibility that requires attention at all times. Recreation facilities that have this option may be more attractive to parents with young children. Recreation facility managers must realize to what extent a facility may need to provide such a service. When thinking in terms of options for child care, three age levels can be considered: infant, preschool, and school age.

Infant

Infant care provides care for children between the ages of birth and 3 years of age. This is a challenging age for child care staff. Parents are concerned about leaving infants in the care of others. Also, the ratio of staff assigned per child may be regulated by local ordinances. It is critical that management be meticulous in fulfilling the various child care requirements and responsibilities. Each infant's schedule and care should be designed on an individual basis. Care of this nature is usually provided for a large portion of the day and can be demanding work requiring strict regulations and caution for the child's health and safety at all times.

Preschool

A preschool operation provides care for children from 3 to 5 years of age. These operations can

© Digital Vision

▶Childcare at recreation facilities is a supplemental service for both users and employees that could provide additional revenue.

be observed in public and private organizations where there is a need to extend services to employees and users of the facility. This type of operation usually parallels the daily schedule and annual calendar of the local schools. Similar to infant care, there are many rules and regulations that must be complied with (available from the DCFS), not to mention public impression if the preschool is not run properly and according to guidelines.

School Age

School-age care centers are typically for children and early adolescents from 6 to 14 years of age, providing after-school care. Child supervision is important to understand because staff-to-child ratios increase due to children having greater flexibility and opportunity to participate in programs offered. For this age level, managers should focus on providing recreational and educational activities that are designed to stimulate the children's physical, mental, social, and emotional growth. This focus should include providing quality supervision, nutrition, and programs in a safe environment. Attention should be paid to making arrangement for parents' drop-off and pickup areas and children's activity areas. School-age child care should be directly related to local grade school schedules. DCFS rules and regulations are in place for licensed school-age child care as well.

Child Care Functions

Although the types of child care operations may differ, there are some common operations that apply to all situations. These operations may vary within the technique and methods depending on the ages of the children. When possible, parents should have the opportunity to be informed of operational practices through observation and conferences.

Health

The most important production area in child care operations is the children's health and well-being. No matter what the age or activity level, a child's physical and emotional health is the top priority. Operational policy should direct staff to wash their hands and environment surfaces frequently. This policy is even more critical if diaper changing is involved. Every effort should be made to avoid the risk of infection that could result from activities or environmental conditions. Staff should disinfect toilets or potty chairs after each use to avoid spreading germs. Where snacks or meals are provided, attention should be paid to the cleanliness of the preparation, storage, serving, and eating areas. Depending on the age, some children should have naps. Quiet times, including listening to stories, can be included during rest breaks to provide a settling time for active children. Management must be fully aware of local and state health requirements and should be prepared for an inspection from health agencies.

Education

Another key function of child care is providing educational programs to help children develop their intellectual capacities. Fundamental to learning is creating meaningfulness about information and a sense of comfort. This can be accomplished by the staff showing care, patience, and understanding for each child's individual differences. For example, depending on the age of the children, staff members can read stories to help them learn to read in addition to influencing their appreciation of the importance of reading.

Playing games can help children learn to think spontaneously and creatively. Because of the unique developmental nature of children, they can learn motor skills, discipline, and other skills through low-level sport or creative play. Child care centers can also provide a setting that allows children freedom to explore their surroundings and interact in informal social situations. Even watching educational television programs, if properly monitored, can expand the minds of children by exposing them to unique places, concepts, and experiences. Parents place a high priority on their children's ability to learn new things. Child care operations that provide this opportunity can create and maintain parental support.

Recreation

Recreation activities, offered for fun and entertainment, also emphasize the learning component of child care. Children like to be active and they should have the freedom to express themselves through recreational activities. These activities may include noncompetitive sports, cultural activities such as music and dance, or simply playing in an open area where they explore and interact with one another. Quiet play, such as reading books, exploring arts and crafts, and playing with toys, can also be important recreational activities. Recreation and education programs can help to keep children meaningfully engaged in physically and intellectually stimulating activities.

Coordination

All of the previously mentioned functions of child care should be coordinated in an efficient and effective fashion. Coordination influences the positive or negative experience of children and their parents' perceptions. Haphazard scheduling not only creates control problems, but it can also be counterproductive to the growth and development of children. Functions should be coordinated into a meaningful schedule to provide the best experience possible for children and to reflect positively on the facility.

Safety

No matter what kind of child care is being delivered, management should be concerned for children's safety. Every precaution should be taken to avoid injuries. All space, equipment, access areas, and activity areas should be constantly monitored to ensure that hazardous situations do not develop. Staff should know the location of all children at all times. If an injury does occur, first aid supplies should be available along with emergency telephone numbers and parental con-

▸Recreation activities allow children to be active, express themselves, and learn how to get along with other children.

tact information. All electrical sockets should be checked for appropriate covers so that children cannot insert fingers, pencils, pens, paper clips, and other objects. Safety cannot be overstated and represents the greatest responsibility for caregivers.

Security

When parents leave their child in a child care environment, they expect every precaution to be taken for their child's security and well-being. Appropriate fences should be in place in the outdoor activity areas so that children are not able to leave the premises. Although the technology is expensive, some child care centers may have surveillance cameras connected to a monitoring system so that parents or staff members are able to observe the children either from home or at the site. Access control could be important depending on the location of the center. Unauthorized people should not be allowed access to the premises. A strict sign-in and sign-out policy should be implemented to monitor who is allowed to enter a facility and who is allowed to take children out of the facility. Emergency lighting should be in place

in the event of an electrical outage, along with appropriate fire prevention equipment, alarms, and properly functioning exits. Emergency exit and severe weather plans should be in place and practiced regularly.

Child Care Operations

In the delivery of a child care operation, certain functions relating to general management should be understood and appreciated. Parents want to know that the child care service is suitable and that their child is in attentive hands at all times. Recreation facility managers should be concerned with the child care delivery functions of staffing, training, and policies.

Staffing

The child care industry uses the term caregivers for people who provide this type of service. They are considered a substitute for and representative of parents. Management should make sure that staff are educated and have the skills and knowledge required. Depending on the children and the center, caregivers can vary in age. Management

▶Proper safety precautions, such as utilizing a strict sign-in and sign-out system for monitoring who can check out children from the area, should prevent unauthorized personnel from accessing a childcare area.

must be aware of caregivers' ages and experiences and assign responsibilities to staff accordingly. Training is a crucial component for all staff at a child care operation. Supervising staff should know basic concepts about child development and information about age-level needs. An appropriate number of caregivers, as dictated by state departments of children and family services, should be on duty to observe and control activities at all times. Staff should have an aptitude for working with children, knowing that children will not always be obedient and will often challenge their patience. Staff should be certified in CPR and first aid because a quick and appropriate response to emergencies is crucial. All staff should be personable and have the ability to communicate well with children and their parents.

Training

Recreation facility managers should pay attention to the training of both child care administrators and hourly wage caregivers. The employee selection process should focus on applicants' experience, credentials, interest, and commitment to the concept of child care. In addition, before an employee is hired, reference and background checks should be conducted. Training should be provided that includes developmentally appropriate activities for children, activity limitations, rest requirements, special arrangements related to mental or physical health, nutrition, facilities and equipment, hygiene, maintenance, and food service. All caregivers should have job descriptions that outline their specific responsibilities. Where necessary, training should be completed to verify that the staff is prepared to handle unique problems that might occur.

Policies

Statements that direct staff and the operations of a child care operation are called *policies*. Policies help staff properly run the center and let parents know appropriate information. Recreation facility administrators should establish policies that incorporate the following:

- **Fees**—How much will the center cost to operate? How much will be charged per participant? Are there special fees for certain services? What can parents expect for their fee?

- **Food**—Will food be served? What kind of food? What procedures will be followed in food service?
- **Hours**—What hours will the center be open? Are those hours flexible? Is early and late pickup available? Is the facility open during holidays? Can parents make vacation and holiday arrangements?
- **Emergency**—Who should be contacted in case of an emergency? What are the emergency procedures?
- **Infant supplies**—Will the caregiver or the parents provide infant supplies and other necessities required for an infant? Do certain children require special supplies for their stay?
- **Nap**—Will children have the opportunity to nap during the day? What conditions will be available for napping? Will parents need provide a blanket and pillow for napping, or will these be provided?
- **Discipline**—How will the child be disciplined? How will parents be notified in the case of a behavioral problem?
- **Spare clothing**—Will parents need to leave spare clothing in the event that additional clothing is necessary?
- **Medical**—Are there medical conditions, such as allergies or illnesses, that staff should be aware of? What permission do staff members have regarding medical treatment? What doctor should be called in the event of a problem? What is the protocol for dispensing medication?

Regulations

Regulations for child care operations vary from state to state. These regulations can include the following:

- One staff person must be present for every five children.
- Only a certain number of children are allowed per room.
- No more than two children under 30 months of age are allowed per caregiver.

Group size in child care centers can be regulated because the smaller the group, the better

the care and control. Some safety codes that affect child care operations include fire emergency procedures, food presentation and consumption, lighting levels, equipment, and use of chemicals. Some regulations also affect the size of certain areas, including restrooms, play areas, and fence heights and types. These regulations should be understood and enforced by management and should be included in any training of administrative staff.

Insurance

Recreation facility managers should be aware of the liability associated with child care. Facilities usually do not operate under the premise that they are going to be sued, but unfortunately that potential exists, especially when taking care of children. Child care providers are liable and can be sued by parents if the parents feel the caregivers were negligent or failed to exercise reasonable care and an accident, injury, or even death resulted. An insurance company should be found to help the facility maintain appropriate liability, accident, and property insurance.

Maintenance

The maintenance of a child care operation requires greater emphasis than facilities where only adults are involved. All facilities should be kept clean and functioning properly, but child care facilities even more so, especially for infants. Every effort to keep all toys, equipment, and surfaces as hygienic as possible should be exerted. A regular cleaning schedule should be established, disinfectant should be used, and all repairs that would pose safety concerns should be taken care of as soon as possible. Equipment, locks, sprinkler systems, exits, and security equipment should be inspected routinely. Debris, water, and snow should be removed as soon as possible to prevent children and parents from slipping, tripping, and falling.

Cost

The cost of providing a child care operation will vary by facility. Some recreation facilities may subsidize the cost of the operation, which may entice users. Where possible, child care should be inexpensive because it is a service needed at a time for families when income may present challenges to affording child care at a recreation facility. Parents are more often likely to pay for a child care service that is monitored by state regulations; however, unregulated or private individual operations can cost less. The cost of a child care operation is often similar to the cost of other facility programs. A more extensive recreation facility will likely have a more involved and expensive child care service. Child care should receive special review in determining fees for the services provided. Wherever possible, parents' ability to pay should be considered, and if possible, scholarships or payment arrangements should be made to accommodate special circumstances.

Child Care Design

Similar to other core product extensions, child care center have unique design requirements. Attention should be directed toward design, appearance, functionality, and maintenance needs that are important to daily operations.

The location of a child care center should always provide access for parents with appropriate control of all entrances and exits. The location should be visible and provide easy access for par-

ents to pick up and drop off their children. There should be minimum pedestrian traffic so that children are safe from potential problems created by outsiders. Sensitivity to such problems should be heightened depending on the crime rate and other factors related to the location.

The dimensions of a child care facility must be planned for in a recreation facility. The general guideline is 35 square feet (3.25 square meters) of activity space per child. In some situations, size and space can determine whether a child care operation can attain DCFS licensing. This can affect the existence and success of a child care center. The design should accommodate the number of children in the facility at any one time. Extra space should be designed for isolating children with behavior or health concerns. Large areas can be a nuisance, create noise problems, and be difficult to staff when trying to meet a proper ratio of children to staff. When space is too large, it can lead to reduced attention span on the part of children and increased supervisory personnel. Areas that

© Jim West

▶Indoor play areas should be designed to stimulate children's creativity and encourage creative play and social opportunities.

are too small with a high density of children can be associated with aggression and a decrease in satisfactory solitary time for children. Production space size is a key component of a child care operation. Ideally, size parameters are considered in the design stage of a facility.

Because of the nature of a child care operation, administrative space sometimes is limited and can be integrated into the general production space of the facility. Wherever possible, an administrative area should be separated with easy access to the child care area and adequate space for work and conferences with parents. Ideally, there should be space for an assistant, office equipment, and a lobby and reception area. Sometimes recreation facility administrators could be directly involved in the delivery of programs or activities. Administrative space should have appropriate viewing capacity and access to child care operational space.

Indoor Play Area

Many auxiliary child care areas are primarily indoor play areas. This is often the case if they are associated with recreation centers, resorts, or private fitness facilities. Indoor play areas should be designed to help children remain occupied and to encourage creative play and social opportunities. Recreation facility managers should determine the number of children that may be in this area at any one time, leading to an appropriate amount of space. The area should be large enough so that children can run and play without congestion or interfering with children involved in other activities or trying to take a nap. The indoor play area should also receive design attention for children who need to be alone, especially if they are experiencing stress, discomfort, or behavior problems. This area should be configured in such a way that it can be supervised with as little intrusion as possible. All equipment and furniture in the indoor play area should be arranged so as to avoid potential injuries or accidents.

Outdoor Play Area

Most states require that children play outdoors for a certain number of hours per week. An outdoor play area should have a fence surrounding it so that outsiders' access is limited and children cannot leave the area on their own. The layout should allow staff to observe the entire play area from a central location.

Depending on the age of the children, the outdoor area should be large enough that they can participate in different activities. The surface should be object free and act as a cushion for falls. The three most common playground surfaces are sand, bark mulch, and poured-in-place rubber. Because of weather elements and possible deterioration, equipment should be monitored for any developments that could cause injury. The outdoor play area should be located away from driveways, roads, and any other hazardous conditions. See chapter 16 for more information on how to develop and design a playground area, as well as the surfaces required for outdoor playground areas.

Kitchen and Cafeteria

The design of a kitchen area in a child care center will depend on the type of facility it is in, as well as the length of stay for the children. The kitchen should be centralized for easy access and distribution of food. It could include the potential for on-site food preparation as well as food delivery. There should be adequate tables and chairs for children to eat at. Ideally, kitchen areas include the following: receiving area, food storage, cooking area, cleanup area, equipment storage, refrigeration, and separate waste storage and removal area. The kitchen area must adhere to health codes, laws, and standards discussed in the previous section on food-service regulations.

Restrooms

Child care centers need two separate restrooms, one for adults and one for children. The children's restroom should have lower fixtures and include a changing area for infants. Lights should always be on during operational hours, and light switches should be out of the reach of children. Restroom areas should be frequently inspected for cleanliness, restocking of supplies, and the general safety of children.

Storage

Most child care centers are designed with inadequate storage space. This is unfortunate because storage is needed for administrative purposes, play equipment, and other objects. Equipment that is improperly stored can create a hazard. Adequate storage allows for items to be put away out of the reach of children. Additional storage is needed for children's backpacks and personal belongings. Often, specially designed cubicles are installed to create storage space for these and other items.

EQUIPMENT CHECKOUT OR RENTAL

Many recreation facilities offer equipment rental or equipment checkout as a core product extension. Equipment checkout or rental systems must ensure that the equipment goes out and is returned properly. Equipment distribution operations can be costly if poorly managed with no systems in place to monitor distribution.

One option for equipment distribution is a simple checkout system for facility users with a requirement to return the equipment after use. The other is a more involved approach where equipment is rented with certain rules and regulations that state what is expected. Both systems require managers to apply fundamental policies and procedures.

Equipment Checkout or Rental Operations

A thorough system that controls the equipment exchange is essential whether a facility maintains a checkout or rental system for distributing equipment. The nature of the facility and the equipment to be distributed usually dictates the system. Some facilities exist solely for the purpose of distributing equipment. For example, the primary purpose of a dive shop may be renting scuba gear to potential customers. Other facilities, such as golf courses, have rental clubs, range balls, and golf carts that are directly related to the core product. Some basic points that could be incorporated in an equipment checkout or rental operation include exchange, policies and procedures, waivers, insurance, and tracking.

Exchange

Any equipment checkout or rental area creates an exchange between the equipment owner (the facility) and the customer. This exchange requires an understanding of the expectations between the owner and the customer. Often, a form is completed that provides pertinent information such as name, address, telephone number, signature to verify understanding of return policy, deposit, and equipment condition. The form could include a statement of understanding that explains the con-

▶Equipment checkout and rental areas should be located in a highly visible area of a facility where users have easy access to their equipment needs.

sequences of equipment damage, breakage, use, or theft. Often the customer must provide proof of identification, such as a facility identification card, picture identification card, driver's license, or credit card.

Policies and Procedures

Sometimes equipment operations need formal policies and procedures to help manage equipment distribution.

- Where rental fees are involved, the prices for using equipment need to be established, printed, and posted.
- It may be necessary to establish time stipulations regarding
  - length of time between when a request is received and responded to by the agency,
  - length of time equipment can be out,
  - deadlines for returning the equipment, or
  - user requirements or any experience required before use.

Written policies often include a statement of consequences for equipment that is lost, stolen, or damaged. A policy statement should also stipulate any penalties for late returns of equipment. Additionally, a policy statement may be required to establish a priority system when equipment is in high demand. A common priority system provides access to equipment on a first come, first served basis. Other priority systems may restrict equipment use to certain classifications such as adults only or facility members only.

Some equipment may require previous user experience. A policy could require proof of experience through certification, license, letters of reference, or similar documentation. This is a common requirement in the car rental business. In the recreational setting, scuba equipment rental often includes the requirement of previous licensing or experience. Sometimes the distribution of equipment could require identification before the exchange, such as showing a membership card, verifying age, or providing other pertinent information. Fundamental to any distribution system is posting all policies and procedures for potential users to read before an exchange. Often these policies and procedures are outlined in a signed waiver.

© Janet Horton

▸It is common for recreation facilities to post policies and procedures for renting or checking out equipment.

Waiver

Some equipment inherently holds the potential for injury. In these cases there may need to be an identifiable means of communicating that risk. Immature or inexperienced users should be advised of the hazards that could be associated with the use of the equipment. This is usually accomplished through a written statement (liability waiver) that expresses the dangers involved. A waiver must be read and signed by users indicating that they recognize the risk they are accepting. Waivers do not relinquish the responsibility of the facility. They do reflect the intent to care for user safety while also informing users of potential risk. Risk levels can vary depending on the type of equipment that is being distributed. Generally, potential for injury is minimal and any harm is usually a result of improper equipment usage.

Insurance

Some equipment exchanges could require users to provide proof of insurance that covers potential injury and damage to the equipment. This situation usually exists with expensive equipment that requires certain control and demonstrated ability. Sometimes insurance is included in the usage, rental, or deposit fee that is charged for the equipment. All equipment presents some risks of injury that could have negative implications for management. Insurance needs should be evaluated and appropriate coverage obtained based on the specific risks posed by whatever equipment is exchanged.

Tracking

An inventory system should identify available equipment for distribution as well as the status of equipment that has been rented or checked out. An inventory system should identify what equipment is available, what has been checked out, when it was checked out, what condition it was when it was checked out, and when it will be returned. User information, including name, address, and phone numbers, should also be recorded and maintained. Computer software can be helpful with both inventorying and monitoring equipment. It is important to have a system that accounts for all equipment in order to minimize lost, missing, or stolen equipment.

Equipment Checkout and Rental Design

A major issue to consider with an equipment area is its location in the overall recreation facility. Users should automatically be aware of and have easy access to the equipment area. An equipment area should be located where the flow or circulation of facility users through a facility creates traffic to the area.

In addition to location, the size of the equipment checkout and rental area is important. This area should always have ample space to fulfill its functions as well as provide for the comfort of employees assigned to the area. Far too often,

©Human Kinetics/Les Woodrum

▶Adequate equipment storage areas are critical for securing, protecting, and accessing equipment to be rented or checked out to the users.

equipment areas are too small to meet equipment distribution needs. However, a more common problem is providing adequate space for the storage of equipment.

A variety of methods can be used to assist with equipment storage, including cabinets, shelving, bins, racks, and hanging devices. Some equipment may require humidity and temperature control to protect it from deterioration. A well-thought-out and accessible storage area facilitates efficient distribution of equipment. Providing easy access to equipment can contribute greatly to getting the equipment to users in a timely fashion.

Some facilities may need to consider laundry of items such as towels or uniforms in relation to equipment checkout and rentals. This can be a service and a convenience to users, eliminating the need to bring towels. Facilities may even provide cleaning services for personal clothing. Obviously this function requires advance planning and will be contingent on available funds and the type of facility services expected by customers.

SUMMARY

Core product extensions not only support the core product, they can also be additional sources of revenue. Commodity outlets, food services, child care, and equipment checkout areas have unique design requirements as well as functions and operations that must be considered in planning the design of a recreation facility.

Appendix A: Associations and Accredited Academic Programs

The appendix contains a list of associations and certified academic programs to use as resources in your daily routine as well as for hiring students graduating from certified academic programs.

ASSOCIATIONS

American Alliance for Health, Physical Education, Recreation and Dance (AAHPERD)

American Camping Association (ACA)

American Mountain Guides Association (AMGA)

American Therapeutic Recreation Association (ATRA)

Association for Experiential Education (AEE)

Association of Outdoor Recreation and Education (AORE)

Canadian Parks and Recreation Association (CPRA)

Canadian Therapeutic Recreation Association (CTRA)

Centers for Disease Control and Prevention (CDC)

Climbing Wall Association (CWA)

Consumer Product Safety Commission (CPSC)

Environmental Protection Agency (EPA)

International Association of Assembly Managers (IAAM)

International Association of Convention and Visitor Bureaus (IACVB)

International Council on Hotel, Restaurant, and Institutional Education (CHRIE)

International Festivals and Events Association (IFEA)

International Special Event Society (ISES)

Leadership in Energy and Environmental Design (LEED)

National Association for Interpretation (NAI)

National Association of State Park Directors (NASPD)

National Collegiate Athletic Association (NCAA)

National Council for Therapeutic Recreation Certification (NCTRC)

National Education Association (NEA)

National Intramural-Recreational Sports Association (NIRSA)

National Park Service (NPS)

National Recreation and Park Association (NRPA)

National Sanitation Foundation (NSF) International

National Society for Experiential Education (NSEE)

North American Society for Sport Management (NASSM)

Occupational Safety and Health Administration (OSHA)

Outdoor Industry Association (OIA)

Professional Convention Management Association (PCMA)

Resort and Commercial Recreation Association (RCRA)

Society for Accessible Travel and Hospitality (SATH)

Student Conservation Association (SCA)

United States Green Building Council (USGBC)

Wilderness Education Association (WEA)

World Leisure and Recreation Association (WLRA)

World Tourism Organization (WTO)

World Travel and Tourism Council (WTTC)

ACCREDITED ACADEMIC PROGRAMS

Arkansas

Arkansas Tech University Department of Parks, Recreation and Hospitality Administration

Arizona

Arizona State University School of Community Resources and Development

Arizona State University West Department of Recreation and Tourism Management Northern Arizona University Parks and Recreation Management Program

California

California Polytechnic State University at San Luis Obispo Recreation Administration Program, Natural Resources Management Department California State University at Chico Department of Recreation and Parks Management

California State University at Fresno Recreation Administration and Leisure Studies

California State University at Long Beach Department of Recreation and Leisure Studies California State University at Sacramento Department of Recreation and Leisure Studies

San Diego State University Department of Recreation San Francisco State University Department of Recreation and Leisure Studies

San Jose State University Department of Recreation and Leisure Studies

Colorado

Metropolitan State College of Denver Department of Health Professions

Florida

Florida International University Park and Recreation Management Curriculum, HPER Florida State University Recreation and Leisure Studies Program University of Florida Department of Tourism, Recreation and Sport Management

Georgia Georgia Southern University Department of Recreation and Sport Management University of Georgia Department of Counseling and Human Development Services

Idaho

University of Idaho College of Education, Recreation Program Unit, Division of HPERD

Illinois

Aurora University School of Experiential Leadership and Recreation Administration

Chicago State University Recreation Program Eastern Illinois University Department of Recreation Administration Illinois State University Recreation and Park Administration Program

Southern Illinois University Department of Health Education and Recreation

University of Illinois Department of Recreation, Sport and Tourism

University of St. Francis Recreation Administration Department

Western Illinois University Department of Recreation, Park, and Tourism Administration

Indiana

Indiana State University Department of Recreation and Sport Management

Indiana University Department of Recreation, Park, and Tourism Studies

Iowa

University of Northern Iowa Health, Physical Education and Leisure Services

Kansas

Kansas State University Recreation Resources Division, Department of Horticulture, Forestry and Recreation Resources Pittsburg State University Department of Health, Physical Education and Recreation

Kentucky

Eastern Kentucky University Department of Recreation and Park Administration Western Kentucky University Recreation and Park Administration Curriculum

Louisiana

Grambling State University Recreation Careers Program, Department of HPELS

Maine

University of Maine at Machias Program in Recreation Management, Division of Professional Studies

Maryland

Frostburg State University Recreation Program, HPER

Massachusetts

Springfield College Department of Sport Management and Recreation

Michigan

Central Michigan University Department of Recreation, Parks and Leisure Services Ferris State University Recreation Leadership and Management Program

Minnesota

Minnesota State University at Mankato Department of Recreation, Parks and Leisure Services

Mississippi

University of Mississippi Department of Exercise Science and Leisure Management University of Southern Mississippi Recreation Program, School of Human Performance and Recreation

Missouri

Southeast Missouri State University Recreation Program, Department of Health and Leisure Missouri State University Recreation and Leisure Studies, HPER Department University of Missouri Department of Parks, Recreation and Tourism

Montana

University of Montana Recreation Management Program

New Hampshire

University of New Hampshire Department of Recreation Management and Policy

New York

Ithaca College Department of Recreation and Leisure Studies State University of New York at Brockport Recreation and Leisure Studies Department

State University of New York at Cortland Department of Recreation and Leisure Studies

North Carolina

Appalachian State University Department of Health, Leisure, and Exercise Science East Carolina University Recreation and Leisure Studies Department

North Carolina Central University Parks and Recreation Management Department PER North Carolina State University Department of Parks, Recreation and Tourism Management

University of North Carolina at Greensboro Department of Recreation, Parks, and Tourism

University of North Carolina at Wilmington Parks and Recreation Management, Department of HPER

Winston-Salem State University Recreation Program

Ohio

Bowling Green State University Sport Management, Recreation and Tourism Division, HPER Kent State University Leisure Studies Program, School of Exercise, Leisure and Sport Ohio University Recreation Studies Program, School Recreation and Sport Science University of Toledo Division of Recreation and Leisure Studies

Oklahoma

Oklahoma State University Program in Leisure Studies, School of AHEP

Pennsylvania

California University of Pennsylvania Earth Sciences Department

East Stroudsburg University Department of Recreation and Leisure Services Management Lock Haven University Department of Recreation and Park Administration

Slippery Rock University Department of Parks and Recreation and Environmental Education

Temple University Sport and Recreation Management

York College Recreation and Leisure Administration Program

South Carolina

Benedict College Recreation and Leisure Services Program

Tennessee

Middle Tennessee State University Program in Recreation, Department of HPER University of Tennessee at Knoxville Recreation and Tourism Management Department

Texas

Texas State University at San Marcos Recreation Administration Division, Department of HPER Texas A&M University Department of Recreation, Park and Tourism Sciences

University of North Texas Recreation and Leisure Studies, Department of KHPR

Utah

Brigham Young University Department of Recreation Management and Youth Leadership

University of Utah Department of Parks, Recreation and Tourism

Utah State University Parks and Recreation Program, Department of HPER

Vermont

Green Mountain College Department of Recreation and Leisure Studies

Virginia

George Mason University Department of Health, Fitness and Recreation Resources

Longwood University Therapeutic Recreation Program

Old Dominion University Recreation and Tourism Studies Program

Radford University Department of Recreation, Parks and Tourism

Virginia Wesleyan College Recreation and Leisure Studies Program

Washington

Eastern Washington University Program in Recreation and Leisure Services

Western Washington University Recreation Program, PEHR Department

Washington, D.C.

Gallaudet University Recreation and Leisure Studies, PER Department

Appendix B:
Accreditation Standards and Certified Park and Recreation Professional Study Guide Criteria

This book addresses several accreditation standards for the Council on Accreditation (COA) and the Commission for Accreditation of Park and Recreation Agencies (CAPRA). Many components of the Operations Management section of the Certified Park and Recreation Professional (CPRP) certification exam are also covered. Following are the standards and content areas addressed in this book:

STANDARDS FOR PROGRAMS IN RECREATION, PARK RESOURCES, AND LEISURE SERVICES

The NRPA Council on Accreditation for Recreation, Park Resources, and Leisure Services Education is sponsored by the National Recreation and Park Association (NRPA). The NRPA Council on Accreditation has established professional competencies for all students. The standards listed are addressed in the chapters.

Standard 7.04 addresses the ability of graduates to stage experiences for guests, recreationists, visitors, or clients. It consists of three substandards:

7.04.01 Students graduating from the program shall demonstrate the ability to design experiences clearly reflecting application of knowledge from relevant facets of contemporary professional practice, science, and philosophy. **Suggested evidence of compliance:** Student portfolios containing examples of planning and design (e.g.,

needs assessment, program plan, treatment plan, or interpretive master plan).

7.04.02 Students graduating from the program shall demonstrate the ability to facilitate recreation and leisure experiences among diverse clientele, settings, cultures, and contexts. **Suggested evidence of compliance:** Evidence of facilitating participation with a minimum of four different populations (clientele), contexts, or settings, at least one of which specifically addresses personal and cultural dimensions of diversity (e.g., age, ethnicity, gender, religion, and physical and mental challenges). Settings might include a resort, national park, wilderness area, community center, stadium, park, or hospital. Contexts may vary from individual to group, family to intergenerational, and single to multifaceted venues.

7.04.03 Students graduating from the program shall demonstrate the ability to evaluate service and experience offerings and to use evaluation data to improve the quality of offerings. **Suggested evidence of compliance:** Student portfolios containing examples of evaluations and how the information was used for improvement

Standard 7.05 addresses students' ability to manage recreation, park resources, leisure services, and other organizations in the experience industry.

7.05.01 Students graduating from the program shall be able to recognize basic facts, concepts, principles, and procedures of management or administration, infrastructure management, financial and human resource management, and marketing or public relations. **Suggested evidence of compliance:** Results of departmental or professional examinations (e.g., CTRS [NCTRC] exam, CPRP [NCB] exam).

7.05.02 Students graduating from the program shall be able to apply entry-level concepts, principles, and procedures of management or administration, infrastructure management, financial and human resource management, and marketing or public relations to a specific setting. **Suggested evidence of compliance:** Internship supervisor evaluations of management skills or student portfolios containing examples (e.g., budget, marketing plan and products, employee manual, tax plans).

Adapted, by permission, from National Recreation and Park Association, 2008, *Council on accreditation: Outcome standards and assessment* (Ashburn, PA: Author).

COMMISSION FOR ACCREDITATION OF PARK AND RECREATION AGENCIES STANDARDS

Charged with providing high-quality recreation services and experiences, an increasing number of park and recreation agencies are applying for the Agency Accreditation Program through the Commission for Accreditation of Park and Recreation Agencies (CAPRA).

CAPRA administers a rigorous program based on a self-assessment and peer review using national standards of best practice to promote the quality of agency services and delivery systems.

Agency accreditation is available to all entities administering park and recreation systems, including municipalities, townships, counties, special districts and regional authorities, and government and school councils.

Agency accreditation is voluntary but an essential piece to producing good environments for communities to play, live, and grow.

2.0 Planning

2.2 Community Planning

2.2.1 Personnel Part of Community Planning Team

2.2.2 Involvement in Community Planning Groups

2.2.3 Community Planning Agencies

2.4.2 Resource Management and Land Use Planning

2.4.2.1 Feasibility Studies

2.4.2.2 Master Site Plan

2.4.2.3 Resource Management Plan

2.4.2.4 Competent Planning Personnel

2.4.2.5 Citizen Involvement

2.4.2.6 Phased Development

7.0 Facility and Land Use Management

7.1 Acquisition of Park and Recreation Lands

7.2 Development of Lands

7.5 Maintenance and Operations Management

7.6 Facilities Management

7.6.1 Legal Requirements

7.6.2 Building Security Plans

7.6.3 Preventive Maintenance

7.8 Agency-Owned Equipment and Property

7.9 Natural Resource Management

7.10 Maintenance Personnel Assignment

Adapted, by permission, from National Recreation and Park Association, 2007, *NRPA certified park and recreation professional examination candidate handbook* (Ashburn, PA: Author).

CONTENT AREAS OF CERTIFIED PARK AND RECREATION PROFESSIONAL CERTIFICATION EXAM

The exam is one of the principal requirements as a certified park and recreation professional (CPRP). It assesses the base knowledge of job-related tasks common to entry-level professionals. The exam is administered under the auspices of the NRPA and the National Certification Board (NCB). A national job analysis was conducted in 1989, and again in 1999 and 2006, to identify the core components of the leisure service profession. The NCB-appointed Job Analysis Advisory Committee conducted the study, which culminated in the test specifications. The test content outline serves as the blueprint for constructing the examination. There are three core components of the examination: general administration, programming, and operations management. The detailed test specifications for the operations management component are included in this publication. For the most recent criteria, visit www.nrpa.org. For more information about becoming certified for the examination, contact the NRPA at 800-626-6772 or www.nrpa.org.

A. Planning and Management

1. Conduct needs assessment for resource development.
2. Maintain inventory of organization's assets.
3. Provide input for capital improvements programs.
4. Inspect sites for hazardous materials and conditions.
5. Assess infrastructure (e.g., utilities, parking, flood plain).
6. Review site plans.
7. Comply with physical accessibility requirements.
8. Adapt equipment and facilities for use by people with disabilities.
9. Provide input for an emergency action plan.
10. Provide input for a general security and safety plan.

B. Maintenance Management

1. Implement maintenance standards.
2. Develop maintenance procedures.
3. Develop handling procedures for hazardous materials.
4. Maintain records on equipment use.
5. Implement energy-efficient procedures.
6. Ensure compliance with state and federal regulations.
7. Conduct scheduled inspections of facilities and equipment.
8. Supervise preventive maintenance program.
9. Initiate repair and replacement of facilities or equipment.
10. Supervise routine maintenance operations (e.g., areas, facilities, landscapes, and equipment).
11. Monitor construction, renovation, and repairs (minor projects).

C. Facility Operations

1. Implement procedures for opening and closing facilities.
2. Provide direct supervision of specific facility or area.
3. Manage security procedures.
4. Conduct security and safety inspections.
5. Manage retail sales and rentals.
6. Implement an emergency action plan.
7. Implement a general security and safety plan.

Adapted, by permission, from National Recreation and Park Association, 2001, *The self-assessment manual for quality operation of park and recreation agencies,* 3rd ed. (Ashburn, PA: Author).

Glossary

adequate use zones—areas beneath a structure that should have a surface that provides fall protection

access control—A concept in security in which appropriate steps to influence who and what can enter an area or a facility are enacted.

accessibility—The ability of all participants to access and use facilities.

accounting—The documentation of incomes and expenditures associated with operating a facility.

acoustics—The science of sound and its impact within an area or room environment.

administrative equipment—Equipment that supports the administrative and executive operation of the facility.

administrative functions—The ultimate executive system that influences the desired results or outcome of an organization; includes planning, organizing, directing, and controlling.

ancillary space—Areas in a facility that support the core product.

aquatic facilities—facilities where the core product revolves around aquatics

aquatic parks—aquatic facilities with features such as water slides, wave attractions, spray features, slow-moving water attractions (for example, a lazy river), toddler play areas, and shallow entries.

area impact—The effect the area will have on a facility as well as the effect a facility will have on the area.

assessment—Used in determining the need for a facility and is critical in influencing a facility's construction. A variety of methods can be used in assessing the need for a facility development project ranging from very informal to very formal.

assessment fee—fees collected for a short duration by members, customers, or patrons for an improvement to a facility.

asset management—The concept of documenting the age and predicted life span of various facility components.

assignable square footage (ASF)—The total number of usable square feet that can be occupied or assigned for actual use or space that is required for delivering the core product and core product extensions.

assumption of risk—assuming of any risk that may be involved in a facility or activity

attractive nuisance—A condition that exists when a product or service that is not currently open or available is considered inviting or attractive to a potential user.

auxiliary space—space in a facility where ancillary spaces and core product extensions are delivered

back washing—A process used in an aquatic facility that involves putting the pump on in reverse to stir up the sand in the filter and get the buildup out of the system.

being green—Term that is commonly used in describing ways that a facility can be more efficient and lessen its impact on the environment.

bond—a method of raising funds for public facilities involving the selling of bonds to be paid back by the recreation agency at a later time

bond issue—A method of raising funds for public facilities. It is often the primary source of funds for local or state capital construction projects. The process incorporates the issue of tax-exempt bonds for the general public to buy with a return of the principal amount plus interest after a certain time or investment period.

bottom line—A result that shows a net profit.

budgeting—A systematic effort to project all income and expenses for a given period.

building maintenance—The upholding, repairs, and cleaning of indoor facilities or structures, including rooms, corridors, stairwells, lobbies, lounges, and offices.

change order—An actual or written design order that authorizes the contractor to make the proposed change in the work at the construction site.

circulation—The ability for a user to get from one place to another easily and safely.

codes—Control guidelines or systems that set limitations or control mechanisms pertaining to recreation facilities and equipment usage.

commodity outlet—A core product extension that can provide unique support and enhance revenue generation for a recreation facility.

community park—A park that is larger than either a neighborhood or an urban park. Typical size of this type of park can range from 15 acres to several hundred acres. This type of park consists of a broader range of amenities that will attract users or residents from a greater geographic area. Also called a regional park.

construction manager—Employee from the construction management firm who ensures that contractors are performing the work as described in the blueprints and specifications for a project.

contingency—An amount of money set aside in the overall project cost to take care of unexpected developments that can come up after design and during construction.

control—The practices that management implements for taking charge and ultimately being responsible for every person at their recreation facility.

controlling—The process of supervising, assessing, and correcting employee performance and resources to ensure successful delivery of the product.

core product—The organizational directive and primary service delivered by an agency.

core product extension—Directives that exist to complement or supplement the core product and generate revenue.

cost analysis—The process of reviewing, comparing, and dissecting costs associated with delivering a recreation product or service in an effort to determine the true costs of delivering the product and applying ways to save money.

cost containment—Assessing space in order to make it as efficient as possible from a revenue versus expense perspective.

customer relations—The recreation professional's ability to relate, share, and interact with users; also called user relations.

cyclical maintenance—Nonroutine maintenance that incorporates various steps over time in order to complete a full process or cycle.

delivery operations—Presenting the product to the user or participant.

depreciation—The process whereby the value of recreation facilities and equipment decreases by a certain percentage each year.

design stage—Early stage of a facility development project that involves bringing together all relevant details of assessment and planning and integrating them into documents that diagram and describe the design of the construction.

design team—Consists of a team leader or architect, administrators from the recreation agency, and the construction manager. This group works together in a cooperative and professional fashion to bring the project to reality.

directing—The process of guiding or channeling people or groups within an overall management system.

economic impact—Refers to money that will be spent by users and employees at the facility directly or indirectly at other businesses or agencies in the community.

efficiency—Relates to how well management uses a facility and other resources in maximizing revenue opportunities while minimizing expenses.

efficiency systems—The electrical and mechanical equipment that supports the overall use of the facility.

elasticity—The amount of give in a surface.

employee—A person hired to work for a recreation agency.

employee relations—The recreation professional's ability to relate, share, and interact with staff.

environmental impact—Considered to be negative and relates to the damage that the facility may have on the environment.

equipment—Any item, object, or thing, mechanical or otherwise, that enhances the production process of the product.

equipment diversity—The variety of purposes and functions that can be served by equipment specifically designed to meet the needs of delivering a specific product.

expendable equipment—Equipment related to the delivery process that is used with the expectation that it may get lost, broken, or worn out. Usually is replaced within 2 years.

extensiveness—Number of various products or services provided at a facility. It indicates the complexity of recreation facility management, which encompasses everything from risk management to maintenance, not to mention unexpected disruption in product delivery.

external support systems—Responsibilities and tasks accomplished outside the organization by partnering or contracting with outside agencies.

facility—Refers to the leisure services environments where activities occur.

fall protection—Safety characteristics that refer to how absorbent a surface is or how much give there is in a surface when there is a fall.

feasibility study—Formal assessment used to determine if a facility design project is financially viable for an agency.

final blueprints—The actual drawings or design documents with which contractors will communicate to subcontractors and craft workers the specifics on what is to be constructed.

finishing stage—Represents work done by the contractors that includes painting walls, installing light fixtures, hanging doors, and installing windows and floor coverings. This is one of the last stages of construction.

fixed equipment—Equipment that is firmly attached as part of the structure of a facility and is usually installed during construction.

fixed price bid—A system where all designs and specifications for the project are awarded to one general contractor to complete all the work. A lump sum option results in a single sum of money paid for all work to be accomplished. Also referred to as a lump sum bid.

flexibility—A recreation professional's awareness of the possibility of the need for adjustment in facility usage and management.

focus group—a group process for gathering information consisting of 5-9 people who represent various segments of users and stakeholders. These users are simply asked to share their thoughts on subjects related to facility development. Focus groups generally range in size from 5 to 12 participants. A facilitator guides the group through questions regarding facility needs.

foot-candle—Units of measure of the calculated supply of energy required to brighten an area with light.

gravity effect—Having multiple businesses in the same area where various types of people are drawn to and may end up spending additional money at nearby establishments.

greenways—When two or more linear parks are connected.

gross income—The total amount of money generated over a specified period.

gross square footage (GSF)—The total number of square feet of a facility established by measuring the outside (perimeter) of a facility and multiplying that by the number of levels.

groundbreaking—Before the actual construction process begins, a ceremony is held to symbolize and recognize the official start of the project.

grounds maintenance—Keeping outdoor spaces clean, functional, and safe. This can include an outdoor facility and the exterior of an indoor facility.

illumination—The amount of light given off by a light source.

in-kind gifts—Where a contractor or other interested party provides labor or materials to a facility at no cost in exchange for a tax deduction or tax write-off for the amount of labor or materials donated.

influence—The act or power to affect an outcome.

internal support systems—Responsibilities and tasks accomplished within the organization.

job announcement—An official posting of a job used to solicit applicants.

job classification—Places a value on each job that is required to fulfill the mission and goals of a recreation agency. This process results in a hierarchical compilation of the type, number, and responsibilities of each job necessary to deliver the products of a specific recreation organization.

job description—A detailed document that includes all of the responsibilities and tasks of the position.

leisure pool—An aquatics area that can have any variety of shapes and does not include areas for competitive swimming.

linear park—A park that is generally found along a stream, river, or wetland area or an abandoned railroad bed. It tends to be long or linear and may connect to other similar parks.

loose-fill surface—A surface that can be displaced.

lump-sum bid—A system where all designs and specifications for the project are awarded to one general contractor to complete all the work. A lump-sum option results in a single sum of money paid for all work to be accomplished. Also referred to as a fixed-priced bid.

maintenance—The concept of keeping facilities and equipment in proper, safe, and functional condition; can be considered a support function.

maintenance equipment—Equipment that contributes to the purpose of keeping both recreation facilities and equipment in proper working condition.

management—The process of working with people and resources to achieve agency.

man-made structures—Facilities that are conceived, planned, designed, constructed, and ultimately occupied by a management system to deliver a recreation product or service.

master plan—A formal comprehensive document that identifies the agency's facility needs and establishes the priority in which construction of new or the renovation of existing recreation facilities will occur.

master schedule—Records of the various uses of the facility by date, time, and space and contact information of the user group.

market segmentation—Targeting a particular segment of users by recognizing their particular needs and interests and then attempting to meet them.

marketing—Management's efforts to obtain and reach an audience in order to deliver a product to them.

multipurpose facility—A facility that incorporates two or more products that differ in their makeup and potential.

national park—A park that has many characteristics similar to a state park. National parks are usually owned and operated by a national government unit and serve all those within that nation and others who visit from other areas of the world. In the United States a national park is operated by the National Park Service, a division of the Department of the Interior.

natural environment—Where little about the attraction or environment has been built or constructed by humans.

needs assessment—Formal assessment that helps an agency understand additional services and facilities that users would like to have provided.

neighborhood parks—Parks intended to serve relatively small areas of a community. They are often located in a densely populated area.

net income—The remaining funds after all expenses, including taxes, have been paid.

organizing—Involves recognition and assignment of specific tasks and responsibilities to employees and resources, as well as designing areas and time assignments that relate to the product.

operational costs—Costs involved in running a facility.

outsourcing—Contracting services to outside vendors.

park—An outdoor space made available to the public and often provided by a public agency for the benefit and enjoyment of the citizens of a respective community, state, or country.

performance appraisal—A formal process resulting from the observation and evaluation of an employee in an effort to assess how the employee is meeting expectations and standards.

permanent equipment—Facility equipment not affixed to the facility but is necessary as part of the structure in order for the facility to operate or fulfill its intended purpose.

petition—A document stating that people are in agreement on a certain issue or need. The petition usually has a formal statement that demonstrates a real or sincere interest or commitment by the petitioners in support of a project.

place—Where a product is distributed and allocated to target consumer markets.

planning—To anticipate through thought and, when appropriate, documentation, all facets that should take the organization to an expected level of success.

policies—Administrative guidelines that formally state limitations on what individuals are allowed to do while using a recreation facility.

preventive maintenance—Maintenance practices that avoid unforeseen maintenance. This preventive system recognizes potential problems and then attends to them, adding longevity to areas and equipment and ensuring they are protected.

preventative supervision—supervision designed to prevent incidents from occurring

price—Cost to the consumer to acquire a product or service. This expense goes beyond the product's sticker price and may also include time and opportunity costs, psychological costs, personal effort costs, and indirect financial costs.

primary space—areas in a facility where the core product is delivered

private sector—Designed to provide a product based on profit-oriented goals.

procedures—Administrative statements that help individuals know how to use a facility and its equipment.

product—The organizational directive and primary service delivered by an agency; same as the core product. It is what the consumer receives from the business transaction or exchange. The product can be a tangible good or intangible service.

product delivery equipment—Relates specifically to the delivery of the product for which the facility was designed.

production—Creating the basis of how the product is delivered. It includes communicating basic information to recreation facility users and allocating the human and physical resources and other elements critical to the delivery of the product.

profit—Generating sufficient net income to exceed expenses.

programming—Designing and manipulating of leisure environments in an effort to promote the desired leisure experiences of participants.

progress meetings—Meetings scheduled on a regular basis by the construction management team with key people involved in the project to discuss the project schedule, provide updates on progress, and resolve issues or problems affecting construction.

project planning—A systematic anticipation of information through careful thought and documentation to develop a facility project.

project schedule—A conceptual plan that ideally reflects every phase of the project.

project statement—A formal planning document that assists in the architect's design of the facility. It serves as a transitional document between planning and design.

promotion—The advancement or appreciation of the status, position, or value of a product or idea. Promotion includes various strategies in delivering information, such as public relations, personal selling, sales promotions, publicity, and advertising.

prospectus—A formal summary of a business venture or facility project that may be used to justify funding or attract investors.

psychographics—Lifestyle information used in target marketing.

public sector—Designed to provide a product based on service-oriented goals.

punch list—Near the conclusion of a facility construction project, a system of assessing and recording everything that is to be finalized or corrected.

purchase order—A formal written request initiated for ordering equipment and arranging for delivery.

purchase requisition—A written request to administration to indicate a need for a particular piece of equipment.

recreation facility—A structure that exists and creates space for the core product and core product extensions.

recreation facility equipment—Items, objects, and things (mechanical and otherwise) provided by management to enhance, make functional, and complete a recreation product's administrative and delivery operations.

recreation facility management—Supervising staff, operating a facility, maintaining equipment, or running an event.

referendums—an issue voted on by the general public

regional park—A park that is larger than either a neighborhood or an urban park. Typical acreage of this type of park can range from 15 acres to several hundred acres. This type of park consists of a broader range of amenities that will attract users or residents from a greater geographic area. Also called a community park.

renovation—The rehabilitation of an existing facility with steps taken to rearrange the space within an existing structure.

resource management—Managing employees, money, equipment, and facilities.

resources—Employees, money, equipment, and facilities.

retrofitting—The addition of new systems of technology to an existing facility.

security equipment—Equipment that is in place to protect the employees and users as well as the facility and its equipment.

self-parking—When the owner parks his or her own vehicle. It is the most common parking option.

separate-bid pricing—Quotes solicited from different general contractors for different elements of the construction process.

service area—Refers to the people within a certain distance of a facility who will be served by the facility. Depending on the type of facility, distance can be measured in actual geographic distance from a facility or it can be measured in the amount of time it takes to get to a facility.

shop drawings—Interpretations of the blueprints by the contractor, or subcontractor, for approval by the architect. They support the blueprints and specification books in a project.

single-purpose facility—A facility that typically has only one product that is developed and delivered.

site analysis—Identifying a variety of factors related to the specific location being considered for a facility.

slide characteristics—How much a surface allows people to slide when participating in activities.

space relationships—Description of how all the areas of a facility will relate to one another.

specification book—Important part of communicating the details of a project to the various contractors. It provides written detailed references to the blueprints.

sponsorships—when an outside entity provides funds to a leisure service agency funds so that their business receives recognition of some type at the facility.

sport park—A park that features some type of sport or a combination of sport facilities as the core product.

staffing—The recruitment, hiring, and training of appropriate individuals who can facilitate the requirements for the product's success.

standard of care—A legal concept that is usually established as a result of previous legal action or precedence.

state park—A park that is usually larger than a community or regional park but may have similar amenities. State parks are usually owned and operated by a large government unit.

strategic planning—A detailed, comprehensive process with several people involved in planning for an organization.

structural equipment—Items that are permanent or attached to the structure and are critical to the core product and core product extension.

structural expenses—Expenses associated with maintaining or improving the physical structure of the facility.

structural material—Refers to the makeup of the materials that are used in constructing the facility.

structures—Any recreation facility; all recreation facilities are considered structures.

supervisor—Job classification in which a person is responsible for reviewing the work of one or more subordinate employees.

supplies—Considered expendable items that are consumed or used up during the production process.

support—Represents activities that take place behind the scenes by personnel who are typically not out front or in contact with facility users.

surface parking—A parking area consisting of a single level surface.

surfaces—the outer area of a boundary such as a wall, floor, or ceiling.

stakeholder—a person that has a vested interest in an agency or facility

surfacing—the type of material used to cover a surface

surveys—A common method for obtaining information; can be considered internal or external. An internal survey can be used in obtaining user or employee feedback regarding an agency's own facility or facilities. An external survey can be used in obtaining comparative information from other facilities with similar products. This type of external comparative survey is often called a benchmark survey.

sustainability—Refers to operating a facility while minimizing the long-term impact on the environment.

synthesizing—Bringing the recreation product and space together as a useful experience for the user.

target market—A population with specific demographic or statistical descriptions or characteristics that are used in order to analyze and ensure the product's success. Some characteristics that can be evaluated in establishing the target market are age, sex, socioeconomic background, and geographic location.

tax levy—A portion of local taxes is collected and earmarked for a specific recreation facility project. A tax levy occurs in the public sector.

tear space—The difference between the gross square footage and the assignable square footage.

theme park—A park with a specific attraction that is designed to appeal to customers or visitors from an entertainment or unique experience perspective.

topography—The natural condition of the land.

unitary surface—A surface that cannot be displaced.

uniqueness—The design, product being delivered, administrative styles, management philosophy, staff composition, and leadership qualities that make each facility different from others.

urban parks—Parks intended to serve the most urban and densely developed area of a community. An urban park is generally fairly small in size and is likely to be bordered by a combination of residences and businesses in a community.

use zones—The area required for participation in an activity and the areas beneath a structure that should have a surface that provides fall protection.

user patterns—monitoring specific times of the day, days of the week, and times of the year that areas of a facility are used.

user relations—The recreation professional's ability to relate, share, and interact with users. Also called customer relations.

users—People who come to a facility to have a positive experience while using the product or service.

valet parking—Parking service where staff members greet customers at the facility entrance and take the vehicle to a different location or parking area to park it.

value engineering—When a recreation administrator and the contractor seek assistance from architects, engineers, and specialists to make sure bid prices accurately reflect details in the project specifications.

vendors—entities that sell their product or services in a recreation facility

water parks—Aquatic facilities that incorporate various water features designed for maximum entertainment of participants.

waterfront—An outdoor aquatic facility located at a lake, beach, river, or quarry.

Bibliography

Access Board. (2002). ADA accessibility guidelines for recreation facilities. www.access-board.gov/recreation/final.htm.

Adkins, C. (1994, October-December). Developing evacuation plans. *Crowd Management*, 18-20, 32.

American Society for Testing Materials International. (2007). *Standard consumer safety performance specification for playground equipment for public use (F1487-07ae1)*. West Conshohocken, PA: Author.

Balenske, K. (1989, October). Building a facility 1-2-3. *Parks and Recreation*, 76-81.

Barnard, A. (1992, March). Locker room logistics. *Athletic Business*, 35-40.

Barnard, A.W. (1997, August). What recreation facilities cost. *Athletic Business*, 32-34, 36, 38-41.

Berg, R. (1990, December). A broader support base. *Athletic Business*, 66-70.

Berlonghi, A.E. (1994, July-September). What is crowd management: Understanding and planning different spectator crowds. *Crowd Management*, 4-9.

Bessler, D. (2006, June). Park management: A systems approach to managing parks infrastructure. *Parks and Recreation Business*, 22-25.

Bigelow, C. (1997, November). Tasty opportunities. *Athletic Business*, 59-65.

Bridges, F.J., & Roquemore, L.L. (2004). *Management for athletic/sport administration: Theory and practice* (4th ed.). Decatur, GA: ESM Books.

Brown, S.S. (1993, February). Selecting safe equipment: What do we really know? *Journal of Physical Education, Recreation, and Dance*, 33-35.

Burkhardt, R. (2006, June). Douglas county regional parks: Turf alternatives. *Parks and Recreation Business*, 28-30.

Campus recreation: A look at trends in recreation at colleges and universities. (2007). *Recreation Management*, 8(6), 52-58.

Carman, D. (2007, July). Complete guide to sports and recreation surfaces. *Recreation Management*, 1-17.

Christiansen, M.L., & Vogelson, H. (1996). *Play it safe: An anthology of playground safety* (2nd ed.). Arlington, VA: National Recreation and Park Association.

Ciancutti, R.D. (2005, August). Happy trails. *Parks and Recreation Business*, 42-43.

Cohen, A. (1995, March). Lockup. *Athletic Business*, 47-50.

Cohen, A. (1997, August). Keeping track of everything. *Athletic Business*, 43-46, 48.

Cohen, A. (1998, September). Beneath the surface. *Athletic Business*, 56-58, 60-62, 64, 66.

Cohen, A. (2003, April). Out of the box. *Athletic Business*, 71-76, 78.

Crompton, J.L. (1999). *Financing and acquiring park and recreation resources*. Champaign, IL: Human Kinetics.

Dahl, B., & Molnar, D.J. (2003). *Anatomy of a park* (3rd ed.). Prospect Heights, IL: Waveland Press.

Dahnert, R., & Pack, A. (2007). Behind the scenes. *American School and University*, 31(7), 48-50, 52, 54-56.

Daly, J. (1995). *Recreation and sport planning and design* (2nd ed.). Champaign, IL: Human Kinetics.

Dillon, J. (1996, August/September). Changes in the changing room. *Athletic Management*, 45-49.

Dolan, T. (2007). Restrooms and locker rooms. *School Planning and Management*, 46(6), 30, 32, 34, 36-38.

Drysdale, A.C. (1973). Food service: The trend is leasing. *Recreation Canada*, 13(4), 18-20.

Flynn, R.B. (1993). *Facility planning for physical education, recreation, and athletics*. Reston, VA: American Alliance for Health, Physical Education, Recreation and Dance.

Fogg, G.E. (2000). *A site design and management process*. Ashburn, VA: National Recreation and Park Association.

Fried, G. (2005). *Managing sport facilities*. Champaign, IL: Human Kinetics.

Gabrielsen, M.A. (1987). *Swimming pool: A guide to their planning, design, and operation* (4th ed.). Champaign, IL: Human Kinetics.

Griffin, P. (1997, August/September). Winning the management game. *Athletic Management*, 30-33.

Hawkins, B., Voreis, J., Hill, J., Myllykangus, S., & Spangler, K. (2007, March). CEPEA: A tool for change. *Parks and Recreation*, 71-76.

Hilkemeyer, F. (1993, May). Food for thought. *Athletic Business*, 39-43.

Horine, L. (2004). *The administration of physical education and sport programs* (5th ed.). Madison, WI: McGraw-Hill.

Hughes, W.L. (1997, August). The aesthetic effect. *Athletic Business*, 69-72.

Introduction to recreation and leisure. (2006). Champaign, IL: Human Kinetics.

Kessler, L., & Wright, S. (1995, April). Baseline smash. *Athletic Business*, 41-46.

Kirkpatrick, R. (1989, June). Playground design and maintenance. *Parks/Grounds Management*, 8-10.

Kocher, E. (1996, April). Gymnasium facelifts. *Athletic Business*, 39-42, 44.

Krenson, F. (1997, April). Making it multipurpose. *Athletic Business*, 67-68, 70-71, 75-76.

LaRue, R.J. (2004, October). The facility audit. *Parks and Recreation Business*, 82-85.

Mertes, J.D., & Hall, J.R. (1996). *Park, recreation, open space and greenway guidelines*. Ashburn, VA: National Recreation and Park Association.

Miller, D. (1990, October). User populations multiply. *Athletic Business*, 44-46.

Miller, D., & Corrington, D. (1995, August). Breaking ground. *Athletic Business*, 63-66.

Morris, B.A. (1999, January). A done deal. *Club Industry*, 20-26.

Morrison, T.A. (Spring, 1989). The influence of building codes on recreation facility design. *NIRSA Journal*, 22-26.

Mull, R.F., Bayless, K.G., & Jamieson, L.M. (2005). *Recreational sport management* (4th ed.). Champaign, IL: Human Kinetics.

Murray, J.E. (1994, September). Where's the contract. *Purchasing*, 34-35.

Musco Sports Lighting. (1990). *The facts of light*. Oskaloosa, IA: Author.

———. (2007). *Sports lighting: Answers to 7 common questions*. Oskaloosa, IA: Author.

Neff, T., & Miller, K. (2007). Building blueprints: Outdoor athletic facilities. *School Planning and Management*, 46(8), 48-49.

Olson, J.R. (1997). *Facility and equipment management for sport directors*. Champaign, IL: Human Kinetics.

Osgood, H. (1997, May). Hey, turn off those lights. *Parks and Recreation*, 98-103.

Patton, J.D. (1997, April). Fitness in flux. *Athletic Business*, 51-54.

Patton, J.D. (1997, August). Mission: Control. *Athletic Business*, 63-68.

Pearce, B. (1998, January). Sign sense. *Athletic Business*, 39-44.

Peterson, J.A., & Tharrett, S.J. (1997). *ACSM's health/fitness facility standards and guidelines* (2nd ed.). Champaign, IL: Human Kinetics.

Phillips, L.E. (1996). *Parks: Design and management*. New York: McGraw-Hill.

Potential and possibilities. (2004, October). *Parks and Recreation Business*, 26, 28-35. Potter, W. (2005, August). Grounded in safety. *Parks and Recreation Business*, 24-26.

Potter, W. (2005, November). Perfect facility designs. *Parks and Recreation Business*, 8, 10-11.

Rogers, J. (1996, May). Light out. *Athletic Business*, 51-54.

Rogers, J.G., & Greer, T.P. (1999, January). Space case. *Athletic Business*, 47-48, 50, 52-53.

Rogers, J.N., & Siter, J.C. (1995, May). Sowing seeds. *Athletic Business*, 49-54, 56.

Sawyer, T.H. (2005). *Facility design and management for health, physical activity, recreation, and sports facility development* (11th ed.). Champaign, IL: Sagamore.

Seidler, T.L. (2006, May/June). Facility design and development: Planning and designing safe facilities. *Journal of Physical Education, Recreation, and Dance*, 77(5), 33-37, 48.

Shalley, W., & Barzdukas, A. (1997, March). Dive right in. *Athletic Business*, 41-42, 44-46, 48, 50-51.

Shaver, J. (2006, March). Schools of thought. *Fitness Business Pro*, 22-25, 31.

Shing, C.C., & Marafa, L.M. (2006, January). Research update: Components of urban park systems. *Parks and Recreation*, 26-30.

Simmons, B. (1995, November). Positioning community bond issue for success. *Parks and Recreation*, 48-54.

Slack, T. (1997). *Understanding sport organizations: The application of organization theory*. Champaign, IL: Human Kinetics.

St. Clair, D. (1996, May). Unlocking the locker room. *Athletic Business*, 67-70.

Teague, T.L. (1996, April). Playgrounds: Managing your risk. *Parks and Recreation*, 54-60.

Tharrett, S., & Peterson, J.A. (2006, June). What makes a great facility manager? *Fitness Management*, 54-57.

Thompson, D., Hudson, S.D., & Olsen, H.M. (2007). *S.A.F.E. play areas: Creation, maintenance, and renovation*. Champaign, IL: Human Kinetics.

Viklund, R. (1995, July). High-performance floors. *Athletic Business*, 41-42, 44-47.

Viklund, R., & Coons, J. (1997, September). Locker rooms: The durable design. *Athletic Business*, 63-68, 70-71.

Visani, D.H. (1995, December). Frontline design. *Athletic Business*, 67-70.

Waldo, B., & Murray, W. (1996, October). Hungry. *Athletic Business*, 58-62.

Walsh, M. (1993, July). Filter out your pool problems. *Parks and Recreation*, 58-63.

Wiggins, D.K. (1995). *Sport in America: From wicked amusement to national obsession*. Champaign, IL: Human Kinetics.

Zagrodnik, J. (2006, March/April). Universal design 101: Seven elements of ageless design. *Journal on Active Aging*, 84-85.

Zamengo, E. (1995, November). Spotlight on security. *Parks and Recreation*, 28-30.

Index

Note: The letters *f* and *t* after page numbers indicate figures or tables, respectively.

A

accidents
    insurance 126
    reports 157*f*
accounting 12. *See also* finances
accreditation 27
administration
    controlling 8
    directing 7
    organizing 6-7
    planning 6
administrators 59, 139. *See also* employees
Americans With Disabilities Act (ADA) 22, 77, 224
ancillary space 238
aquatic facilities 96*f*, 222*f*
    accessibility 223-224
    construction 223
    emergency services 234
    equipment 229-231, 230*f*
    food services 234
    hygiene 227-228
    leisure pools 64*f*, 223
    liability 51*f*
    maintenance 227-228, 235
    mechanical systems 228-229
    opening checklist 158*f*
    pool rental agreement 171*f*
    preventive supervision 227
    product delivery areas 231-233
    safety 226-227
    staffing 224-226, 234, 235
    types 208, 222
    waterfront 222
    water parks 223
asset management 55, 115

B

Boys & Girls Club 14*f*
budgeting 11. *See also* finances

C

caves 18*f*
child care
    access 262*f*
    age levels 259-260
    area design 264-265
    caregiver training 262

    functions 260-261
    insurance 263
    licensing 264
    maintenance 263
    operating costs 263-264
    policies 262-263
    regulations 263
    security 261
    staffing 261-262
circulation 150*f*
    areas 150
    facility directory 151*f*
    and signage 150-151
    and user comfort 151-152
clients. *See* users
commodity outlets 53*f*, 252
    design of 255-256
    displays 254
    enhancements 254-255
    merchandising 253
    pricing 253
    sales 254
    staffing 254
    vendors 253
construction 63*f*. *See also* construction management; project costs
    alternate bids 93
    aquatic facilities 223
    bid process 91, 93
    bonds 93
    codes 77
    conventional option 90
    demolition 76*f*
    design-build option 90-91
    documents 102-103
    excavation 35*f*
    fast-track option 91
    finishing stage 107
    furniture/equipment installation 108-109
    groundbreaking 102*f*
    key system 107-108, 108*f*
    manager 69, 86*f*
    materials 70*f*
    new 63-64
    occupancy 109
    opening ceremony 109-110
    owner acceptance 109

project schedule 103
punch list 108
quotations 92
renovation 63, 124
repairs 62-63, 124
retrofitting 63, 124
ribbon cutting 109*f*
shop drawings 103
turnkey option 91
construction management 103-104
changes 106
coordination 104
inspection 105-106
legal requirements 105
progress meetings 104
project schedule 104
quality check 104-105
security 106-107
site safety 106-107
visitation 107
consultants 59-60, 142
contractors 62, 69, 77, 94*f*, 142. *See* construction
bidding 91, 92, 93
for maintenance 186
contracts 95
controlling costs 95
financing plans 95
insurance coverage 94
signing 95
value engineering
control
codes 161
liabilities 160-161
policies 159
procedures 159
rules and regulations 159
standards 162
coordinating 166. *See also* scheduling
leadership 166
by place 168
seasonality 167
and stakeholders 167
usage and time of day 167-168
core product 4
delivery of 18, 24, 64
disruption in 20
number per facility 20
synthesizing with space 19
core product extensions 238, 255. *See also* commodity outlets
auxiliary space for 65
defined 5
types 6, 65

cost containment 24-25
costs. *See* operational costs; project costs
Council on Accreditation (NRPA) 27
custodial services 65
customer relations 25
customers. *See* users

D
delivery operations 6
auxiliaries 9-10
maintenance 10
production 8
support 8-9
Department of Natural Resources (DNR) 205
design. *See* facility design
disruptions. *See* emergencies

E
economic impact 62
emergencies
aquatic facilities 234
catalysts 190-191
chemical spills 192
CPR training 155*f*
crowds 194
degree of disruption 190
disruptive behaviors 194
fire 193
injuries 191, 192
maintenance 192
product disruption 191
service disruption 191
threats 193-194
weather 192-193
emergency responses 194
action steps 198
evacuation 197-198
exit routes 198*f*
law enforcement 196-197
leadership 195-196
medical assistance 197
taking action 196-197
warnings 196
employee relations 25, 145
employees. *See also* staffing
administrative 139-140
certification 23, 140
compensation 134
coordinator 140
external 141
feedback from 54-55
grievances 139, 145
influence on organization 23
maintenance 141, 185, 186, 187
on-the-job training 137

employees *(continued)*
  performance appraisals 137-139, 138*f*, 139*f*
  recognitions 145
  safety of 144
  specialists 140-141, 185-186
  supervisory 140
  termination of 139
  work environment 144-145
environmental impact 62, 66
Equal Employment Opportunity Act 22
equipment 12
  checkout 266-269
  complexity 114
  costs 127
  depreciation 125
  distributing 121-122
  diversity 114
  functional classification 116-119
  furniture 118
  installation 108-109, 121*f*
  instructions on use 22*f*
  insurance 268
  inventory 121, 268
  key form 119*f*
  leasing 122
  maintenance 87*f*, 181
  operator training 107
  park rentals 210-211
  planning list 66
  playgrounds 214-215
  purchase requisition form 120*f*
  purchasing 119-121
  receiving 121
  rental 122, 266-269
  scheduling 172
  scoreboards 116*f*
  status 115
  storage 65, 268*f*
  and technology 21
  types 115-116
  use 114-115, 122

F
facilities 12, 18, 30-31. *See also* aquatic facilities;
    construction; facility assessment; facility
    design; indoor facilities; outdoor facilities;
    planning
  codes 21-22
  complexity 21
  defined 18
  development options 62-64
  development stages 33-34
  extensiveness 20
  functionality 21, 22-23, 32-33

image 53, 128, 141, 179
  management model 20*f*
  man-made 18, 19
  multipurpose 33
  natural environments 18, 31
  operation costs 22
  product influence 32
  public *versus* private 33
  purpose of 32-33
  service area 62
  sustainability 21, 22
  and technology 21
  uniqueness 21, 31
facility assessment 33, 50
  asset management 55
  benchmarking 53
  efficiency 52-53
  feedback 54-55
  focus groups 54
  gaining support 54
  initial proposal 55-56
  modernization 53-54
  participation (accommodation) 51-52
  petitions 55
  and safety 50-51
  satisfaction 51
  site visits 54
facility design 21-22, 31, 33-34, 69. *See also* con-
    tracts
  aesthetics 74
  assigned square footage (ASF) 87
  blueprints 75-76, 77-83, 103
  child care area 264-265
  commodity outlets 255-256
  finish plan 77
  gross square footage (GSF) 87
  legal requirements 77
  mechanical systems 73-74
  modeling 74, 75*f*
  schedule 77
  schematics 74*f*
  specification book 77, 103
  stage 68
  structural equipment 77
  structural materials 69-70
  structure conceptualization 62, 69
  team 68-69
  tear space 87
finances 11-12. *See also* funding; operational costs;
    project costs
  accountability 22
  accounting 130
  budgeting 130
  cost analysis 130-131

cost assessment assistance 60
cost containment 24-25
cost projections 62
cost savings 22
income 127
structural expenses 124-126
tax dollars 58
food services 256
at aquatic facilities 234
cafeteria 257
catering 257
health codes 257-258
liquor licensing 258
local ordinances 258-259
restaurant 257
snack bars 256
vending machines 256-257
funding
bond issue 97
campaign 99
combination 99
contributions 97-98
donations 97f, 128-129
grants 98
in-kind gifts 98
investments 129
investors 129
mandatory fees 95-96
rentals 128
revenue bond 97
sponsorships 98-99, 129-130
tax levy 96
tax support 130
user fees 96-97
fundraising. See funding

G
golf courses 32f, 98f, 129, 166, 257, 266
gravity effect 62

H
human resources. See employees; staffing

I
ice arenas 114, 115f, 167, 253
indoor facilities 30f, 31
access 39, 40
acoustics 37
climate control 38
electrical systems 36-37, 38
finishes 37
irrigation 38-39
landscape 38
lighting 36
parking 39-40

plumbing 37
production space 35
service needs 65
site selection 34-35
structural appearance 38
surfaces 35-36
utilities 38
injuries 144, 145. See also safety
emergencies 191, 192
medical assistance 9f, 143f, 197
insurance 124, 125-126
for child care 263
at construction site 94
coverage 125-126, 175, 238
on equipment 122, 266, 268

J
job applicants. See staffing

L
landscape 39f
indoor facilities 39
maintenance 181
outdoor facilities 42-43
parking areas 242-243
leadership 6, 166-167. See also management
for emergency responses 195-196
liability
assumption of risk 160
attractive nuisance 161
insurance 126
negligence 160
at pools 51
protection against 22
standard of care 161
waivers 267
lighting 72, 73f
fluorescent 73
high-density 73
incandescent 73
indoor facilities 36
night games 37
outdoor facilities 44
locker rooms 70, 71, 227, 247-249

M
maintenance 141
aquatic facilities 227
assessment 183-184
building 180-181
contracting 186
costs 126-127
cyclical 183
daily checklist 182f
of efficiency systems 187-188

maintenance *(continued)*
   emergencies 192
   employees 141
   of equipment 181
   and facility image 179
   grounds 11*f*, 182*f*, 181
   importance of 178-179
   inspection 187
   inventory 183
   manuals 107, 186-187
   of parking areas 240
   at parks 213
   planning for 65, 183
   planning representatives 60
   at playgrounds 218-219
   preventative 182-183
   priority 178
   projects 182
   record-keeping 186
   routine 181
   and safety 179-180
   shops 187
   storage facilities 187
   supervision 186
   systems 183-184
   task identification 184
   unforeseen 182
   work assignments 185-186
   work orders 184-185
   work request form 184*f*
management 4, 15, 19-20. *See also* administration;
    coordination
   defining 6
   directive 4
   efficiency 24
   flexibility 24
   goal setting 13
   influence 6
   mission 4, 15
   organizational chart 7*f*
   philosophy 58
   profit-oriented goals 14-15
   responsibilities of 24-25
   service-oriented goals 14
   values 4, 15
   vision 4, 15
managers. *See* recreation professionals
marketing 12-13
   with structural design 31
master plans 60-61

N
national parks 206-207
National Park Service (NPS) 206

National Recreation and Park Association (NRPA)
   26, 140
Negligence 22
NRPA. *See* National Recreation and Park Association (NRPA)

O
operational costs 89-90
   contractual services 127
   employees 126
   equipment 127
   maintenance 126-127
   utilities 127
operations. *See* delivery operations
outdoor facilities 30*f*, 31
   access 43
   barriers 42, 43*f*, 151, 161*f*
   conveniences 44
   drainage 42
   equipment storage 65
   irrigation 44
   landscape 42
   land topography 41*f*
   layout 41
   lighting 37*f*, 43
   orientation 41, 42*f*
   seating 44, 44*f*
   service needs 65
   site selection 40-41
   surfaces 42, 52*f*, 71-72
   theater 13*f*
   utilities 43
outsourcing 127, 141-142

P
parking areas 239*f*
   access 240
   accessible parking requirements 243*f*
   aisles 242*f*
   angles 241
   area shape 241
   codes 241
   drainage 243
   indoor facilities 40
   landscaping 242-243
   maintenance of 240
   options for 238
   ordinances 241
   safety 241*f*
   security 240
   sidewalks 242
   signage 240
   spaces 241-242
parks 202. *See also* aquatic facilities; playgrounds

access control 212
amenities 209
design 208-209
equipment rental 210-211
fees 212
food service 210
greenways 205
linear 204, 205
maintenance 213
national 206-207
neighborhood 203
programs 209
regional 203, 204
restrooms 210
retail outlets 211
safety 213
security 213
shelters 209-210
sport 208
state 205-206
theme 207
trails 204, 205, 211
urban 203
welcome centers 209, 210f
participants. See users
planning. See project planning; strategic planning
planning committees 58
administrators 59
architects 60
consultants 59-60
maintenance representatives 60
production representatives 59
staff representatives 59
user representatives 59
playgrounds 179f, 211-212, 214f
equipment 214-215, 215f, 216f
maintenance 218-219
safety 215
supervision 217-218, 218f
surfaces 72f, 216-217
use zones 215-217, 217f
policies
cancellation 173
child care 262-263
communication of 145, 153, 159, 246
damage 174
equipment use 267
fees 173
food-service 175
prioritization 173
refund request form 174f
refunds 173
violation of 23

pools. See aquatic facilities
private sector 14, 15f, 58, 91f
and bidding the project 91-92
product. See core product
professionals. See recreation professionals
profit 4, 14
project costs. See also contracts
architectural fees 88
construction 87
construction management 87-88
consultant fees 88
contingencies 89
controlling 95
engineering fees 88
equipment 88
financing plans 95
furniture 88
hard 86-88
insurance coverage 94
permits 88-89
reimbursable 89
of repairs 62
signage 88
soft 88-89
project planning 6, 33, 58. See also planning committees; site analysis
administrative approach 58
area impact 62, 66
assessment review 61
comparisons 65
cost projections 62
input sources 58
participative approach 58
in private sector 58
project statement 64-66
request for proposal (RFP) 60
service needs 65
spaces 65
trends 64
project statement 64
auxiliary space 65
basic assumption 64
comparison 65
environmental impact 66
equipment list 66
furniture list 66
objective 64
primary space 65
service needs 65
space relationships 65-66
trends 64-65
proposals
initial 55-56
pro shop. See commodity outlets

public sector 14, 58, 90*f*
    and bidding the project 91-92

R
reception area 10*f*, 243, 244*f*
    administration offices 247
    appearance 243
    attitude 244
    design 247
    efficiency 243-244
    functions of 244-247
    lobby 247
recreation facility managers 139, 166
recreation professionals
    associations for 26
    careers for 25
    certifications 23, 140
    employment 25-26
    on-the-job training 137
    professional development 23
    publications 27
    training 26-27
rentals. *See* equipment
resource management 26
resources. *See also* employees; equipment
    fiscal 11-12
    managing 10-11
    maximizing 21
retail areas. *See* commodity outlets
risk management 22, 159. *See also* safety
    analysis 155
    education 155-156
    inspections 156
    leadership 155
    reporting 156, 157, 158, 159
Rock and Roll Hall of Fame (Seattle) 31*f*

S
safety
    accident report 157*f*
    and activity 152
    aquatic facilities 226-227
    citizen report 158*f*
    environmental conditions 154
    and experience level 152-153
    facility assessment 50-51
    and maintenance 179-180
    at parks 213
    at playgrounds 215
    pool checklist 158*f*
    precaution 154-155, 154-156
    and user age 152
    vandalism/trouble report 159*f*
    in work environment 144-145
scheduling. *See also* policies

cancellations 173
    and core product 168-170
    equipment 172
    master schedule 175
    overcrowding 167*f*
    prioritization 173
    procedures 170-171
    reservations 173
    responsibilities 171-173
    space 169
    special events 169-170
    techniques 175
security
    access control 43*f*, 163-164, 163*f*
    child care 261
    construction site
    crowd control 191
    equipment 118
    key system 107-108, 164
    parking areas 240
    at parks 213
    and scheduling 171-172
    staff 163
    surveillance cameras 162-163
    watchdogs 163
service specialists 60
signage 88, 108, 119, 160*f*
    and circulation 150-151
    for parking areas 240
site analysis
    indoor facilities 34-35
    outdoor facilities 40-42
    in planning phase 61
social impact 62
softball complex 4*f*, 19*f*
sport parks 36*f*, 208
staffing. *See also* contractors; employees
    aquatic facilities 224-226
    child care 261-262
    hiring process 135-136
    interviews 136-137
    job classification 134, 135
    job description 135
    job postings 136
    organizational chart 135*f*
    recruitment 134
    by referral 136
    screening applicants 136
    skill assessment 137
    volunteers 143, 144
state parks 205-206
strategic planning 6
structures. *See* facilities
supplies. *See* equipment

surfaces
    indoor facilities 35-36, 71
    outdoor facilities 42, 52*f*, 71-72
    at playgrounds 216-217

T
technology 21, 53, 54, 63, 118, 235

U
users 23-24, 25
    age and safety 152
    behaviors 23, 24, 153-154
    disruptive behaviors 194
    feedback 54-55
    incident reports 153*f*
    influence on facility 23-24
    needs of 23

patterns 23
    planning representatives 59
utilities
    costs 127
    indoor facilities 38-39
    outdoor facilities 44

V
vendors 127, 142, 235, 253, 256. *See also* contractors
volunteers 143, 144

W
water parks. *See* aquatic facilities

Y
YMCA 32*f*

About the Authors

Richard F. Mull, MS, was an assistant professor in the School of Health, Physical Education, and Recreation (HPER) at Indiana University in Bloomington from 1972 to 2006. He has also served as the director of the Center for Student Leadership Development, director of Indiana University's tennis center and outdoor pool, and special assistant to the dean for the auxiliary unit of the school of HPER. From 1972 to 1992, he served as the director of campus recreational sports at Indiana University.

Mull brings the practical experience of over 40 years spent managing recreational sports to his work with students and his writing of numerous publications and books. His professional contributions to the field led to his receipt of the 1989 Honor Award from the National Intramural-Recreational Sports Association (NIRSA). In 1994, he was inducted into the Professional Hall of Fame in the School of Physical Education at West Virginia University.

For more than 35 years, Mull has served as a consultant and advisor in the field of recreational sports. He also served as chairperson of the NIRSA's Professional Development Committee, assistant chairperson of the NIRSA Standards Committee, and vice president of NIRSA. Throughout his career, Mull's special interests have included professional preparation, student development, management, and leadership.

Mull resides in Bloomington, Indiana. In his free time, he enjoys playing golf, cycling, and reading.

Brent A. Beggs, PhD, is an associate professor in the School of Kinesiology and Recreation at Illinois State University in Normal, where he teaches facility planning and design. He also consults for various leisure service agencies in the planning and design of playgrounds and recreation centers. As a practitioner, Beggs was involved in the planning, design, and operation of park expansions, community centers, water parks, and multiple sport complexes.

A certified park and recreation professional, Beggs is a member of the National Recreation and Parks Association, National Intramural-Recreational Sports Association (NIRSA), North American Society of Sport Management, and the Society of Parks and Recreation Educators.

Beggs received his doctorate in leisure behavior from Indiana University in 2002. In 2006 and 2008 he was awarded NIRSA's President's Award for Outstanding Writing in the *Recreational Sports Journal.*

Beggs and his wife, Jeri, reside in Bloomington, Illinois, where he enjoys playing golf, coaching youth basketball and baseball, and participating in fantasy sports.

Mick Renneisen, MS, is director of the City of Bloomington Parks and Recreation Department in Bloomington, Indiana. He is also an adjunct instructor at Indiana University teaching courses in recreation facility management for the School of Health, Physical Education, and Recreation.

Renneisen has more than 25 years of experience in managing and developing a variety of recreation facilities. In 2007, his department received the Gold Medal Award from the National Recreation and Parks Association (NRPA), an award given for excellence in management of resources for a parks and recreation agency. He also received the Willard W. Patty Distinguished Alumni Award for outstanding personal and professional achievement from Indiana University in 2008. He was responsible for the design and management of the award-winning Twin Lakes Sports Park, which received the Daniel Flaherty Best Facility Award (Great Lakes Region) in 1993 and the Amateur Softball Association (ASA) Complex of the Year Award in 1994.

Renneisen is a member of NRPA and the Indiana Parks and Recreation Association. He serves on the Indiana University School of Health, Physical Education, and Recreation Alumni Board; the Bloomington/Monroe County Convention and Visitors Bureau Board; and the YMCA of Monroe County Board. He was also a member of the School of Sports Management Board of Regents.

Renneisen and his wife, Brenda, reside in Bloomington, Indiana. He enjoys traveling, cycling, and playing golf.

You'll find other outstanding recreation resources at
www.HumanKinetics.com